C-3338

THIS IS YOUR **PASSBOOK**® FOR ...

FLIGHT ATTENDANT SKILLS TEST (FAST)

NATIONAL LEARNING CORPORATION®
passbooks.com

COPYRIGHT NOTICE

This book is SOLELY intended for, is sold ONLY to, and its use is RESTRICTED to individual, bona fide applicants or candidates who qualify by virtue of having seriously filed applications for appropriate license, certificate, professional and/or promotional advancement, higher school matriculation, scholarship, or other legitimate requirements of educational and/or governmental authorities.

This book is NOT intended for use, class instruction, tutoring, training, duplication, copying, reprinting, excerption, or adaptation, etc., by:

1) Other publishers
2) Proprietors and/or Instructors of «Coaching» and/or Preparatory Courses
3) Personnel and/or Training Divisions of commercial, industrial, and governmental organizations
4) Schools, colleges, or universities and/or their departments and staffs, including teachers and other personnel
5) Testing Agencies or Bureaus
6) Study groups which seek by the purchase of a single volume to copy and/or duplicate and/or adapt this material for use by the group as a whole without having purchased individual volumes for each of the members of the group
7) Et al.

Such persons would be in violation of appropriate Federal and State statutes.

PROVISION OF LICENSING AGREEMENTS. — Recognized educational, commercial, industrial, and governmental institutions and organizations, and others legitimately engaged in educational pursuits, including training, testing, and measurement activities, may address request for a licensing agreement to the copyright owners, who will determine whether, and under what conditions, including fees and charges, the materials in this book may be used them. In other words, a licensing facility exists for the legitimate use of the material in this book on other than an individual basis. However, it is asseverated and affirmed here that the material in this book CANNOT be used without the receipt of the express permission of such a licensing agreement from the Publishers. Inquiries re licensing should be addressed to the company, attention rights and permissions department.

All rights reserved, including the right of reproduction in whole or in part, in any form or by any means, electronic or mechanical, including photocopying, recording, or by any information storage and retrieval system, without permission in writing from the Publisher.

Copyright © 2020 by

National Learning Corporation

212 Michael Drive, Syosset, NY 11791
(516) 921-8888 • www.passbooks.com
E-mail: info@passbooks.com

PUBLISHED IN THE UNITED STATES OF AMERICA

PASSBOOK® SERIES

THE *PASSBOOK® SERIES* has been created to prepare applicants and candidates for the ultimate academic battlefield – the examination room.

At some time in our lives, each and every one of us may be required to take an examination – for validation, matriculation, admission, qualification, registration, certification, or licensure.

Based on the assumption that every applicant or candidate has met the basic formal educational standards, has taken the required number of courses, and read the necessary texts, the *PASSBOOK® SERIES* furnishes the one special preparation which may assure passing with confidence, instead of failing with insecurity. Examination questions – together with answers – are furnished as the basic vehicle for study so that the mysteries of the examination and its compounding difficulties may be eliminated or diminished by a sure method.

This book is meant to help you pass your examination provided that you qualify and are serious in your objective.

The entire field is reviewed through the huge store of content information which is succinctly presented through a provocative and challenging approach – the question-and-answer method.

A climate of success is established by furnishing the correct answers at the end of each test.

You soon learn to recognize types of questions, forms of questions, and patterns of questioning. You may even begin to anticipate expected outcomes.

You perceive that many questions are repeated or adapted so that you can gain acute insights, which may enable you to score many sure points.

You learn how to confront new questions, or types of questions, and to attack them confidently and work out the correct answers.

You note objectives and emphases, and recognize pitfalls and dangers, so that you may make positive educational adjustments.

Moreover, you are kept fully informed in relation to new concepts, methods, practices, and directions in the field.

You discover that you arre actually taking the examination all the time: you are preparing for the examination by "taking" an examination, not by reading extraneous and/or supererogatory textbooks.

In short, this PASSBOOK®, used directedly, should be an important factor in helping you to pass your test.

FLIGHT ATTENDANT SKILLS TEST

DUTIES:
 This test is designed to measure knowledge, aptitudes, skills and abilities of flight attendants on commercial airlines.

SUBJECT OF EXAMINATION
The test may cover some or all of the following areas:
1. Flight attendant duties;
2. Airline and airport operations and terminology;
3. Dealing with the public;
4. First aid and safety;
5. Reasoning and judgment;
6. Understanding and interpreting written material; and
7. Verbal and clerical abilities.

HOW TO TAKE A TEST

I. YOU MUST PASS AN EXAMINATION

A. *WHAT EVERY CANDIDATE SHOULD KNOW*

Examination applicants often ask us for help in preparing for the written test. What can I study in advance? What kinds of questions will be asked? How will the test be given? How will the papers be graded?

As an applicant for a civil service examination, you may be wondering about some of these things. Our purpose here is to suggest effective methods of advance study and to describe civil service examinations.

Your chances for success on this examination can be increased if you know how to prepare. Those "pre-examination jitters" can be reduced if you know what to expect. You can even experience an adventure in good citizenship if you know why civil service exams are given.

B. *WHY ARE CIVIL SERVICE EXAMINATIONS GIVEN?*

Civil service examinations are important to you in two ways. As a citizen, you want public jobs filled by employees who know how to do their work. As a job seeker, you want a fair chance to compete for that job on an equal footing with other candidates. The best-known means of accomplishing this two-fold goal is the competitive examination.

Exams are widely publicized throughout the nation. They may be administered for jobs in federal, state, city, municipal, town or village governments or agencies.

Any citizen may apply, with some limitations, such as the age or residence of applicants. Your experience and education may be reviewed to see whether you meet the requirements for the particular examination. When these requirements exist, they are reasonable and applied consistently to all applicants. Thus, a competitive examination may cause you some uneasiness now, but it is your privilege and safeguard.

C. *HOW ARE CIVIL SERVICE EXAMS DEVELOPED?*

Examinations are carefully written by trained technicians who are specialists in the field known as "psychological measurement," in consultation with recognized authorities in the field of work that the test will cover. These experts recommend the subject matter areas or skills to be tested; only those knowledges or skills important to your success on the job are included. The most reliable books and source materials available are used as references. Together, the experts and technicians judge the difficulty level of the questions.

Test technicians know how to phrase questions so that the problem is clearly stated. Their ethics do not permit "trick" or "catch" questions. Questions may have been tried out on sample groups, or subjected to statistical analysis, to determine their usefulness.

Written tests are often used in combination with performance tests, ratings of training and experience, and oral interviews. All of these measures combine to form the best-known means of finding the right person for the right job.

II. HOW TO PASS THE WRITTEN TEST

A. NATURE OF THE EXAMINATION

To prepare intelligently for civil service examinations, you should know how they differ from school examinations you have taken. In school you were assigned certain definite pages to read or subjects to cover. The examination questions were quite detailed and usually emphasized memory. Civil service exams, on the other hand, try to discover your present ability to perform the duties of a position, plus your potentiality to learn these duties. In other words, a civil service exam attempts to predict how successful you will be. Questions cover such a broad area that they cannot be as minute and detailed as school exam questions.

In the public service similar kinds of work, or positions, are grouped together in one "class." This process is known as *position-classification*. All the positions in a class are paid according to the salary range for that class. One class title covers all of these positions, and they are all tested by the same examination.

B. FOUR BASIC STEPS

1) Study the announcement

How, then, can you know what subjects to study? Our best answer is: "Learn as much as possible about the class of positions for which you've applied." The exam will test the knowledge, skills and abilities needed to do the work.

Your most valuable source of information about the position you want is the official exam announcement. This announcement lists the training and experience qualifications. Check these standards and apply only if you come reasonably close to meeting them.

The brief description of the position in the examination announcement offers some clues to the subjects which will be tested. Think about the job itself. Review the duties in your mind. Can you perform them, or are there some in which you are rusty? Fill in the blank spots in your preparation.

Many jurisdictions preview the written test in the exam announcement by including a section called "Knowledge and Abilities Required," "Scope of the Examination," or some similar heading. Here you will find out specifically what fields will be tested.

2) Review your own background

Once you learn in general what the position is all about, and what you need to know to do the work, ask yourself which subjects you already know fairly well and which need improvement. You may wonder whether to concentrate on improving your strong areas or on building some background in your fields of weakness. When the announcement has specified "some knowledge" or "considerable knowledge," or has used adjectives like "beginning principles of..." or "advanced ... methods," you can get a clue as to the number and difficulty of questions to be asked in any given field. More questions, and hence broader coverage, would be included for those subjects which are more important in the work. Now weigh your strengths and weaknesses against the job requirements and prepare accordingly.

3) **Determine the level of the position**

Another way to tell how intensively you should prepare is to understand the level of the job for which you are applying. Is it the entering level? In other words, is this the position in which beginners in a field of work are hired? Or is it an intermediate or advanced level? Sometimes this is indicated by such words as "Junior" or "Senior" in the class title. Other jurisdictions use Roman numerals to designate the level – Clerk I, Clerk II, for example. The word "Supervisor" sometimes appears in the title. If the level is not indicated by the title, check the description of duties. Will you be working under very close supervision, or will you have responsibility for independent decisions in this work?

4) **Choose appropriate study materials**

Now that you know the subjects to be examined and the relative amount of each subject to be covered, you can choose suitable study materials. For beginning level jobs, or even advanced ones, if you have a pronounced weakness in some aspect of your training, read a modern, standard textbook in that field. Be sure it is up to date and has general coverage. Such books are normally available at your library, and the librarian will be glad to help you locate one. For entry-level positions, questions of appropriate difficulty are chosen – neither highly advanced questions, nor those too simple. Such questions require careful thought but not advanced training.

If the position for which you are applying is technical or advanced, you will read more advanced, specialized material. If you are already familiar with the basic principles of your field, elementary textbooks would waste your time. Concentrate on advanced textbooks and technical periodicals. Think through the concepts and review difficult problems in your field.

These are all general sources. You can get more ideas on your own initiative, following these leads. For example, training manuals and publications of the government agency which employs workers in your field can be useful, particularly for technical and professional positions. A letter or visit to the government department involved may result in more specific study suggestions, and certainly will provide you with a more definite idea of the exact nature of the position you are seeking.

III. KINDS OF TESTS

Tests are used for purposes other than measuring knowledge and ability to perform specified duties. For some positions, it is equally important to test ability to make adjustments to new situations or to profit from training. In others, basic mental abilities not dependent on information are essential. Questions which test these things may not appear as pertinent to the duties of the position as those which test for knowledge and information. Yet they are often highly important parts of a fair examination. For very general questions, it is almost impossible to help you direct your study efforts. What we can do is to point out some of the more common of these general abilities needed in public service positions and describe some typical questions.

1) General information

Broad, general information has been found useful for predicting job success in some kinds of work. This is tested in a variety of ways, from vocabulary lists to questions about current events. Basic background in some field of work, such as sociology or economics, may be sampled in a group of questions. Often these are principles which have become familiar to most persons through exposure rather than through formal training. It is difficult to advise you how to study for these questions; being alert to the world around you is our best suggestion.

2) Verbal ability

An example of an ability needed in many positions is verbal or language ability. Verbal ability is, in brief, the ability to use and understand words. Vocabulary and grammar tests are typical measures of this ability. Reading comprehension or paragraph interpretation questions are common in many kinds of civil service tests. You are given a paragraph of written material and asked to find its central meaning.

3) Numerical ability

Number skills can be tested by the familiar arithmetic problem, by checking paired lists of numbers to see which are alike and which are different, or by interpreting charts and graphs. In the latter test, a graph may be printed in the test booklet which you are asked to use as the basis for answering questions.

4) Observation

A popular test for law-enforcement positions is the observation test. A picture is shown to you for several minutes, then taken away. Questions about the picture test your ability to observe both details and larger elements.

5) Following directions

In many positions in the public service, the employee must be able to carry out written instructions dependably and accurately. You may be given a chart with several columns, each column listing a variety of information. The questions require you to carry out directions involving the information given in the chart.

6) Skills and aptitudes

Performance tests effectively measure some manual skills and aptitudes. When the skill is one in which you are trained, such as typing or shorthand, you can practice. These tests are often very much like those given in business school or high school courses. For many of the other skills and aptitudes, however, no short-time preparation can be made. Skills and abilities natural to you or that you have developed throughout your lifetime are being tested.

Many of the general questions just described provide all the data needed to answer the questions and ask you to use your reasoning ability to find the answers. Your best preparation for these tests, as well as for tests of facts and ideas, is to be at your physical and mental best. You, no doubt, have your own methods of getting into an exam-taking mood and keeping "in shape." The next section lists some ideas on this subject.

IV. KINDS OF QUESTIONS

Only rarely is the "essay" question, which you answer in narrative form, used in civil service tests. Civil service tests are usually of the short-answer type. Full instructions for answering these questions will be given to you at the examination. But in case this is your first experience with short-answer questions and separate answer sheets, here is what you need to know:

1) Multiple-choice Questions

Most popular of the short-answer questions is the "multiple choice" or "best answer" question. It can be used, for example, to test for factual knowledge, ability to solve problems or judgment in meeting situations found at work.

A multiple-choice question is normally one of three types—

- It can begin with an incomplete statement followed by several possible endings. You are to find the one ending which *best* completes the statement, although some of the others may not be entirely wrong.
- It can also be a complete statement in the form of a question which is answered by choosing one of the statements listed.
- It can be in the form of a problem – again you select the best answer.

Here is an example of a multiple-choice question with a discussion which should give you some clues as to the method for choosing the right answer:

When an employee has a complaint about his assignment, the action which will *best* help him overcome his difficulty is to
A. discuss his difficulty with his coworkers
B. take the problem to the head of the organization
C. take the problem to the person who gave him the assignment
D. say nothing to anyone about his complaint

In answering this question, you should study each of the choices to find which is best. Consider choice "A" – Certainly an employee may discuss his complaint with fellow employees, but no change or improvement can result, and the complaint remains unresolved. Choice "B" is a poor choice since the head of the organization probably does not know what assignment you have been given, and taking your problem to him is known as "going over the head" of the supervisor. The supervisor, or person who made the assignment, is the person who can clarify it or correct any injustice. Choice "C" is, therefore, correct. To say nothing, as in choice "D," is unwise. Supervisors have and interest in knowing the problems employees are facing, and the employee is seeking a solution to his problem.

2) True/False Questions

The "true/false" or "right/wrong" form of question is sometimes used. Here a complete statement is given. Your job is to decide whether the statement is right or wrong.

SAMPLE: A roaming cell-phone call to a nearby city costs less than a non-roaming call to a distant city.

This statement is wrong, or false, since roaming calls are more expensive.

This is not a complete list of all possible question forms, although most of the others are variations of these common types. You will always get complete directions for answering questions. Be sure you understand *how* to mark your answers – ask questions until you do.

V. RECORDING YOUR ANSWERS

Computer terminals are used more and more today for many different kinds of exams.

For an examination with very few applicants, you may be told to record your answers in the test booklet itself. Separate answer sheets are much more common. If this separate answer sheet is to be scored by machine – and this is often the case – it is highly important that you mark your answers correctly in order to get credit.

An electronic scoring machine is often used in civil service offices because of the speed with which papers can be scored. Machine-scored answer sheets must be marked with a pencil, which will be given to you. This pencil has a high graphite content which responds to the electronic scoring machine. As a matter of fact, stray dots may register as answers, so do not let your pencil rest on the answer sheet while you are pondering the correct answer. Also, if your pencil lead breaks or is otherwise defective, ask for another.

Since the answer sheet will be dropped in a slot in the scoring machine, be careful not to bend the corners or get the paper crumpled.

The answer sheet normally has five vertical columns of numbers, with 30 numbers to a column. These numbers correspond to the question numbers in your test booklet. After each number, going across the page are four or five pairs of dotted lines. These short dotted lines have small letters or numbers above them. The first two pairs may also have a "T" or "F" above the letters. This indicates that the first two pairs only are to be used if the questions are of the true-false type. If the questions are multiple choice, disregard the "T" and "F" and pay attention only to the small letters or numbers.

Answer your questions in the manner of the sample that follows:

32. The largest city in the United States is
    A. Washington, D.C.
    B. New York City
    C. Chicago
    D. Detroit
    E. San Francisco

1) Choose the answer you think is best. (New York City is the largest, so "B" is correct.)
2) Find the row of dotted lines numbered the same as the question you are answering. (Find row number 32)
3) Find the pair of dotted lines corresponding to the answer. (Find the pair of lines under the mark "B.")
4) Make a solid black mark between the dotted lines.

VI. BEFORE THE TEST

Common sense will help you find procedures to follow to get ready for an examination. Too many of us, however, overlook these sensible measures. Indeed, nervousness and fatigue have been found to be the most serious reasons why applicants fail to do their best on civil service tests. Here is a list of reminders:

- Begin your preparation early – Don't wait until the last minute to go scurrying around for books and materials or to find out what the position is all about.
- Prepare continuously – An hour a night for a week is better than an all-night cram session. This has been definitely established. What is more, a night a week for a month will return better dividends than crowding your study into a shorter period of time.
- Locate the place of the exam – You have been sent a notice telling you when and where to report for the examination. If the location is in a different town or otherwise unfamiliar to you, it would be well to inquire the best route and learn something about the building.
- Relax the night before the test – Allow your mind to rest. Do not study at all that night. Plan some mild recreation or diversion; then go to bed early and get a good night's sleep.
- Get up early enough to make a leisurely trip to the place for the test – This way unforeseen events, traffic snarls, unfamiliar buildings, etc. will not upset you.
- Dress comfortably – A written test is not a fashion show. You will be known by number and not by name, so wear something comfortable.
- Leave excess paraphernalia at home – Shopping bags and odd bundles will get in your way. You need bring only the items mentioned in the official notice you received; usually everything you need is provided. Do not bring reference books to the exam. They will only confuse those last minutes and be taken away from you when in the test room.
- Arrive somewhat ahead of time – If because of transportation schedules you must get there very early, bring a newspaper or magazine to take your mind off yourself while waiting.
- Locate the examination room – When you have found the proper room, you will be directed to the seat or part of the room where you will sit. Sometimes you are given a sheet of instructions to read while you are waiting. Do not fill out any forms until you are told to do so; just read them and be prepared.
- Relax and prepare to listen to the instructions
- If you have any physical problem that may keep you from doing your best, be sure to tell the test administrator. If you are sick or in poor health, you really cannot do your best on the exam. You can come back and take the test some other time.

VII. AT THE TEST

The day of the test is here and you have the test booklet in your hand. The temptation to get going is very strong. Caution! There is more to success than knowing the right answers. You must know how to identify your papers and understand variations in the type of short-answer question used in this particular examination. Follow these suggestions for maximum results from your efforts:

1) Cooperate with the monitor

The test administrator has a duty to create a situation in which you can be as much at ease as possible. He will give instructions, tell you when to begin, check to see that you are marking your answer sheet correctly, and so on. He is not there to guard you, although he will see that your competitors do not take unfair advantage. He wants to help you do your best.

2) Listen to all instructions

Don't jump the gun! Wait until you understand all directions. In most civil service tests you get more time than you need to answer the questions. So don't be in a hurry. Read each word of instructions until you clearly understand the meaning. Study the examples, listen to all announcements and follow directions. Ask questions if you do not understand what to do.

3) Identify your papers

Civil service exams are usually identified by number only. You will be assigned a number; you must not put your name on your test papers. Be sure to copy your number correctly. Since more than one exam may be given, copy your exact examination title.

4) Plan your time

Unless you are told that a test is a "speed" or "rate of work" test, speed itself is usually not important. Time enough to answer all the questions will be provided, but this does not mean that you have all day. An overall time limit has been set. Divide the total time (in minutes) by the number of questions to determine the approximate time you have for each question.

5) Do not linger over difficult questions

If you come across a difficult question, mark it with a paper clip (useful to have along) and come back to it when you have been through the booklet. One caution if you do this – be sure to skip a number on your answer sheet as well. Check often to be sure that you have not lost your place and that you are marking in the row numbered the same as the question you are answering.

6) Read the questions

Be sure you know what the question asks! Many capable people are unsuccessful because they failed to *read* the questions correctly.

7) Answer all questions

Unless you have been instructed that a penalty will be deducted for incorrect answers, it is better to guess than to omit a question.

8) Speed tests

It is often better NOT to guess on speed tests. It has been found that on timed tests people are tempted to spend the last few seconds before time is called in marking answers at random – without even reading them – in the hope of picking up a few extra points. To discourage this practice, the instructions may warn you that your score will be "corrected" for guessing. That is, a penalty will be applied. The incorrect answers will be deducted from the correct ones, or some other penalty formula will be used.

9) Review your answers

If you finish before time is called, go back to the questions you guessed or omitted to give them further thought. Review other answers if you have time.

10) Return your test materials

If you are ready to leave before others have finished or time is called, take ALL your materials to the monitor and leave quietly. Never take any test material with you. The monitor can discover whose papers are not complete, and taking a test booklet may be grounds for disqualification.

VIII. EXAMINATION TECHNIQUES

1) Read the general instructions carefully. These are usually printed on the first page of the exam booklet. As a rule, these instructions refer to the timing of the examination; the fact that you should not start work until the signal and must stop work at a signal, etc. If there are any *special* instructions, such as a choice of questions to be answered, make sure that you note this instruction carefully.

2) When you are ready to start work on the examination, that is as soon as the signal has been given, read the instructions to each question booklet, underline any key words or phrases, such as *least, best, outline, describe* and the like. In this way you will tend to answer as requested rather than discover on reviewing your paper that you *listed without describing*, that you selected the *worst* choice rather than the *best* choice, etc.

3) If the examination is of the objective or multiple-choice type – that is, each question will also give a series of possible answers: A, B, C or D, and you are called upon to select the best answer and write the letter next to that answer on your answer paper – it is advisable to start answering each question in turn. There may be anywhere from 50 to 100 such questions in the three or four hours allotted and you can see how much time would be taken if you read through all the questions before beginning to answer any. Furthermore, if you come across a question or group of questions which you know would be difficult to answer, it would undoubtedly affect your handling of all the other questions.

4) If the examination is of the essay type and contains but a few questions, it is a moot point as to whether you should read all the questions before starting to answer any one. Of course, if you are given a choice – say five out of seven and the like – then it is essential to read all the questions so you can eliminate the two that are most difficult. If, however, you are asked to answer all the questions, there may be danger in trying to answer the easiest one first because you may find that you will spend too much time on it. The best technique is to answer the first question, then proceed to the second, etc.

5) Time your answers. Before the exam begins, write down the time it started, then add the time allowed for the examination and write down the time it must be completed, then divide the time available somewhat as follows:

- If 3-1/2 hours are allowed, that would be 210 minutes. If you have 80 objective-type questions, that would be an average of 2-1/2 minutes per question. Allow yourself no more than 2 minutes per question, or a total of 160 minutes, which will permit about 50 minutes to review.
- If for the time allotment of 210 minutes there are 7 essay questions to answer, that would average about 30 minutes a question. Give yourself only 25 minutes per question so that you have about 35 minutes to review.

6) The most important instruction is to *read each question* and make sure you know what is wanted. The second most important instruction is to *time yourself properly* so that you answer every question. The third most important instruction is to *answer every question*. Guess if you have to but include something for each question. Remember that you will receive no credit for a blank and will probably receive some credit if you write something in answer to an essay question. If you guess a letter – say "B" for a multiple-choice question – you may have guessed right. If you leave a blank as an answer to a multiple-choice question, the examiners may respect your feelings but it will not add a point to your score. Some exams may penalize you for wrong answers, so in such cases *only*, you may not want to guess unless you have some basis for your answer.

7) Suggestions
   a. Objective-type questions
      1. Examine the question booklet for proper sequence of pages and questions
      2. Read all instructions carefully
      3. Skip any question which seems too difficult; return to it after all other questions have been answered
      4. Apportion your time properly; do not spend too much time on any single question or group of questions
      5. Note and underline key words – *all, most, fewest, least, best, worst, same, opposite,* etc.
      6. Pay particular attention to negatives
      7. Note unusual option, e.g., unduly long, short, complex, different or similar in content to the body of the question
      8. Observe the use of "hedging" words – *probably, may, most likely,* etc.
      9. Make sure that your answer is put next to the same number as the question
      10. Do not second-guess unless you have good reason to believe the second answer is definitely more correct
      11. Cross out original answer if you decide another answer is more accurate; do not erase until you are ready to hand your paper in
      12. Answer all questions; guess unless instructed otherwise
      13. Leave time for review

   b. Essay questions
      1. Read each question carefully
      2. Determine exactly what is wanted. Underline key words or phrases.
      3. Decide on outline or paragraph answer

    4. Include many different points and elements unless asked to develop any one or two points or elements
    5. Show impartiality by giving pros and cons unless directed to select one side only
    6. Make and write down any assumptions you find necessary to answer the questions
    7. Watch your English, grammar, punctuation and choice of words
    8. Time your answers; don't crowd material

8) Answering the essay question

Most essay questions can be answered by framing the specific response around several key words or ideas. Here are a few such key words or ideas:

M's: manpower, materials, methods, money, management
P's: purpose, program, policy, plan, procedure, practice, problems, pitfalls, personnel, public relations

    a. Six basic steps in handling problems:
        1. Preliminary plan and background development
        2. Collect information, data and facts
        3. Analyze and interpret information, data and facts
        4. Analyze and develop solutions as well as make recommendations
        5. Prepare report and sell recommendations
        6. Install recommendations and follow up effectiveness

    b. Pitfalls to avoid
        1. *Taking things for granted* – A statement of the situation does not necessarily imply that each of the elements is necessarily true; for example, a complaint may be invalid and biased so that all that can be taken for granted is that a complaint has been registered
        2. *Considering only one side of a situation* – Wherever possible, indicate several alternatives and then point out the reasons you selected the best one
        3. *Failing to indicate follow up* – Whenever your answer indicates action on your part, make certain that you will take proper follow-up action to see how successful your recommendations, procedures or actions turn out to be
        4. *Taking too long in answering any single question* – Remember to time your answers properly

IX. AFTER THE TEST

Scoring procedures differ in detail among civil service jurisdictions although the general principles are the same. Whether the papers are hand-scored or graded by machine we have described, they are nearly always graded by number. That is, the person who marks the paper knows only the number – never the name – of the applicant. Not until all the papers have been graded will they be matched with names. If other tests, such as training and experience or oral interview ratings have been given, scores will be combined. Different parts of the examination usually have different weights. For example, the written test might count 60 percent of the final grade, and a rating of training and experience 40 percent. In many jurisdictions, veterans will have a certain number of points added to their grades.

After the final grade has been determined, the names are placed in grade order and an eligible list is established. There are various methods for resolving ties between those who get the same final grade – probably the most common is to place first the name of the person whose application was received first. Job offers are made from the eligible list in the order the names appear on it. You will be notified of your grade and your rank as soon as all these computations have been made. This will be done as rapidly as possible.

People who are found to meet the requirements in the announcement are called "eligibles." Their names are put on a list of eligible candidates. An eligible's chances of getting a job depend on how high he stands on this list and how fast agencies are filling jobs from the list.

When a job is to be filled from a list of eligibles, the agency asks for the names of people on the list of eligibles for that job. When the civil service commission receives this request, it sends to the agency the names of the three people highest on this list. Or, if the job to be filled has specialized requirements, the office sends the agency the names of the top three persons who meet these requirements from the general list.

The appointing officer makes a choice from among the three people whose names were sent to him. If the selected person accepts the appointment, the names of the others are put back on the list to be considered for future openings.

That is the rule in hiring from all kinds of eligible lists, whether they are for typist, carpenter, chemist, or something else. For every vacancy, the appointing officer has his choice of any one of the top three eligibles on the list. This explains why the person whose name is on top of the list sometimes does not get an appointment when some of the persons lower on the list do. If the appointing officer chooses the second or third eligible, the No. 1 eligible does not get a job at once, but stays on the list until he is appointed or the list is terminated.

X. HOW TO PASS THE INTERVIEW TEST

The examination for which you applied requires an oral interview test. You have already taken the written test and you are now being called for the interview test – the final part of the formal examination.

You may think that it is not possible to prepare for an interview test and that there are no procedures to follow during an interview. Our purpose is to point out some things you can do in advance that will help you and some good rules to follow and pitfalls to avoid while you are being interviewed.

What is an interview supposed to test?
The written examination is designed to test the technical knowledge and competence of the candidate; the oral is designed to evaluate intangible qualities, not readily measured otherwise, and to establish a list showing the relative fitness of each candidate – as measured against his competitors – for the position sought. Scoring is not on the basis of "right" and "wrong," but on a sliding scale of values ranging from "not passable" to "outstanding." As a matter of fact, it is possible to achieve a relatively low score without a single "incorrect" answer because of evident weakness in the qualities being measured.

Occasionally, an examination may consist entirely of an oral test – either an individual or a group oral. In such cases, information is sought concerning the technical knowledges and abilities of the candidate, since there has been no written examination for this purpose. More commonly, however, an oral test is used to supplement a written examination.

Who conducts interviews?

The composition of oral boards varies among different jurisdictions. In nearly all, a representative of the personnel department serves as chairman. One of the members of the board may be a representative of the department in which the candidate would work. In some cases, "outside experts" are used, and, frequently, a businessman or some other representative of the general public is asked to serve. Labor and management or other special groups may be represented. The aim is to secure the services of experts in the appropriate field.

However the board is composed, it is a good idea (and not at all improper or unethical) to ascertain in advance of the interview who the members are and what groups they represent. When you are introduced to them, you will have some idea of their backgrounds and interests, and at least you will not stutter and stammer over their names.

What should be done before the interview?

While knowledge about the board members is useful and takes some of the surprise element out of the interview, there is other preparation which is more substantive. It *is* possible to prepare for an oral interview – in several ways:

1) Keep a copy of your application and review it carefully before the interview

This may be the only document before the oral board, and the starting point of the interview. Know what education and experience you have listed there, and the sequence and dates of all of it. Sometimes the board will ask you to review the highlights of your experience for them; you should not have to hem and haw doing it.

2) Study the class specification and the examination announcement

Usually, the oral board has one or both of these to guide them. The qualities, characteristics or knowledges required by the position sought are stated in these documents. They offer valuable clues as to the nature of the oral interview. For example, if the job involves supervisory responsibilities, the announcement will usually indicate that knowledge of modern supervisory methods and the qualifications of the candidate as a supervisor will be tested. If so, you can expect such questions, frequently in the form of a hypothetical situation which you are expected to solve. NEVER go into an oral without knowledge of the duties and responsibilities of the job you seek.

3) Think through each qualification required

Try to visualize the kind of questions you would ask if you were a board member. How well could you answer them? Try especially to appraise your own knowledge and background in each area, *measured against the job sought*, and identify any areas in which you are weak. Be critical and realistic – do not flatter yourself.

4) Do some general reading in areas in which you feel you may be weak

For example, if the job involves supervision and your past experience has NOT, some general reading in supervisory methods and practices, particularly in the field of human relations, might be useful. Do NOT study agency procedures or detailed manuals. The oral board will be testing your understanding and capacity, not your memory.

5) Get a good night's sleep and watch your general health and mental attitude

You will want a clear head at the interview. Take care of a cold or any other minor ailment, and of course, no hangovers.

What should be done on the day of the interview?

Now comes the day of the interview itself. Give yourself plenty of time to get there. Plan to arrive somewhat ahead of the scheduled time, particularly if your appointment is in the fore part of the day. If a previous candidate fails to appear, the board might be ready for you a bit early. By early afternoon an oral board is almost invariably behind schedule if there are many candidates, and you may have to wait. Take along a book or magazine to read, or your application to review, but leave any extraneous material in the waiting room when you go in for your interview. In any event, relax and compose yourself.

The matter of dress is important. The board is forming impressions about you – from your experience, your manners, your attitude, and your appearance. Give your personal appearance careful attention. Dress your best, but not your flashiest. Choose conservative, appropriate clothing, and be sure it is immaculate. This is a business interview, and your appearance should indicate that you regard it as such. Besides, being well groomed and properly dressed will help boost your confidence.

Sooner or later, someone will call your name and escort you into the interview room. *This is it.* From here on you are on your own. It is too late for any more preparation. But remember, you asked for this opportunity to prove your fitness, and you are here because your request was granted.

What happens when you go in?

The usual sequence of events will be as follows: The clerk (who is often the board stenographer) will introduce you to the chairman of the oral board, who will introduce you to the other members of the board. Acknowledge the introductions before you sit down. Do not be surprised if you find a microphone facing you or a stenotypist sitting by. Oral interviews are usually recorded in the event of an appeal or other review.

Usually the chairman of the board will open the interview by reviewing the highlights of your education and work experience from your application – primarily for the benefit of the other members of the board, as well as to get the material into the record. Do not interrupt or comment unless there is an error or significant misinterpretation; if that is the case, do not hesitate. But do not quibble about insignificant matters. Also, he will usually ask you some question about your education, experience or your present job – partly to get you to start talking and to establish the interviewing "rapport." He may start the actual questioning, or turn it over to one of the other members. Frequently, each member undertakes the questioning on a particular area, one in which he is perhaps most competent, so you can expect each member to participate in the examination. Because time is limited, you may also expect some rather abrupt switches in the direction the questioning takes, so do not be upset by it. Normally, a board member will not pursue a single line of questioning unless he discovers a particular strength or weakness.

After each member has participated, the chairman will usually ask whether any member has any further questions, then will ask you if you have anything you wish to add. Unless you are expecting this question, it may floor you. Worse, it may start you off on an extended, extemporaneous speech. The board is not usually seeking more information. The question is principally to offer you a last opportunity to present further qualifications or to indicate that you have nothing to add. So, if you feel that a significant qualification or characteristic has been overlooked, it is proper to point it out in a sentence or so. Do not compliment the board on the thoroughness of their examination – they have been sketchy, and you know it. If you wish, merely say, "No thank you, I have nothing further to add." This is a point where you can "talk yourself out" of a good impression or fail to present an important bit of information. Remember, *you close the interview yourself.*

The chairman will then say, "That is all, Mr. _____, thank you." Do not be startled; the interview is over, and quicker than you think. Thank him, gather your belongings and take your leave. Save your sigh of relief for the other side of the door.

How to put your best foot forward

Throughout this entire process, you may feel that the board individually and collectively is trying to pierce your defenses, seek out your hidden weaknesses and embarrass and confuse you. Actually, this is not true. They are obliged to make an appraisal of your qualifications for the job you are seeking, and they want to see you in your best light. Remember, they must interview all candidates and a non-cooperative candidate may become a failure in spite of their best efforts to bring out his qualifications. Here are 15 suggestions that will help you:

1) Be natural – Keep your attitude confident, not cocky

If you are not confident that you can do the job, do not expect the board to be. Do not apologize for your weaknesses, try to bring out your strong points. The board is interested in a positive, not negative, presentation. Cockiness will antagonize any board member and make him wonder if you are covering up a weakness by a false show of strength.

2) Get comfortable, but don't lounge or sprawl

Sit erectly but not stiffly. A careless posture may lead the board to conclude that you are careless in other things, or at least that you are not impressed by the importance of the occasion. Either conclusion is natural, even if incorrect. Do not fuss with your clothing, a pencil or an ashtray. Your hands may occasionally be useful to emphasize a point; do not let them become a point of distraction.

3) Do not wisecrack or make small talk

This is a serious situation, and your attitude should show that you consider it as such. Further, the time of the board is limited – they do not want to waste it, and neither should you.

4) Do not exaggerate your experience or abilities

In the first place, from information in the application or other interviews and sources, the board may know more about you than you think. Secondly, you probably will not get away with it. An experienced board is rather adept at spotting such a situation, so do not take the chance.

5) If you know a board member, do not make a point of it, yet do not hide it

Certainly you are not fooling him, and probably not the other members of the board. Do not try to take advantage of your acquaintanceship – it will probably do you little good.

6) Do not dominate the interview

Let the board do that. They will give you the clues – do not assume that you have to do all the talking. Realize that the board has a number of questions to ask you, and do not try to take up all the interview time by showing off your extensive knowledge of the answer to the first one.

7) Be attentive

You only have 20 minutes or so, and you should keep your attention at its sharpest throughout. When a member is addressing a problem or question to you, give him your undivided attention. Address your reply principally to him, but do not exclude the other board members.

8) Do not interrupt

A board member may be stating a problem for you to analyze. He will ask you a question when the time comes. Let him state the problem, and wait for the question.

9) Make sure you understand the question

Do not try to answer until you are sure what the question is. If it is not clear, restate it in your own words or ask the board member to clarify it for you. However, do not haggle about minor elements.

10) Reply promptly but not hastily

A common entry on oral board rating sheets is "candidate responded readily," or "candidate hesitated in replies." Respond as promptly and quickly as you can, but do not jump to a hasty, ill-considered answer.

11) Do not be peremptory in your answers

A brief answer is proper – but do not fire your answer back. That is a losing game from your point of view. The board member can probably ask questions much faster than you can answer them.

12) Do not try to create the answer you think the board member wants

He is interested in what kind of mind you have and how it works – not in playing games. Furthermore, he can usually spot this practice and will actually grade you down on it.

13) Do not switch sides in your reply merely to agree with a board member

Frequently, a member will take a contrary position merely to draw you out and to see if you are willing and able to defend your point of view. Do not start a debate, yet do not surrender a good position. If a position is worth taking, it is worth defending.

14) Do not be afraid to admit an error in judgment if you are shown to be wrong

The board knows that you are forced to reply without any opportunity for careful consideration. Your answer may be demonstrably wrong. If so, admit it and get on with the interview.

15) Do not dwell at length on your present job

The opening question may relate to your present assignment. Answer the question but do not go into an extended discussion. You are being examined for a *new* job, not your present one. As a matter of fact, try to phrase ALL your answers in terms of the job for which you are being examined.

Basis of Rating

Probably you will forget most of these "do's" and "don'ts" when you walk into the oral interview room. Even remembering them all will not ensure you a passing grade. Perhaps you did not have the qualifications in the first place. But remembering them will help you to put your best foot forward, without treading on the toes of the board members.

Rumor and popular opinion to the contrary notwithstanding, an oral board wants you to make the best appearance possible. They know you are under pressure – but they also want to see how you respond to it as a guide to what your reaction would be under the pressures of the job you seek. They will be influenced by the degree of poise you display, the personal traits you show and the manner in which you respond.

ABOUT THIS BOOK

This book contains tests divided into Examination Sections. Go through each test, answering every question in the margin. At the end of each test look at the answer key and check your answers. On the ones you got wrong, look at the right answer choice and learn. Do not fill in the answers first. Do not memorize the questions and answers, but understand the answer and principles involved. On your test, the questions will likely be different from the samples. Questions are changed and new ones added. If you understand these past questions you should have success with any changes that arise. Tests may consist of several types of questions. We have additional books on each subject should more study be advisable or necessary for you. Finally, the more you study, the better prepared you will be. This book is intended to be the last thing you study before you walk into the examination room. Prior study of relevant texts is also recommended. NLC publishes some of these in our Fundamental Series. Knowledge and good sense are important factors in passing your exam. Good luck also helps. So now study this Passbook, absorb the material contained within and take that knowledge into the examination. Then do your best to pass that exam.

———

EXAMINATION SECTION

EXAMINATION SECTION
TEST 1

DIRECTIONS: Each question or incomplete statement is followed by several suggested answers or completions. Select the one that BEST answers the question or completes the statement. *PRINT THE LETTER OF THE CORRECT ANSWER IN THE SPACE AT THE RIGHT.*

1. Any surface of an aircraft, movable or fixed, that is designed to aid in the craft's maneu-verability through its position relative to passing air is known as a(n)

   A. spoiler   B. flap   C. air foil   D. aileron

1____

2. The FAA requires that an emergency evacuation of an aircraft be accomplished in _____ or less, regardless of the size of the aircraft or the number of people on board.

   A. 1 minute   B. 90 seconds
   C. 3 minutes   D. 5 minutes

2____

3. Once a cabin decompression begins, it takes approximately _____ seconds for the greater pressure on the inside of the aircraft to become equalized with the lesser outside pressure.

   A. 5   B. 15   C. 30   D. 60

3____

4. Which of the following is NOT a typical difference between galleys on wide-bodied and narrow-bodied aircraft?

   A. Location of buffets
   B. Countertop work services
   C. Means of boarding food items
   D. Means of refrigeration

4____

5. In 12 hours, 30 minutes, a plane travels 500 miles. What is its average speed, in miles per hour?

   A. 150   B. 200   C. 250   D. 300

5____

6. Jet escape doors are

   A. continually disarmed
   B. used only for emergency purposes
   C. designed to open inward
   D. only used with 727 aircraft

6____

7. For each cabin occupied by through passengers during a stopover, there must be at least _____ flight attendant(s) present.

   A. 1
   B. 2
   C. 3
   D. There is no legal requirement

7____

8. Another term for jet lag is
8____

    A. malaise.
    C. lassitude

    B. dysrhythmia
    D. arrhythmia

9. Blind passengers accompanied by seeing-eye dogs are
9____

    A. typically seated in bulkhead rows
    B. separated from their dogs only throughout the duration of the flight
    C. typically seated in back rows
    D. not permitted on international flights

10. Guidelines concerning a flight attendant's uniform accessories typically include restrictions on each of the following EXCEPT
10____

    A. number   B. color   C. variety   D. size

11. According to FAA regulations, any flight with a passenger load of 50-100 must provide at least _____ flight attendant(s).
11____

    A. 1   B. 2   C. 3   D. 4

12. The airport coded MCI is located in
12____

    A. Kansas City, Missouri
    C. Miami, Florida

    B. Orlando, Florida
    D. Macon, Georgia

13. A passenger's portable first aid oxygen bottle typically contains enough oxygen to last for _____ of continuous use.
13____

    A. 10 minutes
    C. 1 hour

    B. 30 minutes
    D. 2 hours

14. What type of fire extinguisher is used only on Class A fires?
14____

    A. CO_2
    C. Helium

    B. Dry chemical
    D. Water

15. Which of the following is a flight's second officer?
15____

    A. Lead flight attendant
    C. Ground control chief

    B. Flight engineer
    D. Co-pilot

16. During training, flight attendant seniority is determined by
16____

    A. alphabetical listing
    B. birthdate or Social Security number
    C. random drawing
    D. order of enrollment

17. Which of the following is not a guideline for flight attendants in taking authorized meal breaks?
17____

    A. At least one flight attendant must remain in each cabin during a break.
    B. The captain should be notified that a break is being taken.
    C. The meal must be eaten only after all passengers have been served.
    D. The break must be taken out of sight of the passengers.

18. The MOST important item in a passenger's seat-back pocket is probably the   18____

    A. airsickness bag
    B. passenger safety briefing card
    C. route map
    D. flotation device

19. After inflight service has been completed, a flight attendant's FIRST responsibility is to   19____

    A. pick up food and beverage items from passenger tables
    B. clear countertops
    C. secure latches of carrier doors
    D. verify liquor accounting

20. What is the term for the work schedule that shows how trip sequences fall within a month?   20____

    A. Bid package   B. Information sheet
    C. Manifest   D. Line of flying

21. A passenger who displays the symptoms of asthma trouble should be kept in a ____ position.   21____

    A. supine   B. supine with legs elevated
    C. sitting   D. standing

22. Passengers who are transit aliens   22____

    A. must be seated in the last row of the aircraft
    B. are not to be served alcohol at any time
    C. must be accompanied by at least one armed guard
    D. are not allowed to deplane on stopovers

23. The MAIN body of an aircraft, excluding wings, tail and engines, is the   23____

    A. jetway   B. fuselage   C. belly   D. radome

24. A passenger's body temperature should be initially checked by neans of placing the _____ against the passenger's skin.   24____

    A. back of the hand   B. palm
    C. fingertips   D. backs of the fingers

25. What is the length of time between 9:13 A.M. and 3:43 P.M.?   25____

    A. 4 hours, 30 minutes   B. 5 hours, 40 minutes
    C. 6 hours, 30 minutes   D. 7 hours, 50 minutes

KEY (CORRECT ANSWERS)

1. C		11. B
2. B		12. A
3. A		13. C
4. D		14. D
5. B		15. B
6. B		16. B
7. A		17. B
8. B		18. B
9. A		19. A
10. C		20. D

21. C
22. D
23. B
24. D
25. C

TEST 2

DIRECTIONS: Each question or incomplete statement is followed by several suggested answers or completions. Select the one that BEST answers the question or completes the statement. *PRINT THE LETTER OF THE CORRECT ANSWER IN THE SPACE AT THE RIGHT.*

Questions 1-6.

DIRECTIONS: Questions 1 through 6 refer to the figure below, drawings representing different types of commercial airliners. Place the letter that corresponds to each airliner in the space at the right.

1. McDonnell Douglas DC-10

2. Boeing 747

3. Airbus A320

4. Boeing 727

5. McDonnell Douglas DC-9

6. Boeing 757

A

B

C

D

E

F

G

1____

2____

3____

4____

5____

6____

7. Typically, a flight attendant's minimum monthly flight hours on domestic flights range from   7____

    A. 40-65   B. 55-72   C. 67-74   D. 85-100

8. Typically, a flight attendant's minimum monthly flight hours on domestic flights range from   8____

    A. monthly duty hours
    B. next scheduled outbound trip
    C. number of hours flown
    D. distance between hotel and airport

9. Each of the following is a factor that typically determines the number of hours a flight attendant needs for legal rest EXCEPT   9____

    A. 11:00 A.M.   B. 1:00 P.M.
    C. 3:00 P.M.   D. 5:00 P.M.

10. Another term for an aircraft's tail assembly is   10____

    A. rudder   B. empennage
    C. stabilizer   D. radome

11. When there is an excess of air in a person's lungs, and a loss of carbon dioxide in the blood, _____ may occur.   11____

    A. hyperventilation   B. hypoglycemia
    C. hypothermia   D. hypoxia

12. The ideal method for serving a hot drink to a passenger is to   12____

    A. put the cup on a serving tray, bring the tray close for pouring, and return the full cup to the passenger
    B. reach across and pour directly into the cup on the passenger's tray
    C. hand the pitcher over and allow the passenger to fill his or her own cup
    D. pour the drink into the cup and hand the cup to the passenger

13. Under normal circumstances, a flight attendant may not be scheduled for more than _____ domestic duty hours within a 24-hour period.   13____

    A. 8-10   B. 10-14   C. 14-16   D. 16-20

14. Each of the following is a symptom of jet lag EXCEPT   14____

    A. eye sensitivity
    B. flushed face
    C. dehydration
    D. feeling of sluggishness and discomfort

15. What is the term for the act of positioning an emergency slide or exit in the emergency-ready mode?   15____

    A. Tying the lanyard   B. Arming
    C. Fortifying   D. Girting

16. On a 24-hour clock, the time 1:25 P.M. would appear as   16____

    A. 0125   B. 1025   C. 1325   D. 1725

17. During flight, a cabin pressure leak can usually be identified by a(n)　　　　17____

    A.   area of remarkably lower temperature
    B.   high-pitched whistling sound coming from a door or window frame
    C.   sudden rush of a large volume of air
    D.   drafty area near a door or window

18. A passenger is entitled to a specially-requested meal if the request is given _____ in 18____
advance of the flight.

    A. 4   B. 8   C. 12   D. 24

19. When conducting aisle checks during flight, a flight attendant should always 19____

    A.   focus on passengers who have pressed a call button
    B.   move from the front of the plane to the back
    C.   insist that seat belts be fastened
    D.   address passengers by name

20. When lifting heavy objects during inflight service, a flight attendant should 20____

    A.   use flexed knees and leg muscles as support
    B.   use a rigid piece of equipment as a lever
    C.   bend over at the waist and lift with the back muscles
    D.   enlist the help of an able-bodied passenger

21. Which of the following is NOT a guideline to follow for inflight wine service? 21____

    A.   Red wine should be chilled.
    B.   First-class wines should be boarded in fifths and poured for the passenger at his/
        her seat.
    C.   White wine should be chilled.
    D.   *Splits* sold in coach should be handed to the passenger along with the glass.

22. A flight attendant's area of safety responsibility is usually 22____

    A.   assigned in zones before takeoff by the lead flight attendant
    B.   the area near and around the assigned jump seat
    C.   divided by emergency exit rows and bulkheads
    D.   up to ten rows of passenger seats

23. To an observer onboard an airplane facing forward, an *A* seat would be 23____

    A.   immediately adjacent to the right side window
    B.   immediately adjacent to the left side window
    C.   on the right side immediately adjacent to the aisle
    D.   on the left side immediately adjacent to the aisle

24. In preparation for an emergency evacuation, a flight attendant's first instruction to pas- 24____
sengers should be to

    A.   remove and stow shoes
    B.   assume the protective landing position
    C.   loosen restrictive clothing
    D.   remove the safety information card from the seat pocket

25. The downward-acting force on a plane in flight is   25____

    A. thrust   B. weight

    C. compression   D. drag

KEY (CORRECT ANSWERS)

1. C		11. A	
2. F		12. A	
3. G		13. B	
4. D		14. B	
5. A		15. B	
6. E		16. C	
7. B		17. B	
8. A		18. D	
9. B		19. B	
10. B		20. A	

21. A	
22. B	
23. B	
24. D	
25. B	

TEST 3

DIRECTIONS: Each question or incomplete statement is followed by several suggested answers or completions. Select the one that BEST answers the question or completes the statement. *PRINT THE LETTER OF THE CORRECT ANSWER IN THE SPACE AT THE RIGHT.*

1. In preparing for inflight food and beverage service, a flight attendant's first task is to   1____

    A.   verify amount of liquor against accounting sheets
    B.   assemble and unwrap necessary supply packages
    C.   make the galley area ready for use
    D.   verify the correct number of meals and other items correlate with planned passenger load and caterer's checklist

2. The time beginning when the captain first releases the brakes leaving the gate until the   2____
time he sets the brakes at the arrival gate is known as _____ time.

    A.   duty   B.   block   C.   standard   D.   brake

3. Which of the following exhibited by a passenger during flight should NOT be received by   3____
a flight attendant as a warning signal of an emergency health situation?

    A.   Bluish skin tone
    B.   Dilated pupils
    C.   Pain or discomfort in the inner ear
    D.   Incoherence

4. A flight attendant's selection of work schedule is determined by his/her seniority   4____

    A.   at the base of operations
    B.   systemwide
    C.   with the company
    D.   in training

5. Mild turbulence is characterized by each of the following EXCEPT   5____

    A.   light choppiness
    B.   slight changes in attitude
    C.   bumpiness
    D.   changes in altitude

6. According to FAA regulations, recurrent ground training for flight attendants must consist   6____
of at least _____ hours of instruction in Group I reciprocating powered airplanes.

    A.   4   B.   5   C.   8   D.   12

7. A passenger complains of abdominal pain. The pain has begun intermittently, in a gener-   7____
alized area around the navel, and has moved to the right part of the abdomen. The pain
is not severe, but there is a fever present. Most likely, the passenger is experiencing

    A.   appendicitis   B.   stomach upset
    C.   menstrual cramps   D.   bowel obstruction

8. Typically, the number of oxygen masks housed above or in front of passenger's seats is   8____

   A. 3
   B. equal to the number of passengers seated in the row G. equal to the number of passengers seated in the rows
   C. in front and behind
   D. one more than the number of passengers seated in the row

9. In a 24-hour period, a flight attendant should not serve more than _____ international   9____
flight hours.

   A. 6-8   B. 8-10   C. 10-12   D. 12-14

10. Which of the following is NOT a typical cause of flight understaffing?   10____

   A. Increased passenger load
   B. Length of trip
   C. Equipment change
   D. Insufficient reserve pool

11. One flight from takeoff to landing, which may be only a portion of a complete flight   11____
sequence, is known as a

   A. branch   B. leg   C. fragment   D. member

12. The MOST essential part of a flight attendant's grooming begins with   12____

   A. good dental regimen
   B. appropriate use of fragrances
   C. maintenance of healthy skin
   D. general cleanliness

13. At the termination of a flight attendant's last flight for the day, duty time extends for   13____
approximately another _____ minutes before the flight attendant is released for legal
rest.

   A. 15   B. 30   C. 60   D. 90

14. During turbulence, a flight attendant may leave his or her seat   14____

   A. only if permission is obtained from the cockpit
   B. for the purpose of a planned evacuation
   C. to avoid an interruption in inflight services
   D. only if there is a medical emergency

15. Traveling by plane, a family departed San Francisco at 8:00 A.M. and arrived in New York   15____
City six hours later. What time was it in New York when they arrived?

   A. 11:00 A.M.   B. 4:00 P.M.
   C. 5:00 P.M.   D. 7:00 P.M.

16. A flight attendant's bid choices are typically due about _____ after the trip schedule   16____
posting.

   A. 8 hours   B. 24 hours
   C. 1 week   D. 2 weeks

17. Respiratory arrest occurs when a victim's   17____

    A. breathing has stopped and pulse has slowed
    B. breathing and heart action have stopped
    C. airway is partially obstructed
    D. breathing has stopped, but a pulse exists

18. _____ is the term for transport of a nonworking crew member on an airplane or ground   18____
transportation for the purpose of protecting or returning from a flight assignment .

    A. Deadhead   B. Deployment
    C. Dummy transport   D. Ferry flight

19. It is NOT an authority of the FAA to   19____

    A. develop and operate a common system of air navigation and air traffic control for
both civil and military aviation
    B. ensure service to smaller communities through payment of federal subsidies
    C. regulate airport safety
    D. sponsor aviation safety programs on a nationwide basis

20. The yaw of a plane is produced by the   20____

    A. elevators   B. rudder
    C. horizontal stabilizers   D. ailerons

21. White exterior lights on a plane are used to indicate each of the following EXCEPT   21____

    A. right and left outboard trailing edges of the horizontal stabilizers
    B. nose landing gear
    C. right and left outboard trailing edges of the wings
    D. lower flap surfaces

22. In a 7-day period, a flight attendant should not serve more than _____ flight hours on   22____
domestic flights.

    A. 24   B. 30   C. 40   D. 55

23. The delivery of an aircraft without passengers to a destination is known as a   23____

    A. pass flight   B. milk run
    C. ferry flight   D. deadhead

24. What is the code for O'Hare Airport in Chicago, Illinois?   24____

    A. ORD   B. OHX   C. CHI   D. OHI

25. A passenger pays for an item costing $4.20 with three dollar bills, a fifty-cent piece, and   25____
four quarters. The passenger's change will be

    A. $.05   B. $.15   C. $.25   D. $.30

KEY (CORRECT ANSWERS)

1.	D	11.	B
2.	B	12.	D
3.	C	13.	B
4.	A	14.	A
5.	D	15.	C
6.	A	16.	C
7.	A	17.	D
8.	D	18.	A
9.	D	19.	B
10.	D	20.	B

21.	C
22.	B
23.	C
24.	A
25.	D

———

TEST 4

DIRECTIONS: Each question or incomplete statement is followed by several suggested answers or completions. Select the one that BEST answers the question or completes the statement. *PRINT THE LETTER OF THE CORRECT ANSWER IN THE SPACE AT THE RIGHT.*

1. Which of the following statements about flight attendant vacationing is FALSE?   1____

    A. The usual compensation procedure is to pay for the trips missed or credit with flight hours on a daily basis.
    B. The number of days that may be bid is determined by seniority with the company.
    C. Bid days can be divided into one to three periods.
    D. The number of days that may be awarded is determined by seniority at the domicile.

2. A flight attendant's FIRST responsibility in responding to a potential emergency health situation is to   2____

    A. check the patient's temperature
    B. ask the passenger or seat partner about the passenger's medical history
    C. notify the captain that an emergency may exist
    D. check the patient's airway

3. The organized system for the distribution of inflight services is the   3____

    A. service chart   B. flow plan
    C. master grid   D. flight plan

4. By definition, a *heavy* jet is any aircraft weighing _____ pounds or more.   4____

    A. 100,000   B. 200,000   C. 300,000   D. 400,000

5. A flight attendant on layover typically assumes financial responsibility for   5____

    A. meals
    B. uniform cleanings
    C. transport between airport and hotel
    D. telephone charges billed to the hotel room

6. Whenever supplemental oxygen is to be used on a flight, the flight attendant's FIRST responsibility is to   6____

    A. turn on the flow of oxygen
    B. strap the bottle to a fixed object
    C. check the flow meter
    D. make sure nobody is smoking

7. To turn an aircraft laterally, causing one wing to be higher than another, is to   7____

    A. pitch   B. tilt   C. bank   D. grade

8. hich of the following is NOT a condition that would disqualify one for flight attendant service?   8____

    A. Chronic sinus problems   B. Astigmatism
    C. High blood pressure   D. Chronic back problems

9. Which of the following is NOT a difference between an all-coach 727 and one that is full-service?   9____

    A. Aisle space   B. Passenger leg room
    C. Galley space   D. Number of restrooms

10. *Pitoh* is the   10____

    A. movement of an aircraft around its vertical axis
    B. movement of an aircraft on its horizontal axis
    C. movement of an aircraft on its lateral axis
    D. downward-acting force on a plane in flight

11. Each of the following is a symptom of cardiac arrest EXCEPT   11____

    A. dilated pupils   B. lack of pulse
    C. flushed skin   D. unconsciousness

12. _____ is NOT a typical symptom of oxygen deficiency.   12____

    A. Pain and discomfort   B. Vision problems
    C. Headache   D. Sleepiness

13. The recommended method for resting the legs at the end of a day's work is by   13____

    A. elevating the legs and remaining immobile
    B. lying flat on the back and gently flexing toes
    C. elevating the legs and doing exercises to improve circulation
    D. slow stretches with the knees locked

14. Each of the following is an expectation of flight attendants in dealing with non-ambulatory passengers EXCEPT   14____

    A. assisting with lavatory visits
    B. seating with the use of aisle chairs
    C. provision of necessary equipment such as oxygen
    D. assisting with food and beverage items

15. An infant appears not to be breathing. The infant's pulse should be checked   15____

    A. just below either thumb   B. at the neck artery
    C. behind either knee   D. below the left nipple

16. FAA regulations prohibit a person from acting or attempting to act as a crew member of a civil aircraft within _____ hours of the consumption of any alcoholic beverage.   16____

    A. 4   B. 8   C. 12   D. 18

17. A group left on a trip when it was 3:20 P.M. in Chicago. When the group arrived in Salt Lake City, the airport clock read 6:40 P.M. How long did the trip take? 17____

    A. 2 hours, 20 minutes   B. 3 hours, 20 minutes
    C. 4 hours, 20 minutes   D. 5 hours, 20 minutes

18. Which of the following is not a recommended response to external bleeding? 18____

    A. Applying a tourniquet
    B. Keep victim warm by covering with a blanket
    C. Elevation of victim's feet 8-12 inches, unless unconscious
    D. Applying direct pressure

19. Deciding what actions to take with a passenger who is behaving abnormally is the ultimate responsibility of the 19____

    A. captain
    B. lead flight attendant
    C. first officer
    D. ground adviser on public relations

20. Most larger aircraft are equipped with _____ window exits. 20____

    A. 2   B. 4   C. 5   D. 6

21. What is the term for a lack of oxygen in the blood, most prevalent after decompression? 21____

    A. Hematoxia   B. Hypoxia
    C. Anemia   D. Hypothermia

22. Dry chemical fire extinguishers are typically used only with Class _____ fires. 22____

    A. A   B. B   C. C   D. D

23. Most air carriers allow a maximum of _____ pet(s) per cabin on any flight. 23____

    A. 1   B. 2   C. 5   D. 8

24. On an aircraft's left wing tip is mounted a _____ safety light. 24____

    A. green   B. red   C. blue   D. white

25. Systemwide flight attendant seniority typically affects each of the following EXCEPT 25____

    A. pay scale
    B. transfers to other home bases
    C. vacation bids
    D. filling of temporary assignments

KEY (CORRECT ANSWERS)

1.	D		11.	C
2.	B		12.	A
3.	B		13.	C
4.	C		14.	A
5.	D		15.	D
6.	D		16.	B
7.	C		17.	C
8.	B		18.	A
9.	A		19.	A
10.	C		20.	B

21.	B
22.	B
23.	A
24.	B
25.	C

———

EXAMINATION SECTION
TEST 1

DIRECTIONS: Each question or incomplete statement is followed by several suggested answers or completions. Select the one that BEST answers the question or completes the statement. *PRINT THE LETTER OF THE CORRECT ANWER IN THE SPACE AT THE RIGHT.*

1. Which of the following is NOT a preflight safety inspection that is unique to aircraft with buffets below the main cabin deck?

    A. Cart lifts
    B. Restraining devices
    C. Jump seat areas
    D. Escape hatches

1____

2. The dome-shaped protective covering for an aircraft's radar unit is the

    A. pod   B. camber   C. radome   D. cowling

2____

3. Each of the following situations may prevent a junior flight attendant from being *drafted* by an airline to resolve a coverage situation EXCEPT

    A. illegality due to preceding or future trips
    B. senior line-holder is available to take open trips
    C. current leave of absence status
    D. alcohol consumption within 12 hours of report time

3____

4. In preparation for an emergency evacuation, the cabin should be prepared in each of the following ways EXCEPT

    A. provision of pillows and blankets to passengers
    B. unlocking lavatory doors
    C. adjustment of cabin lighting
    D. moving able-bodied passengers to emergency exits to assist

4____

5. The backward-acting force on a plane in flight is

    A. drag   B. shear   C. thrust   D. tailwind

5____

6. According to FAA regulations, initial ground training for flight attendants must consist of at least _____ hours of instruction in Group II airplanes.

    A. 4   B. 8   C. 12   D. 16

6____

7. Calls in the cabin system typically originate from each of the following locations EXCEPT

    A. flight deck
    B. lavatories
    C. emergency exits
    D. jump seats

7____

Questions 8-14.

DIRECTIONS: Questions 8 through 14 refer to the figure shown on the following page, a trip sequence form with an accompanying lines-of-flying form. Use the information on the forms to answer each question.

EFFECTIVE DATES: OCTOBER 1 through OCTOBER 31

ID #	# of F/A	A/C	FLT #	DPTR CITY	ARVL CITY	RPT TIME	DPTR TIME	ARVL TIME	FLT TIME	DUTY TIME	L/O	CREDIT TIME	ACTUAL TIME	RON	MEAN EXP.
100	12	747	2	SFO	BOS	1145	1300	2105	505	635				Boston Park Hotel	
		747	1	BOS	SFO	0805	0905	1210	605	735	1200	1110	1110		$30.00
101	4	DC8	12	SFO	SEA	0700	0800	0948	148		142				
		DC8	23	SEA	SFO		1130	1315	145	645		430	333		$ 6.00
102	4	DC8	58	SFO	SEA	0900	1000	1148	148		242				
		DC8	167	SEA	LAX		1430	1642	212		48				
		DC8	112	LAX	SFO		1730	1836	106	951		506	506		$ 8.00
103	3	737	444	SFO	SMF	0400	0500	0534	31		26				
		737	379	SMF	SFO		0600	0635	35		145				
		727	76	SFO	OMA		0820	1320	300	920	2355			Omaha Plaza	
		727	663	OMA	LAX		1315	1420	305		110				
		737	542	LAX	SFO		1530	1606	106	636		1031	820		$35.00
104	3	727	39	SFO	SAN	1100	1200	1323	123		47				
		727	740	SAN	SFO		1410	1528	118		123				
		737	643	SFO	FAT		1651	1735	44		30				
		737	525	FAT	LAX		1805	1855	50		135				
		737	600	LAX	SFO		2030	2136	106	1036		533	521		$10.00

FLIGHT ATTENDANT WORK SCHEDULES
LINES OF FLYING

Month _____ Equipment _____ Domicile _____

8. Which trip sequence involves the greatest amount of layover time?　　　　8____

    A.　100　　　　B.　102　　　　C.　103　　　　D.　104

9. The duty period begins earliest in the day for trip sequence　　　　9____

    A.　100　　　　B.　101　　　　C.　103　　　　D.　104

10. 0: t.he 8th day of the month, the flight attendant who selects the #1 line of flying will　　10____
depart from

    A.　Seattle　　　　　　　　　　B.　Boston
    C.　Los Angeles　　　　　　　　D.　San Francisco

11. If a flight attendant works line of flying #1, how many flight hours will be accumulated in　　11____
the month shown?

    A.　51 hours, 10 minutes　　　　B.　72 hours, 30 minutes
    C.　78 hours, 10 minutes　　　　D.　88 hours, 20 minutes

12. The trip sequence using the largest aircraft is　　　　12____

    A.　100　　　　B.　101　　　　C.　103　　　　D.　104

13. On the 20th day of the month, the flight attendant who selects the #3 line of flying will　　13____
depart from _____ before terminating his/her trip in San Francisco.

    A.　Los Angeles　　　　　　　　B.　Omaha
    C.　Seattle　　　　　　　　　　　D.　Boston

14. Which trip sequence requires the largest crew of flight attendants?　　　　14____

    A.　100　　　　B.　102　　　　C.　103　　　　D.　104

15. Which of the following persons may, under certain circumstances, be served alcoholic　　15____
beverages on a flight?

    A.　A person carrying a licensed deadly weapon
    B.　A person who appears to be intoxicated
    C.　Transit aliens
    D.　A prisoner in transit to a prison facility

16. Under irregular operating circumstances, a flight attendant may be scheduled for a maxi-　　16____
mum of _____ international duty hours in a 24-hour period.

    A.　10-12　　　　B.　14-16　　　　C.　16-20　　　　D.　20-22

17. If a passenger experiences a nosebleed, a flight attendant should　　　　17____

    A.　pinch the nose closed
    B.　tip the passenger's head backward
    C.　have the passenger blow his/her nose to expel blood
    D.　apply a warm cloth

18. What is the term for the major airport location that serves as a center of operation for the　　18____
dispatch of flight attendants?

    A.　Hub　　　　B.　Domicile　　　　C.　Abode　　　　D.　Quarters

19. A Class _____ fire involves common combustibles such as paper, plastic, and fabric.   19____

    A. A   B. B   C. C   D. D

20. In a financial quarter, a flight attendant should not serve more than _____ international   20____
flight hours.

    A. 67-74   B. 85-100   C. 240-255   D. 275-300

21. When performing cardiopulmonary resuscitation on an adult, approximately how many   21____
breaths should be administered per minute?

    A. 6   B. 12   C. 20   D. 32

22. Hinged panels mounted in the top of the wing forward of the trailing edge flaps can be   22____
raised to function as speed brakes or roll controllers. These devices are known as

    A. leading edge devices   B. spoilers
    C. elevators   D. ailerons

23. In an infant requires supplemental oxygen and the plastic mask provided is too large for   23____
the infant's face,

    A. a wadding of clean, dry cloth should be placed between the mask and the infant's face
    B. the tubing should be inserted into a hole cut into the bottom of a paper drinking cup which will be used as a mask
    C. the oxygen should be bubbled into a container of clean water beneath the infant's mouth and nose
    D. the tubing should be inserted directly into the infant's airway

24. What is the term for the back part of a plane?   24____

    A. Yaw   B. Starboard   C. Avast   D. Aft

25. A flight attendant's flight hours typically begin when the   25____

    A. blocks are removed from the wheels of the nose gear
    B. aircraft has left the ground
    C. aircraft begins takeoff
    D. flight attendant reports for duty

KEY (CORRECT ANSWERS)

1.	B	11.	C
2.	C	12.	A
3.	B	13.	A
4.	B	14.	A
5.	A	15.	C
6.	D	16.	C
7.	C	17.	A
8.	C	18.	B
9.	C	19.	A
10.	D	20.	C

21.	B
22.	B
23.	B
24.	D
25.	A

TEST 2

DIRECTIONS: Each question or incomplete statement is followed by several suggested answers or completions. Select the one that BEST answers the question or completes the statement. *PRINT THE LETTER OF THE CORRECT ANSWER IN THE SPACE AT THE RIGHT.*

1. Which of the following portable electronic devices is NOT included in the FAA operation ban on civil aircraft?

    A. Cellular telephones   B. Portable voice recorders
    C. Laptop computers   D. Radio headsets

1_____

2. On an aircraft's right wing tip is mounted a _____ safety light.

    A. green   B. red   C. blue   D. white

2_____

3. The inflight dinner hour is usually

    A. 0400-0700   B. 0700-0900   C. 1200-1300   D. 1700-1900

3_____

4. When nonstop flights exceed approximately _____ hours, the inflight crew must be granted rest breaks on board the aircraft.

    A. 4-6   B. 8-10   C. 10-12   D. 14-16

4_____

5. The lower lobe of an aircraft, designed to hold cargo containers and landing gear, is called the

    A. hold   B. belly   C. carrier   D. bulkhead

5_____

6. For approximately the first _____ minutes of a flight, communication with the cockpit should be avoided if possible, unless a safety matter is involved.

    A. 10   B. 30   C. 45   D. 60

6_____

7. _____ is the term for the position of an aircraft around one or all of its axes in relation to a fixed point of reference.

    A. Attitude   B. Bearing   C. Demeanor   D. Posture

7_____

8. Each of the following is an immediate effect felt by passengers and crew in a decompression EXCEPT

    A. difficulty breathing
    B. impaired vision
    C. nausea
    D. generalized feeling of pressure against body

8_____

9. To purchase two items, one for $2.75 and the other for $4.25, a passenger gives a flight attendant a $20 bill. How much change is owed the passenger?

    A. $11.00   B. $12.50   C. $13.00   D. $14.00

9_____

10. Which of the following is NOT a step in administering supplemental oxygen to an adult passenger?   10_____

    A. Notify the captain
    B. Plug mask fitting into low-flow outlet
    C. Pinch upper part of mask around passenger's nose
    D. Remove lipstick or protective lip covering

11. A flight attendant's post-flight responsibilities before deplaning typically take about _____ minutes.   11_____

    A. 5   B. 15   C. 30   D. 60

12. The supervisor of inflight crew and services on international flights is the   12_____

    A. purser   B. comptroller
    C. bursar   D. service officer

13. A girt bar is used to   13_____

    A. reinforce cabin bulkheads
    B. lock the cabin doors during flight
    C. open emergency exits during evacuation
    D. secure the evacuation slide pack to the doorsill

14. During flight, an aisle check should be made every _____ minutes.   14_____

    A. 5-10   B. 15-30   C. 30-45   D. 60

15. During flight, the cabins of most commercial airliners are pressurized to simulate an altitude of approximately _____ feet.   15_____

    A. 500 to 1,000   B. 1,000 to 5,000
    C. 5,000 to 7,000   D. 10,000 to 15,000

16. On a 24-hour clock a time is expressed as 2330. What time is it in conventional hours?   16_____

    A. 10:30 A.M.   B. 1:30 P.M.
    C. 3:30 P.M.   D. 11:30 P.M.

17. Which of the following is by definition a large transport aircraft, rather than a heavy jet?   17_____

    A. A-300   B. B-737   C. DC-10   D. L-1011

18. A Class _____ fire starts from an electrical source.   18_____

    A. A   B. B   C. C   D. D

19. Appearance standards and health laws dictate that during food service, long hair   19_____

    A. should be secured by means of a hair net or similar covering
    B. should be secured so that it does not fall forward of the face
    C. should be tucked into the collar behind the flight attendant's neck
    D. is not permitted under any circumstances

20. Which of the following is NOT a means of emergency escape fron galley units beneath   20____
    the main cabin deck?
    A. Built-in ladder   B. Floor hatch
    C. Cart lift   D. Overhead hatch

21. In order to qualify for service, a flight attendant's vision must be correctable to   21____

    A. 20/20   B. 20/30   C. 20/40   D. 20/50

Questions 22-25.

DIRECTIONS: Questions 22 through 25 refer to the figure below, a drawing of a typical airliner
              tail assembly. Place the letter that corresponds to each component in the
              space at the right.

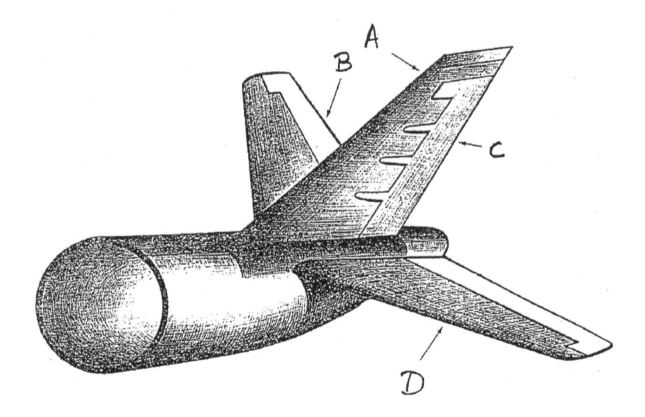

22. Horizontal stabilizer   22____

23. Vertical stabilizer   23____

24. Elevator   24____

25. Rudder   25____

KEY (CORRECT ANSWERS)

1.	B		11.	B
2.	A		12.	A
3.	D		13.	D
4.	B		14.	B
5.	B		15.	C
6.	A		16.	D
7.	A		17.	B
8.	C		18.	C
9.	C		19.	B
10.	B		20.	B

21.	A
22.	D
23.	A
24.	B
25.	C

TEST 3

Each question or incomplete statement is followed by several suggested answers or completions. Select the one that BEST answers the question or completes the statement. *PRINT THE LETTER OF THE CORRECT ANSWER IN THE SPACE AT THE RIGHT.*

1. Movable surfaces on each wing of an aircraft that act to vary the lift around the plane's horizontal axis are
   1_____

   A. ailerons
   B. rudders
   C. stabilizers
   D. spoilers

2. A junior flight attendant on reserve status is considered to be on call for _____ hours a day.
   2_____

   A. 8
   B. 12
   C. 16
   D. 24

3. A child with an extremely high fever should be given a sponge bath until the temperature falls below _____ F.
   3_____

   A. 100
   B. 101
   C. 102
   D. 104

4. Which of the following is NOT advised when dealing with an obviously intoxicated passenger?
   4_____

   A. Speaking firmly and sternly
   B. Cutting off the supply of alcohol
   C. Notifying captain of circumstances
   D. Using tact and discretion

5. The most prominent exception to typical aircraft emergency door exits is the rear door of the
   5_____

   A. 727
   B. 747
   C. DC-10
   D. L-1011

6. Each of the following is a symptom of respiratory arrest EXCEPT
   6_____

   A. dilated pupils
   B. bluish skin
   C. labored breathing
   D. unconsciousness

7. The airport coded LGA is located in
   7_____

   A. Long Beach, California
   B. New Orleans, Louisiana
   C. Lansing, Michigan
   D. Flushing, New York

8. Which of the following is not a recommended means of fighting the effects of jag lag?
   8_____

   A. When traveling as a passenger, sleep, if possible, on the plane
   B. Eating larger meals than normal
   C. Keeping activity at a slow pace
   D. Drinking large amounts of liquids

9. Company seniority, or the length of service with the entire airline, is a factor that can affect a flight attendant's
   9_____

   A. rank among all flight attendants at the airline
   B. passes and reduced travel
   C. work schedules
   D. transfer to home bases

10. The last U.S. city from which an international flight departs is known as a(n)   10____

    A. portal   B. corridor   C. gateway   D. casement

11. A change purse contains 4 half dollars, 12 quarters, 8 dimes, 5 nickels, and 25 pennies.   11____
How much money is in the purse?

    A. $5.50   B. $6.30   C. $6.80   D. $7.25

12. Systemwide flight attendant seniority is usually determined by   12____

    A. length of service among all flight attendants at the home base
    B. birthdate among active flight attendants
    C. length of service with the airline
    D. graduation date from flight attendant training

13. If supplemental oxygen is not obtained within the first _____ of a decompression,   13____
unconsciousness will result.

    A. 5 seconds   B. 15 to 30 seconds
    C. 30 seconds to 1 minute   D. 1 to 2 minutes

14. If a plane is traveling at a speed of 300 miles per hour, how long will it take the plane to   14____
fly a distance of 1000 miles?

    A. 2 hours, 40 minutes   B. 3 hours, 20 minutes
    C. 3 hours, 50 minutes   D. 4 hours, 10 minutes

15. A flight attendant suspects that a passenger has suffered a second-degree burn from a   15____
hot liquid. The flight attendant should

    A. apply ice to the burned area
    B. drain any visible blisters
    C. apply cold-water compresses
    D. apply any available burn ointments to the burned area

16. In tense emergency situations, a passenger is sometimes dazed, immobile, docile, and   16____
unthinking, and may be very difficult to deal with. This phenomenon is known as

    A. negative panic   B. quandary
    C. stupefaction   D. catatonia

17. A junior flight attendant's probationary period typically lasts for a period of   17____

    A. 60-90 days   B. 3-4 months
    C. 6-8 months   D. 12-18 months

18. The outer covering of an engine is known as a(n)   18____

    A. radome   B. cowling   C. mantle   D. pylon

19. Each of the following is a recommendation associated with the delivery of emergency   19____
instructions to passengers, EXCEPT

    A. speaking in a loud voice
    B. avoiding the use of negatives such as *do not*
    C. avoiding a tone that is too demanding
    D. using concise phrases

20. An engine is attached to the wing of an aircraft by a part known as the 20____

    A. pylon   B. fixer   C. cowling   D. bollard

21. In a 24-hour period, a flight attendant should not serve more than _____ domestic flight 21____
hours.

    A. 6   B. 8   C. 10   D. 12

22. Flight attendant schedulers typically rotate shifts on a(n) _____ -hour basis. 22____

    A. 8   B. 12   C. 16   D. 24

23. Which of the following should NOT be done by a flight attendant during an emergency 23____
evacuation?

    A. Shouting at passengers
    B. Begin moving as soon as the plane has landed and is taxiing on the ground
    C. Giving reluctant passengers a shove
    D. Using a strict, commanding tone

24. *Yaw* is the 24____

    A. movement of an aircraft around its vertical axis
    B. movement of an aircraft on its horizontal axis
    C. movement of an aircraft on its lateral axis
    D. centrifugal force on a plane in flight

25. Which of the following is not a policy concerning the service of alcoholic beverages to 25____
passengers?
The passenger

    A. must be of legal age in the territory whose airspace is occupied by the aircraft
    B. may not drink alcohol from his or her own supply
    C. must consume the beverage on board the plane
    D. may not be served a drink if he/she is intoxicated

_____

KEY (CORRECT ANSWERS)

1.	A		11.	B
2.	D		12.	D
3.	C		13.	B
4.	A		14.	B
5.	A		15.	C
6.	C		16.	A
7.	D		17.	C
8.	B		18.	B
9.	B		19.	C
10.	C		20.	A

21.	B
22.	D
23.	B
24.	A
25.	A

———

TEST 4

DIRECTIONS: Each question or incomplete statement is followed by several suggested answers or completions. Select the one that BEST answers the question or completes the statement. *PRINT THE LETTER OF THE CORRECT ANSWER IN THE SPACE AT THE RIGHT.*

1. Different portions of a passenger cabin interior are referred to as   1____

   A. zones   B. districts   C. bulkheads   D. segments

2. Upon boarding, a passenger requests that a flight attendant place his medication in a   2____
   refrigerated unit in the aircraft galley. The flight attendant should

   A. prevent the passenger from boarding until a physician can be consulted to verify
      the request
   B. offer a container, such as a motion sickness bag, filled with ice, and request that
      the passenger keep the medicine at his seat
   C. leave the medicine unrefrigerated for flights of under two hours in duration
   D. place the medication in the refrigerated unit nearest the passenger

3. Under normal circumstances, preflight cabin preparation is usually completed in approxi-   3____
   mately _____ minutes.

   A. 5-10   B. 10-20   C. 30-40   D. 45-60

4. To check the flow of supplemental oxygen, the flight attendant should   4____

   A. inhale a small amount
   B. pinch or tap the end of the tube while listening
   C. question the passenger
   D. check the pressure gauge

5. Another term for trip advisory is   5____

   A. maintenance   B. bill of lading
   C. bidding   D. manifest

6. An authority of the Civil Aeronautics Board is to   6____

   A. conduct research to improve air traffic control and environmental procedures
   B. monitor the fare structure for passenger transportation
   C. certify flight schools according to government safety standards
   D. provide for development and improvement of aircraft

7. Which of the following is not a characteristic or resulting cabin condition of a rapid   7____
   decompression?

   A. Extremely warm flow of air
   B. A loud, sudden, explosive noise
   C. Loose objects, dust, and debris flying through cabin
   D. Dense fog

8. Any person escorting a severely mentally disturbed passenger must advise the airline _____ before a flight, and offer assurance that medical authorities have sanctioned air travel.

   A. 30 days   B. 48 hours   C. 24 hours   D. 6 hours

8_____

9. What is the condition called for irritation to the eardrum during descent, caused by congestion in the Eustachian tube?

   A. Auricula   B. Cochleitis
   C. Linatrium   D. Aerotitis

9_____

10. The airport coded PDX is located in

    A. Providence, Rhode Island
    B. Portland, Oregon
    C. Portland, Maine
    D. Philadelphia, Pennsylvania

10_____

11. Items close to the center line of an aircraft are described as

    A. amidst   B. median   C. essential   D. inboard

11_____

12. A flight attendant's portable oxygen bottle typically contains enough oxygen to last for _____ of continuous use.

    A. 10 minutes   B. 30 minutes
    C. 1 hour   D. 2 hours

12_____

13. A flight attendant's duty hours typically begin when the

    A. pre-flight cabin check begins
    B. aircraft has left the ground
    C. flight attendant checks in with the crew desk
    D. blocks have been removed from the nose gear

13_____

14. _____ traffic is the term for passengers brought to a major airline by regional or commuter airlines.

    A. Bottleneck   B. Feed
    C. Deadhead   D. Ferry

14_____

15. What type of fire extinguisher can be used on any type of fire?

    A. CO_2 B. Dry chemical
    C. Liquid nitrogen   D. Water

15_____

16. What is the term for a wall or partition used to divide the passenger cabin?

    A. Bulwark   B. Cleaver   C. Bulkhead   D. Rampart

16_____

17. Typically, a flight attendant is scheduled to be on board from _____ prior to takeoff.

    A. 15 to 30 minutes   B. 30 minutes to 1 hour
    C. 45 minutes to 1 1/2 hours   D. 1 to 2 hours

17_____

31

18. _____ serve primarily to increase an aircraft's lift. 18____

    A. Ailerons   B. Leading edge devices
    C. Spoilers   D. Rudders

19. What is the term for the movement of an aircraft on a horizontal axis, as when one wing is higher than another? 19____

    A. Drag   B. Pitch   C. Yaw   D. Roll

20. Each of the following is a protocol involved with the transport of a passenger who is being extradited or transported to prison facilities EXCEPT the 20____

    A. passenger is accompanied by at least one armed guard
    B. prisoner and escort(s) are the first to deplane
    C. captain and the airline decide whether the passenger is to be handcuffed
    D. prisoner and escort(s) are seated in the last row of the aircraft

21. In preparing for inflight food and beverage service, the object is to begin serving passengers 21____

    A. as soon as all passengers are seated
    B. as soon as the aircraft is airborne
    C. within 40 minutes of takeoff
    D. as soon as the aircraft has achieved cruising altitude

22. What is the code for the Orange County Airport in Santa Ana, California? 22____

    A. OCX   B. ORN   C. SNA   D. IRV

23. Each of the following is a potential sign of extreme mental and physical fatigue EXCEPT 23____

    A. headaches
    B. decrease in attention span
    C. insomnia
    D. loss of appetite

24. A seated passenger is choking badly enough that she cannot breathe. An immediate response should be to 24____

    A. apply four quick, forceful blows on the back between the shoulder blades
    B. apply four quick, forceful abdominal thrusts
    C. roll the passenger onto her back on the floor
    D. avoid interfering with the passenger

25. The Airline Deregulation Act of 1978 was designed to do each of the following EXCEPT 25____

    A. limit the scope of the Civil Aeronautics Board's authority
    B. increase competition among carriers
    C. allow carriers more freedom in choosing new routes and markets
    D. encourage entry into air commerce by new carriers

KEY (CORRECT ANSWERS)

1.	A		11.	D
2.	B		12.	A
3.	B		13.	C
4.	B		14.	B
5.	D		15.	A
6.	B		16.	C
7.	A		17.	B
8.	C		18.	B
9.	D		19.	D
10.	B		20.	B

21.	B
22.	C
23.	B
24.	A
25.	A

EXAMINATION SECTION
TEST 1

DIRECTIONS: Each question or incomplete statement is followed by several suggested answers or completions. Select the one that BEST answers the question or completes the statement. *PRINT THE LETTER OF THE CORRECT ANSWER IN THE SPACE AT THE RIGHT.*

1. The intended direction of a flight in the horizontal plane is referred to as its   1._____

    A. course   B. route   C. bearing   D. arc

2. The primary disadvantage associated with an open mechanized system of cargo han-   2._____
dling at an airport is a

    A. need for skilled labor
    B. very large space requirement
    C. lack of clear handling standards
    D. high level of container damage

3. Airport operations change from landside to airside in nature when a passenger or freight   3._____
travels from

    A. apron to taxiway   B. gate to apron
    C. pier to gate   D. concourse to pier

4. In terms of air traffic control, the positive control area, where all flights must be con-   4._____
ducted under air traffic control rules and directions, extends from the altitudes of _____
feet.

    A. 1,000-12,000   B. 5,000-25,000
    C. 6,000-18,000   D. 11,000-29,999

5. In the electrical shop of a Category II airport, the lighting systems typically require   5._____
_____ employees in addition to the foreman.

    A. 5   B. 9   C. 18   D. 41

6. The FAA's Index C of its aviation regulations applies to aircraft that are _____ feet long.   6._____

    A. more than 90 feet long and not more than 126
    B. more than 126 and not more than 160
    C. more than 160 and not more than 200
    D. more than 200

7. Which of the following is NOT a significant factor in determining the peaking characteris-   7._____
tics of airport traffic?

    A. Domestic/international ratio
    B. Reliability
    C. Geographical location
    D. Long haul/short haul

8. On a flight plan, an aircraft's *operating weight* is defined as the   8._____

   A. operating weight plus the payload
   B. sum of the weights of the various types of loads (passengers, baggage, cargo, mail) and also the weight of any additional ULDs
   C. sum of dry operating weight and takeoff fuel
   D. weight of the basic aircraft, fully equipped, together with crew and their baggage, pantry/commissary supplies, and flight spares, but not including fuel and payload

9. An aircraft is equipped with four engines. On takeoff, what gradient reduction, in percent, will give the aircraft *net* climb performance?   9._____

   A. 0.5   B. 0.8   C. 1.0   D. 1.5

10. According to the policies of the International Air Transport Association (IATA), the aims of schedule coordination include each of the following EXCEPT to   10._____

   A. arrange for regular appraisal of declared applied limits
   B. provide guidelines and recommendations for such elements as curfews and tariffs
   C. ensure all operators have an equitable opportunity to satisfy their scheduling requirement within existing constraints
   D. resolve problems without recourse to governmental intervention

11. In most United States airports, it is common practice to provide mechanized assistance to terminal users when walking distances exceed _____ feet.   11._____

   A. 750   B. 1500   C. 3000   D. 5000

12. The airport passenger and freight terminal is a facility that has three distinct functions. Which of the following is NOT one of these?   12._____

   A. Change of movement type   B. Processing
   C. Support   D. Change of mode

13. _____ cargo rates are typically applied to items such as gold, bullion, flowers, and live animals.   13._____

   A. Classified   B. Specific commodity
   C. Consolidation   D. Container

14. The height above the earth's surface of the lowest layer of clouds or obscuring phenomena that are reported as *broken, overcast,* or *obscuration,* and not classified as *thin* or *partial,* is referred to as the   14._____

   A. ceiling   B. nimbus   C. threshold   D. brink

15. On a flight plan, a figure appears that is labeled *takeoff weight*. The weight indicated is the   15._____

   A. landing weight + trip fuel
   B. zero fuel weight + takeoff fuel
   C. dry operating weight
   D. maximum takeoff weight

16. The preventive maintenance program for a medium-intensity approach lighting system requires that checks on the electrical distribution equipment should be performed   16.____

    A. monthly   B. bimonthly
    C. semiannually   D. annually

17. At an airport, the braking radius of 1000 feet is acceptable at 50 mph in good weather. In slippery conditions, this same radius would be acceptable *only* if the aircraft's speed is reduced to _____ mph.   17.____

    A. 5   B. 10   C. 20   D. 30

18. The *break-even* load factor for long-haul operations of a modern wide-bodied passenger aircraft is typically _____%.   18.____

    A. 60   B. 70   C. 80   D. 90

19. In normal operation, it is generally assumed that bags can be unloaded from an aircraft onto a claim device at a rate of approximately _____ per minute.   19.____

    A. 10   B. 20   C. 30   D. 45

20. Tow tractors in use at airports must generally be capable of moving an aircraft at a speed of approximately _____ mph.   20.____

    A. 5   B. 12   C. 20   D. 32

21. According to FAA recommendations, the figure representing Typical Peak Hour Passengers (TPHP) at an airport with approximately 15,000,000 annual passengers should be about _____% of the annual flow.   21.____

    A. 1   B. 0.12   C. 0.05   D. 0.035

22. Which of the following stages in the exportation of freight typically occurs LAST?   22.____

    A. Preparation of flight manifest
    B. Allocation to flight and/or ULD
    C. Receipt of airway bill documents
    D. Preparation of flight tally

23. When a three-bar VASIS system is used for runway lighting, a large aircraft on approach will use the   23.____

    A. upwind bar *only*
    B. downwind bar *only*
    C. upwind and middle bars
    D. downwind and middle bars

24. The runways at an airport are iced over to a depth of 1/2 to one inch. The outdoor air temperature is less than 10°F.
The application rate of traditional de-icing solution that would be recommended would be one gallon per _____ square feet.   24.____

    A. 750   B. 500   C. 300   D. 100

25. What is the term for the track over the ground of an aircraft flying at a constant distance   25.____
from an air navigation facility by reference to distance measuring equipment?

   A. Trip   B. Glide   C. Route   D. Arc

—————

KEY (CORRECT ANSWERS)

1.	A	11.	B
2.	D	12.	C
3.	C	13.	A
4.	C	14.	A
5.	B	15.	B
6.	B	16.	D
7.	B	17.	C
8.	C	18.	B
9.	C	19.	B
10.	B	20.	B

21. D
22. A
23. C
24. C
25. D

—————

TEST 2

DIRECTIONS: Each question or incomplete statement is followed by several suggested answers or completions. Select the one that BEST answers the question or completes the statement. *PRINT THE LETTER OF THE CORRECT ANSWER IN THE SPACE AT THE RIGHT.*

1. The most critical aspect of an aircraft's approach performance is the ability to climb after a missed approach has been declared. It must, therefore, be possible to demonstrate an adequate climb performance in several flight conditions.
    Which of the following is NOT one of these conditions?   1.____

    A. Gross gradient not less than 3.2% at airfield altitude with all engines at maximum takeoff power in the final landing configuration
    B. Maximum gross climb gradient at the airfield altitude with all but the critical engine out, and the critical engine at maximum takeoff power in the final landing configuration but with the gear up
    C. Minimum gross climb gradient at the airfield altitude with the critical engine out and all others at maximum takeoff power in the final landing configura-. tion but wlth the gear up
    D. Positive net gradient at 1500 ft. above airfield in the cruise configuration with one engine out

2. Which of the following types of ULDs (Unit Load Devices) has the highest volume?   2.____

    A. M-1   B. M-2   C. A-1   D. L-3

3. Of the following airline personnel, which would typically have the LATEST input into airline scheduling?   3.____

    A. Operations control   B. Current planning
    C. Commercial economist   D. Schedules planning

4. For which of the following aircraft would it take the longest to unload passenger baggage?   4.____

    A. B747   B. B757   C. L-1011   D. BAC111

5. Which of the following is NOT a noise abatement procedure commonly used to reduce the noise of aircraft on approach?   5.____

    A. Low drag approaches with reduced flap settings and lower engine power settings
    B. Interception of glide slope at higher altitudes when interception is from above the slope
    C. Two-segment approaches flaring to a reduced angle for final approach and touch-down
    D. Use of continuous descent approaches, utilizing secondary surveillance radar for height information

6. A primary radar system used as a landing aid should provide solid coverage to an altitude of around _____ feet.   6.____

    A. 5,000-8,000   B. 10,000-12,000
    C. 15,000-21,000   D. 25,000-30,000

7. Which of the following typically accounts for the greatest percentage of revenue for an airport facility?   7.____

    A. Air carrier landing fees
    B. Hangar and building area
    C. Terminal area
    D. Airport parking (automobiles)

8. The primary determinant of revenue for an airport is   8.____

    A. peak flows
    B. average monthly flows
    C. landing tariffs
    D. annual flows

9. Each of the following is an advantage associated with the use of centralized search procedures at airport security stations EXCEPT   9.____

    A. minimization of necessary personnel and equipment
    B. favored by passengers
    C. minimization of the risk of collusion
    D. encouragement of passenger spending in restaurants and shops

10. For demonstrating takeoff distance in the United States, a pilot may not rotate the aircraft nose up before the speed has reached the highest of several variables.
Which of the following is not one of these variables?   10.____

    A. 0.75 times the minimum control speed in the air
    B. A speed which allows 1.2 times the stall speed
    C. A speed below 1.10 times the minimum unstick or lift-off speed
    D. Decision speed

11. For which of the following pairs of airport areas is adjacency considered *essential?*   11.____

    A. Transit lounge and ramp area
    B. Maintenance facilities and aircraft loading section
    C. Aircraft stands and post office
    D. Visitor/greeter area and customs check

12. At airports, time as a variable has been found to influence the subjective evaluation in noise in terms of each of the following EXCEPT the   12.____

    A. time of day at which the noise occurs
    B. amount of time between noise occurrences
    C. duration of the sound
    D. number of times the sound is repeated

13. In determining an aircraft's approach performance, it is important to remember that an extra knot of airspeed at the threshold converts to an extra _____ feet of runway.   13.____

    A. 50   B. 100   C. 200   D. 350

14. In inclement weather, it is typical to place a limit of _____ knots on the crosswind velocity acceptable for wet runway conditions.   14.____

    A. 3   B. 5   C. 7   D. 10

15. In ramp handling, *marshaling* includes the positioning and removal of each of the follow-   15.____
ing EXCEPT

    A. wheel chocks   B. airstart power units
    C. engine blanking covers   D. surface control locks

16. In describing the peaking hours of passenger flow at an airport facility, the method of the   16.____
Standard Busy Rate (SBR) is usually defined as

    A. the twentieth highest hour of passenger flow, or that rate of flow that is surpassed
        by only 19 hours of operation at higher flows
    B. the hourly rate above which 5 percent of the traffic at the airport is handled
    C. the thirtieth highest hour of passenger flow, or that rate of flow that is surpassed by
        only 29 hours of operation at higher flows
    D. 1.2 x the absolute peak hour volume

17. An airway, a type of ATC control area, is typically about _____ wide, starting at varying   17.____
heights and extendingthrough a range of height bands.

    A. 1,000 yards   B. 1 mile
    C. 5 miles   D. 10 miles

18. The FAA requires that an airport have runways sufficient both in number and orientation   18.____
to permit use by the aircraft for which it is designed, with a usability factor of at least
_____% with reference to wind conditions.

    A. 89.9   B. 92   C. 95   D. 98.9

19. Which of the following steps in *arrival* baggage operations is typically performed FIRST?   19.____

    A. Transport to terminal airside
    B. Presentation
    C. Conveyance to reclaim
    D. Sortation

20. After an airline's scheduling operations have passed into the hands of the schedules   20.____
planning unit, which of the following factors will affect the planning procedure?

    A. Competition
    B. Currently available route capacity
    C. Fare structure
    D. Acceptability of service schedule to the airport

21. Typical aircraft servicing standards (ground handling) are _____minutes for all transit   21.____
operations.

    A. 30   B. 60   C. 90   D. 120

22. The preventive maintenance inspection schedule for centerline and touchdown zone   22.____
lighting systems requires that checks on the torque of mounting bolts be performed

    A. weekly   B. monthly
    C. bimonthly   D. semiannually

23. On a flight plan, an aircraft's *dry operating weight* is defined as the   23.____

    A. operating weight plus the payload
    B. sum of the weights of the various types of loads (passengers, baggage, cargo, mail, and also the weight of any additional ULDs)
    C. sum of dry operating weight and takeoff fuel
    D. weight of the basic aircraft, fully equipped, together with crew and their baggage, pantry/commissary supplies, and flight spares, but not including fuel and payload

24. The MOST significant improvements in noise impact that can be achieved when aircraft are on runways is   24.____

    A. reduced engine power
    B. sound absorbing material in the inlet and outlet engine ducts
    C. control of the use of thrust reversal
    D. the development of minimum noise routings (MNRs)

25. Most of the baggage handling irregularities at United States airports are the result of   25.____

    A. loss   B. pilferage
    C. mishandling   D. damage

———

KEY (CORRECT ANSWERS)

1.	B		11.	D
2.	B		12.	B
3.	A		13.	B
4.	C		14.	D
5.	B		15.	B
6.	B		16.	C
7.	A		17.	D
8.	D		18.	C
9.	C		19.	A
10.	A		20.	D

21.	B
22.	C
23.	D
24.	C
25.	A

———

EXAMINATION SECTION
TEST 1

DIRECTIONS: Each question or incomplete statement is followed by several suggested answers or completions. Select the one that BEST answers the question or completes the statement. *PRINT THE LETTER OF THE CORRECT ANSWER IN THE SPACE AT THE RIGHT.*

Questions 1-8.

DIRECTIONS: Questions 1 through 8 refer to the figure below, a diagram of a typical flight plan. In the space at the right, place the letter that corresponds to each column heading next to the description of the information listed in the column.

FLIGHT PLAN

DC10 Los Angeles (LAX) to Chicago - O'Hare (ORD) - 1580 n.m.

Route - LAX .. DAG.J146.GLD.J192.PWE.J64.BDF.V10.VAINS..ORD

[Daggett via Jet Airway 146 to Goodland via Jet Airway 192 to Pawnee City via Jet Airway 64 to Bradford via Victor Airway 10 to Vains and Chicago - O'Hare.]

	[A]	[B]	[C]	[D]	[E]	[F]	[G]	[H]	[I]	[J]	[K]	[L]	[M]
RCA	256	37	828	09	51	486	26045	044	530	36	148	588
DVC	308	37	827	07	50	483	29071	056	539	35	91	497
GUC	98	37	826	07	49	482	29086	056	538	11	28	469
GLD	257	37	825	06	45	480	31094	053	533	28	73	396
PWE	258	37	824	04	40	478	31095	058	536	29	71	325
LMN	105	37	823	04	38	477	30087	056	533	12	29	296
POD	166	37	822	03	37	475	29053	046	521	19	45	251
- ORD	132						27030	028		23	21	230

1. Deviation from standard temperature   1._____

2. True airspeed   2._____

3. Segment time (minutes)   3._____

4. Flight plan checkpoint   4._____

5. Flight level (thousands of feet)   5._____

6. Ground speed   6._____

7. Segment fuel burnoff (hundreds of pounds)   7._____

8. Segment mileage (nautical miles)   8._____

43

9. According to FAA's assessment of aircraft accident probabilities, which of the following is classified as having *reasonable probability* (10^{-5} occurrences per flight)?   9.____

    A. Stall on approach
    B. Ground contact more than 2 km from runway
    C. Ground contact on runway
    D. Double engine failure on turn

10. For most airlines, the most significant factor influencing the development of a schedule for a particular airport facility is   10.____

    A. marketability
    B. long-haul crewing constraints
    C. utilization and load factors
    D. aircraft availability

11. Which of the following is typically a *non-commercial* service offered at an airport facility?   11.____

    A. Insurance   B. Car parking
    C. Portering   D. Hotel reservations

12. What is the term for a geographical location determined by visual reference to the surface, by reference to one or more radio navigational facilities, by celestial plotting, or by another navigational device?   12.____

    A. Fix   B. Bearing
    C. Locus   D. Reporting point

13. Which of the following typically contributes the greatest labor costs associated with baggage handling at United States airports?   13.____

    A. Security and supervision
    B. Check-in
    C. Claim area
    D. Loading/unloading

14. The outer market of an ILS (Instrument Landing System) is typically located at approximately _____ mile(s) from the landing threshold.   14.____

    A. 1   B. 3   C. 5   D. 8

15. Approximately what percentage of an airport's gross terminal area is distributed for public use?   15.____

    A. 15   B. 20   C. 30   D. 40

16. The MAIN *disadvantage* associated with the use of the Busy Hour Rate (BHR) method for determining peaking hours of airport passenger flow is that   16.____

    A. so many data must be collected and analyzed that the method may be beyond the resources of a smaller airport
    B. it is subject to variations in average load factors
    C. the implied level of congestion is considered to be common between airports
    D. it is subject to errors in forecasting

17. For jets, approach performance is measured in the basic case from a 50-foot screen. At target threshold speed on a dry runway, the target threshold speed must not be less than _____ times the stalling speed in the landing configuration.   17.____

   A. 0.8   B.   1.3   C.   1.75   D.   2.1

18. In the event of power failure at an airport, the recommended switchover time to second-   18.____
ary power supply for the ILS localizer of a precision approach Category I runway is
_____ second(s).

   A. 0 (immediate)   B.   1
   C. 10   D.   15

19. Which of the following is a passive means of metal detection at airport security stations?   19.____

   A. Eddy current device   B.   Flux gate magnetometer
   C. Inductive loop   D.   Gamma spectrograph

20. Each of the following is an activity that is included in the procedure of flight dispatch at an   20.____
airport EXCEPT

   A. marshaling
   B. flight crew briefing
   C. flight watch
   D. aircraft weight and balance

21. As a noise abatement procedure, it is recommended that aircraft perform final descents   21.____
at an angle of _____.

   A. 1-2   B.   3-4   C.   5-7   D.   7-10

22. In terms of air traffic control, the United States continental control area covers the United   22.____
States upward from the altitude of _____ feet.

   A. 60   B.   1,000   C.   14,500   D.   21,000

23. On approach to an airport which uses the PAPI (Precision   23.____
Approach Path Indicator) runway lighting system, a pilot sees
the following display of lights below. This is an indication to
the pilot that the approach is

   WRRR   RRRW

   A. slightly high
   B. correct
   C. slightly low
   D. too low

24. In order to facilitate debris removal operations on an airport's paved areas, it is custom-   24.____
ary to divide them into manageable segments of approximately _____ square meters.

   A. 100   B.   250   C.   500   D.   1000

25. When used in the immediate vicinity of the airport in conjunction with instrument approaches, an airport's transition area extends upward from about _____ feet above the surface of the earth.

   A. 60   B. 700   C. 1200   D. 2000

25._____

KEY (CORRECT ANSWERS)

1.	E		11.	C
2.	G		12.	A
3.	K		13.	B
4.	A		14.	C
5.	C		15.	C
6.	J		16.	A
7.	L		17.	B
8.	C		18.	C
9.	A		19.	B
10.	C		20.	A

21.	B
22.	C
23.	C
24.	C
25.	B

TEST 2

DIRECTIONS: Each question or incomplete statement is followed by several suggested answers or completions. Select the one that BEST answers the question or completes the statement. *PRINT THE LETTER OF THE CORRECT ANSWER IN THE SPACE AT THE RIGHT.*

1. Typically, the day of highest cargo flow at an airport facility is   1.____

   A. Wednesday   B. Friday   C. Saturday   D. Monday

2. The line departments of an airport administration typically include each of the following   2.____
   EXCEPT

   A. commercial   B. planning
   C. operations   D. engineering/maintenance

3. For a DC10 aircraft, the MINIMUM number of personnel required for baggage loading/   3.____
   unloading is

   A. 2   B. 4   C. 8   D. 12

4. FAA regulations state that all obstacles within a defined fan at the end of the take-off dis-   4.____
   tance available (TODA) must be cleared by 35 feet by the net flight path, or by 50 feet if
   any turn included in the flight path is greater than

   A. 5°   B. 10°   C. 15°   D. 25°

5. Of the following, which is the most significant source of baggage mishandling at United   5.____
   States airports?

   A. Misconnections due to mischecked bags
   B. Misconnections due to loading error
   C. Interline transfer misconnections
   D. On-line transfer misconnections

6. As cargo makes its way through the cargo terminal toward import output, which of the fol-   6.____
   lowing is generally performed LAST?

   A. Sortation   B. Cleared bond delivery
   C. In-bond storage   D. Customs examination

7. Which of the following is NOT a principle that is typically involved in matching aircraft to   7.____
   an airport infrastructure?

   A. The regulation of operations and performance
   B. Service factors
   C. The use of net performance
   D. The assessment of probability of failure

8. During cargo apron operations, a 100 series 747 is loaded from the side door only. A   8.____
   good turnaround time, within reasonable expectations, would be

   A. 45 minutes   B. 90 minutes
   C. 2 1/2 hours   D. 4 hours

9. The aim of approach visual aid systems is to at least provide information on the glide   9._____
    slope down to _____ feet, and preferably to give a reference throughout the entire final
    approach.

    A. 60   B. 120   C. 200   D. 350

10. Variations in airport demand levels are typically measured in terms of each of the follow- 10._____
    ing EXCEPT

    A. monthly peaks within a particular year
    B. annual variation over time
    C. weekly peaks within a particular month
    D. daily peaks within a particular month or week

11. At most airports, departing passengers typically spend about _____ minutes in the ter- 11._____
    minal facility.

    A. 30   B. 45   C. 60   D. 90

12. To a plane on the ground, a flashing red aerodrome control light means   12._____

    A. general warning signal - exercise caution
    B. taxi clear of landing area
    C. return to starting point on airport
    D. stop

13. What is the term for the flight path of an aircraft over the surface of the earth?   13._____

    A. Track   B. Route   C. Arc   D. Course

14. The primary determinant of physical and operational costs involved in running an airport   14._____
    facility is usually _____ flows.

    A. peak   B. average monthly
    C. average daily   D. annual

15. According to FAA regulations, at least one fire fighting and rescue vehicle required by the   15._____
    applicable Index must be able to reach the midpoint of the farthest runway serving air
    carrier users from its assigned post within

    A. 60 seconds   B. 90 seconds
    C. 2 minutes   D. 4 minutes

16. United States instrument flight rules require that an instrument flight must be conducted   16._____
    at a minimum height of _____ feet above the highest obstacle within 5 miles of the air-
    craft's position, except while landing or taking off.

    A. 700   B. 1000   C. 3000   D. 5000

17. Which of the following types of concession leasing arrangements is most commonly   17._____
    used at United States airports?

    A. Open tender
    B. Closed tender
    C. Private treaty
    D. A combination of open tender and private treaty

18. In order to be considered to have *good* braking action, a runway must provide a friction coefficient of AT LEAST

    A. .25   B. .30   C. .40   D. .50

18.____

19. Which of the following steps in determining an airport's peak profile hour would be performed LAST?

    A. For each hour, the average hourly volume is computed across the month.
    B. The largest hourly value in the average peak day is determined.
    C. The peak month is selected.
    D. The average hourly volume for an average peak day is determined.

19.____

20. NOTAMs, urgent operational codes for the attention of aircrew and operations personnel, always contain a total of five letters. The second letter is always a vowel. If the second letter of a NOTAM code is the vowel J, what is being referred to?

    A. Radio aids   B. Taxiways
    C. Lighting facilities   D. Aerodromes

20.____

21. At an airport, terminal management's final choice of operational procedure will depend primarily on each of the following factors EXCEPT

    A. financial constraints
    B. availability of local labor and skills
    C. organizational structure
    D. local industrial relations

21.____

22. Of the following noise reducing improvements in second-generation high bypass ratio airplane engines, which is most significant?

    A. The use of low flow speeds in the fan, compressor, and exhaust areas of the engine
    B. Elimination of inlet guide vanes
    C. Increased spacing of turbine blade rows
    D. Sound absorbing material in the inlet and outlet engine ducts

22.____

23. The FAA's most common measure of single-event noise occurrences at airports is

    A. day/night average sound level (DNL)
    B. sound exposure level (SEL)
    C. noise and number index (NNI)
    D. effective perceived noise level (EPNL)

23.____

24. For reasons of safety, the speeds of automated pedestrian walkways used in airport terminals must be limited to approximately _____ mph.

    A. 1.5   B. 3   C. 7.5   D. 12

24.____

25. An instrument runway served by ILS and visual aids, intended for use in operations down   25.____
    to a decision height of 100 feet and an RVR of 1200 feet, would be classified as

    A. a precision approach runway - Category II
    B. a precision approach runway - Category III
    C. Category IIIA
    D. Category IIIC

————

KEY (CORRECT ANSWERS)

1.	B		11.	C
2.	B		12.	B
3.	B		13.	A
4.	C		14.	A
5.	C		15.	D
6.	B		16.	B
7.	B		17.	B
8.	B		18.	C
9.	C		19.	B
10.	C		20.	C

21. C
22. A
23. B
24. A
25. A

————

EXAMINATION SECTION
TEST 1

DIRECTIONS: Each question or incomplete statement is followed by several suggested answers or completions. Select the one that BEST answers the question or completes the statement. *PRINT THE LETTER OF THE CORRECT ANSWER IN THE SPACE AT THE RIGHT.*

1. Assume that you are called on to render first aid to a man injured in an accident. You find he is bleeding profusely, is unconscious, and has a broken arm. There is a strong odor of alcohol about him.
   The FIRST thing for which you should treat him is the   1._____

   A. bleeding   B. unconsciousness
   C. broken arm   D. alcoholism

2. In applying first aid for removal of a foreign body in the eye, an important precaution   2._____
   to be observed is:
   Do not

   A. attempt to wash out the foreign body
   B. bring the upper eyelid down over the lower
   C. rub the eye
   D. touch or attempt to remove a speck on the lower lid

3. The one of the following symptoms which is LEAST likely to indicate that a person   3._____
   involved in an accident requires first aid for shock is that

   A. he has fainted twice   B. his face is red and flushed
   C. his skin is wet with sweat   D. his pulse is rapid

4. When giving first aid to a person suffering from shock as a result of an auto accident, it is   4._____
   MOST important to

   A. massage him in order to aid blood circulation
   B. have him sip whiskey
   C. prop him up in a sitting position
   D. cover the person and keep him warm

5. Assume that you are about to apply artificial respiration to a person.   5._____
   The LEAST useful of the following items is a(n)

   A. blanket   B. inhalator
   C. hot water bottle   D. radiant heater

6. Assume that you are called on to render first aid to a man injured in an accident. You find   6._____
   he is bleeding profusely in spurts, has a rash indicating food poisoning, has a broken leg,
   and is not breathing.
   The FIRST thing for which you should treat him is

   A. profuse bleeding   B. not breathing
   C. the broken leg   D. food poisoning

7. Assume that you are called to render first aid to a person who is unconscious. Your first glance indicates that the victim's face is cherry red.
You would IMMEDIATELY start treatment for

    A. heat exhaustion   B. sunstroke
    C. gas asphyxiation   D. red unconsciousness

7.___

8. Of the following statements concerning the treatment of wounds with severe bleeding, the LEAST accurate is:

    A. The chief duty of the first aider is to stop the bleeding at once
    B. Application of digital pressure in most severe venous bleeding may well be recommended
    C. In all serious bleeding, the first aider should think first of pressure
    D. Stimulants should be given so that the patient will not go into shock

8.___

9. Of the following statements concerning the use of tourniquets, the LEAST accurate is:

    A. Tourniquets are most frequently used in cases of severe venous bleeding
    B. It is preferable to use a pad over the artery with a tourniquet
    C. A tourniquet is correctly applied in only two places
    D. A tourniquet should be loosened every fifteen or twenty minutes

9.___

10. Suppose that you are called to administer first aid to an unconscious person.
Of the following, the BEST reason for not attempting to administer a liquid stimulant to this person is that

    A. he may have poor circulation of blood
    B. he may choke on the liquid
    C. stimulants affect the heart
    D. stimulants should be administered at the direction of a physician

10.___

11. Assume that it is necessary for you to apply a tourniquet in order to stop serious bleeding.
The one of the following MOST properly used for this purpose is

    A. thin cord   B. thick rope
    C. a necktie   D. wire

11.___

12. Suppose than an elderly man has met with an accident and is lying on the floor awaiting the arrival of a doctor. Of the following, the BEST action to take in order to prevent shock is to

    A. raise him to a sitting position   B. apply a wet cloth to his head
    C. apply artificial respiration   D. cover him with a coat

12.___

13. While you are on duty, a fellow officer suddenly turns pale and his breathing becomes rapid and shallow. He is apparently suffering from heat exhaustion.
Of the following, the LEAST desirable action for you to take under the circumstances is to

    A. apply cold cloths to his head   B. place him in a reclining position
    C. give him a stimulant   D. have him sip salt water

13.___

14. Assume that a fellow officer is in contact with an electrically charged wire.   14._____
    Of the following, the BEST reason for not grasping the victim's clothing with your bare
    hands in order to pull him off the wire is that

    A. his clothing may be damp with perspiration
    B. his clothing may be 100% wool
    C. you may be standing on a dry surface
    D. you may be wearing rubber-soled shoes

15. The recommended first aid procedure for a person who has fainted is to lay him down   15._____
    with his head lower than his body.
    Such a position is used because it

    A. quickly relieves exhaustion
    B. is the most comfortable position
    C. speeds the return of blood to his head
    D. retards rapid breathing

16. If an ambulance is required for an injured passenger, all subway employees including   16._____
    railroad clerks are instructed to call the transit police department and have them call the
    ambulance.
    An important reason for such a procedure is to

    A. enable the clerk to concentrate on his regular duties
    B. provide faster service
    C. fix responsibility
    D. avoid possible duplication of calls

17. According to the latest recommended first aid practice, a cut finger should be cleaned   17._____
    with

    A. soap and water   B. phenol
    C. mercurochrome   D. iodine

18. If a clerk has to telephone for an ambulance for an injured person, the MOST important   18._____
    information he must transmit is

    A. where the ambulance is needed
    B. the name of the injured person
    C. how the accident occurred
    D. what part of the body has been injured

19. When an ambulance arrives to take away an unconscious person, it would probably be   19._____
    MOST difficult for an officer to obtain the name of the

    A. station   B. ambulance attendant
    C. hospital   D. injured person

20. The first aid procedure of not moving a person unless absolutely necessary is MOST   20._____
    important in the case of a person who has

    A. fainted   B. collapsed from heat
    C. fractured his leg   D. broken a finger

21. Shock, a condition often brought on by a serious injury to any part of the body, is dangerous MAINLY because   21.____

    A. body temperature rises too high
    B. blood pressure becomes very high
    C. the injured person remains unconscious for a long time
    D. there is a reduction in the flow of blood to the vital organs

22. If a little *battery fluid* accidentally gets into a person's eye, the FIRST thing to do is to   22.____

    A. call a doctor or ambulance
    B. find out what safety rule was broken
    C. put several drops of clean olive oil in the eye
    D. wash the eye with large quantities of plain water

23. If an unconscious person is found on the sidewalk, the BEST of the following to do right away is to   23.____

    A. cover him to keep him warm
    B. give him sips of hot tea or coffee
    C. move him into the nearest building
    D. shake him gently to arouse him

24. To keep germs from entering a wound, it is BEST to   24.____

    A. apply a sterilized dressing to the wound
    B. put an antiseptic on the wound
    C. squeeze the wound gently to make it bleed
    D. wash the wound with soap and hot water

25. If several persons are injured in an accident, the one who should be treated FIRST is the person who   25.____

    A. has a compound fracture   B. has severe burns
    C. is bleeding seriously   D. is in the greatest pain

KEY (CORRECT ANSWERS)

1.	A	11.	C
2.	C	12.	D
3.	B	13.	A
4.	D	14.	A
5.	B	15.	C
6.	A	16.	D
7.	C	17.	A
8.	D	18.	A
9.	A	19.	D
10.	B	20.	C

21.	D
22.	D
23.	A
24.	A
25.	C

TEST 2

DIRECTIONS: Each question or incomplete statement is followed by several suggested answers or completions. Select the one that BEST answers the question or completes the statement. *PRINT THE LETTER OF THE CORRECT ANSWER IN THE SPACE AT THE RIGHT.*

1. An injured person who is unconscious should *not* be given a liquid to drink MAINLY because

    A. cold liquid may be harmful
    B. he may choke on it
    C. he may not like the liquid
    D. his unconsciousness may be due to too much liquid

1.___

2. The MOST important reason for putting a bandage on a cut is to

    A. help prevent germs from getting into the cut
    B. hide the ugly scar
    C. keep the blood pressure down
    D. keep the skin warm

2.___

3. In first aid for an injured person, the MAIN purpose of a tourniquet is to

    A. prevent infection
    B. restore circulation
    C. support a broken bone
    D. stop severe bleeding

3.___

4. Artificial respiration is given in first aid MAINLY to

    A. force air into the lungs
    B. force blood circulation by even pressure
    C. keep the injured person awake
    D. prevent shock by keeping the victim's body in motion

4.___

5. The aromatic spirits of ammonia in a first aid kit should be used to

    A. clean a dirty wound
    B. deaden pain
    C. revive a person who has fainted
    D. warm a person who is chilled

5.___

6. Suppose that you come upon an old man with blood on his face, seated on the sidewalk leaning against the tire of a parked car.
Of the following, the BEST action for you to take FIRST is to

    A. ask the man for identification
    B. call a policeman to move him from his dangerous position
    C. examine him to see what first aid help you can give
    D. look up and down the block to find a witness to the accident

6.___

7. A person trips on a station stairway, striking his head so severely that his breathing is stopped.
First aid treatment should consist of the IMMEDIATE application of

    A. a bandage
    B. a compress
    C. cold water
    D. artificial respiration

7.___

8. When a passenger becomes seriously ill, it is advisable to call an ambulance PRIMA-RILY to   8.____

    A. save expense for the city
    B. provide adequate treatment
    C. save money for the passenger
    D. remove him from city property

9. The procedure of not moving a person unless absolutely necessary is MOST essential in the case of a person who has   9.____

    A. fainted
    B. collapsed from heat exhaustion
    C. fractured his leg
    D. a severe nose bleed

10. A railroad clerk sees a passenger, apparently ill, fall to the floor some distance from his booth during a quiet period.   10.____
The railroad clerk should

    A. immediately close the booth and go to the passenger
    B. not leave the booth since a hold-up may be planned
    C. remain in the booth and call the nearest hospital
    D. send the next passenger to the person's assistance

11. If an artery has been cut, you can tell by the   11.____

    A. quick clotting of the blood
    B. RH factor of the blood
    C. slow, steady flow of blood
    D. spurting of the blood

12. The BEST material to be used directly over a wound or burn is   12.____

    A. absorbent cotton   B. adhesive tape
    C. sterile gauze   D. tourniquet

13. Aromatic spirits of ammonia is used as a(n)   13.____

    A. antidote for arsenic poisoning   B. stimulant
    C. sedative drug   D. sterilizing solution

14. A compound fracture is one in which   14.____

    A. broken bones protrude through the skin
    B. bones are broken and shattered
    C. a large bone and its adjoining smaller bones are broken
    D. two or more bones are broken

15. If you accidentally get a liquid chemical into your eye, the FIRST thing you should do is   15.____

    A. try to rub the chemical out of your eye
    B. rinse your eye with cold water
    C. bandage your eye
    D. put eye drops in your eye

16. If the label on a bottle of cleaning fluid has the word *flammable* on it, it means that the fluid   16.____

    A. is strong enough to remove grease stains
    B. must be mixed with water before use
    C. can easily be set on fire
    D. is used to kill germs

17. When a fire occurs in or near electrical equipment, the MOST suitable method of extinguishing it is to   17.____

    A. drench it with water
    B. use rags to beat it out
    C. use a fire extinguisher of the proper type
    D. smother it with grease

18. The BEST way to treat a person who has fainted is to   18.____

    A. place him gently on his back
    B. give him a cold glass of water to drink
    C. give him artificial respiration
    D. revive him immediately by placing him in a sitting position

19. The BEST thing to do immediately for a person who has suffered a severe blow to his head in a fall is to   19.____

    A. have him lie down and remain quiet until medical attention is obtained
    B. quickly transport him to a bed
    C. have him sit down and give him a glass of water
    D. get him up and walk him around

20. Of the following, the one which is LEAST likely to be a symptom of shock is that the victim   20.____

    A. feels cold
    B. feels weak
    C. has a rapid but weak pulse
    D. looks flushed

21. In attempting to revive a person who has stopped breathing after receiving an electric shock, it is MOST important to   21.____

    A. start artificial respiration immediately
    B. wrap the victim in a blanket
    C. massage the ankles and wrists
    D. force the victim to swallow a stimulant

22. Artificial respiration after a severe shock is ALWAYS necessary when the shock results   22.____
    in

    A. unconsciousness   B. a burn
    C. stoppage of breathing   D. bleeding

23. If a maintainer makes contact with a 600-volt conductor and remains in contact, your   23.____
    FIRST action should be to

    A. search for the disconnecting switch
    B. ground the conductor with a bare wire
    C. pull him loose by his clothing
    D. cut the conductor

24. Assume that you have burned your hand accidentally while on the job.   24.____
    The POOREST first aid remedy for the burn would be

    A. tannic acid   B. iodine
    C. vaseline   D. baking soda

25. Small cuts or injuries should be   25.____

    A. taken care of immediately to avoid infection
    B. ignored because they are seldom important
    C. ignored unless they are painful
    D. taken care of at the end of the day

KEY (CORRECT ANSWERS)

1.	B		11.	D
2.	A		12.	C
3.	D		13.	B
4.	A		14.	A
5.	C		15.	B
6.	C		16.	C
7.	D		17.	C
8.	B		18.	A
9.	C		19.	A
10.	A		20.	D

21.	A
22.	C
23.	C
24.	B
25.	A

EXAMINATION SECTION
TEST 1

DIRECTIONS: Each question or incomplete statement is followed by several suggested answers or completions. Select the one that BEST answers the question or completes the statement. *PRINT THE LETTER OF THE CORRECT ANSWER IN THE SPACE AT THE RIGHT.*

1. Companies with successful customer service organizations *usually* experience each of the following EXCEPT

    A. fewer customer complaints
    B. greater response to advertising
    C. lower marketing costs
    D. more repeat business

1.____

2. To be MOST useful to an organization, feedback received from customers should be each of the following EXCEPT

    A. centered on internal customers
    B. ongoing
    C. focused on a limited number of indicators
    D. available to every employee in the organization

2.____

3. Instead of directly saying *no* to a customer, service representatives will usually get BEST results with a reply that begins with the words:

    A. I'll try
    B. I don't believe
    C. You can
    D. It's not our policy

3.____

4. Once a customer problem is identified, each of the following should become a part of the service recovery process EXCEPT

    A. following up on the problem resolution
    B. making whatever promises are necessary
    C. providing the customer with what was originally requested
    D. listening and responding to every complaint given by the customer

4.____

5. The percentage of an organization's annual business that involves repeat customers is CLOSEST to _____%.

    A. 25   B. 45   C. 65   D. 85

5.____

6. Of the following, the _____ is NOT generally considered to be a major source of *service promise.*

    A. customer service representative
    B. organization
    C. particular department that delivers product to the customer
    D. customer

6.____

7. A customer appears to be mildly irritated when lodging a complaint.　　　　7._____
    The MOST appropriate action for a service representative to take while attempting res-
    olution is to

    A. allow venting of frustrations
    B. enlist the customer in generating solutions
    C. show emotional neutrality
    D. create calm

8. If an organization loses one customer who normally spends $50 per week, the projected　　8._____
    result of reduction in sales for the following year will be APPROXIMATELY

    A. $2600　　　　B. $12,400　　　　C. $124,000　　　　D. $950,000

9. The majority of *service promises* originate from　　　　9._____

    A. organizational management
    B. customer service professionals
    C. the customers' expectations
    D. organizational marketing

10. To arrive at a *fair fix* to a service problem, one should FIRST　　　　10._____

    A. offer an apology for the problem
    B. ask probing questions to understand and confirm the nature of the problem
    C. listen to the customer's description of the problem
    D. determine and implement a solution to the problem

11. Which of the following is NOT generally considered to be a function of *open questioning*　　11._____
    when dealing with a customer?

    A. Defining problems
    B. Confirming an order
    C. Getting more information
    D. Establishing customer needs

12. When dealing with a customer, service representatives should generally use the pronoun　　12._____

    A. *they*, meaning the company as a whole
    B. *they*, meaning the department to whom the complaint will be referred
    C. *I*, meaning themselves, as representatives of the organization
    D. *we*, meaning themselves and the customer

13. A customer service representative demonstrates product and service knowledge by　　13._____

    A. anticipating the changing needs of customers
    B. soliciting feedback from customers about customer service
    C. studying the capabilities of the office computer system
    D. knowing what questions are asked most by customers about a product or service

14. When listening to a customer during a face-to-face meeting, the MOST appropriate non-verbal gesture is
    14.____

    A. clenched fists
    B. leaning slightly toward the customer
    C. hands casually in pockets
    D. standing with crossed arms

15. Before breaking or bending an existing service rule in order to better serve a customer, a representative should be aware of each of the following EXCEPT the
    15.____

    A. reason for the rule
    B. location of a written copy of the rule and policy
    C. consequences of not following the rule
    D. situations in which the rule is applicable

16. The LEAST likely reason for a dissatisfied customer's failure to complain about a product or service is that the customer
    16.____

    A. does not think the complaint will produce the desired results
    B. is unaware of the proper channels through which to voice his/her complaint
    C. does not believe he/she has the time to spend on the complaint
    D. does not believe anyone in the organization really cares about the complaint

17. Most research shows that _____% of what is communicated between people during face-to-face meetings is conveyed through entirely nonverbal cues.
    17.____

    A. 10   B. 30   C. 50   D. 80

18. When a customer submits a written complaint, the representative should write a response that avoids
    18.____

    A. addressing every single component of the customer's complaint
    B. a personal tone
    C. the use of a pre-formulated response structure
    D. mentioning future business transactions

19. A customer service representative spends several hours practicing with the various forms and paperwork required by the company for handling customer service situations. Which of the following basic areas of learning is the representative trying to improve upon?
    19.____

    A. Interpersonal skills
    B. Product and service knowledge
    C. Customer knowledge
    D. Technical skills

20. If a customer service representative must deal with other members of a service team in order to resolve a problem, the representative should avoid
    20.____

    A. developing personal relationships
    B. giving others credit for ideas that clearly were not theirs
    C. circumventing uncooperative team members by quietly contacting a superior
    D. involving customers in the resolution of a complaint

21. A customer service representative is willing to help customers promptly.   21.____
    Which of the following service factors is the representative able to demonstrate?

    A. Assurance   B. Responsiveness
    C. Empathy   D. Reliability

22. A service representative begins work in a specialized order entry job and soon learns   22.____
    that many customers call in with orders at the last minute, causing her routine to be
    thrown out of balance and creating stress.
    After studying the ordering patterns of all clients, the MOST effective resolution to the
    problem would be to

    A. mail reminder notices to habitually late customers in advance of typical ordering
        dates to establish lead time
    B. telephone habitually late customers a few days before their typical ordering dates
        to establish lead time
    C. place the orders of habitually late customers in advance, changing them later if
        necessary
    D. establish and enforce a rigid lead-time deadline to create more manageable client
        behavior

23. For BEST results, customer service representatives will improve service by considering   23.____
    themselves to be representative of

    A. the entire organization
    B. the department receiving the complaint
    C. the customer
    D. an adversary of the organization, who will fight along with the customer

24. Of all the customers who stop doing business with organizations, _____ percent do so   24.____
    because of product dissatisfaction.

    A. 15   B. 40   C. 65   D. 80

25. When using the *problem-solving* approach to solve the problem of a dissatisfied cus-   25.____
    tomer, the LAST step should be to

    A. double check for customer satisfaction
    B. identify the customer's expectations
    C. outline a solution or alternatives
    D. take action on the problem

KEY (CORRECT ANSWERS)

1.	B	11.	B
2.	A	12.	C
3.	C	13.	D
4.	B	14.	B
5.	C	15.	B
6.	C	16.	C
7.	B	17.	C
8.	A	18.	C
9.	B	19.	D
10.	C	20.	C

21.	B
22.	B
23.	A
24.	A
25.	A

———————

TEST 2

Each question or incomplete statement is followed by several suggested answers or completions. Select the one that BEST answers the question or completes the statement. *PRINT THE LETTER OF THE CORRECT ANSWER IN THE SPACE AT THE RIGHT.*

1. Of the following, the LEAST likely reason for a customer to telephone an organization or department is to
   1.____

   A. voice an objection   B. make a statement
   C. offer praise   D. ask a question

2. Customer service *usually* requires each of the following EXCEPT
   2.____

   A. product knowledge
   B. friendliness and approachability
   C. problem-solving skills
   D. company/organization knowledge

3. According to research, a typical dissatisfied customer will tell about _____ people how dissatisfied he/she is with an organization's product or service.
   3.____

   A. 3   B. 5   C. 10   D. 20

4. When a service target is provided by a manager, it is MOST important for a service representative to know the
   4.____

   A. nature of the customer database associated with the target
   B. formula for achieving the target
   C. methods used by other service personnel for achieving the target
   D. purpose behind the target

5. Typically, customers cause about _____ of the service and product problems they complain about.
   5.____

   A. 1/5   B. 1/3   C. 1/2   D. 2/3

6. When a dissatisfied customer complains to a service representative, making a sale is NOT considered to be good service when the
   6.____

   A. customer appreciates being changed to a different service or product
   B. the original product or service is in need of additional parts or components to be complete
   C. the customer remains angry about the original complaint
   D. the original product or service is in need of repair

7. As service representatives, personnel would be LEAST likely to be responsible for
   7.____

   A. service   B. marketing
   C. problem-solving   D. sales

8. When writing a memorandum on a customer complaint, _____ can be considered 8.____
    optional by a service representative.

    A. the date the complaint was filed and/or the problem occurred
    B. a summary of the customer's comments
    C. the address of the customer
    D. a suggestion for correcting the situation

9. In most successful organizations, customer service is considered PRIMARILY to be the 9.____
    domain of the

    A. entire organization   B. sales department
    C. complaint department   D. service department

10. According to MOST research, the cost of attracting a new customer, in relation to the 10.____
    cost of retaining a current customer, is about

    A. half as much   B. about the same
    C. twice as much   D. five times as much

11. If a customer service representative is unable to do what a customer asks, the represen- 11.____
    tative should avoid

    A. quoting organizational policy regarding the customer's request
    B. explaining why it cannot be done
    C. making specific statements
    D. offering alternatives

12. When a customer presents a service representative with a request, the representative's 12.____
    FIRST reaction should *usually* be a(n)

    A. apology
    B. friendly greeting
    C. statement of organizational policy regarding the request
    D. request for clarifying information

13. It is NOT a primary reason for written communication with customers to 13.____

    A. create documentation   B. solidify relationships
    C. confirm understanding   D. solicit business contact

14. Of the following, which would be LEAST frustrating for a customer to hear from a service 14.____
    representative?

    A. You will have to
    B. I will do my best
    C. Let me see what I can do
    D. He/she should be back any minute

15. A customer appears to be mildly irritated when lodging a complaint. 15.____
    It is MOST appropriate for a service representative to demonstrate _____ in reaction
    to the complaint.

    A. urgency   B. empathy
    C. nonchalance   D. surprise

16. The _____ would be indirectly served by an individual who takes customer orders at an organization's telephone center.

    A. customer   B. management personnel
    C. billing agents   D. warehouse staff

16._____

17. Based on the actions of a customer service representative, customers will be MOST likely to make judgments concerning each of the following EXCEPT the

    A. kind of people employed by the organization
    B. company's value system
    C. organization's commitment to advertised promises
    D. value of the organization's product

17._____

18. When dealing with customers, a service representative's apologies, if necessary, should NOT be

    A. immediate   B. official   C. sincere   D. personal

18._____

19. Of all the customers who stop doing business with organizations, approximately _____ percent do so because of indifferent treatment by employees.

    A. 20   B. 45   C. 70   D. 95

19._____

20. If a customer service representative is aware that the organization is not capable of meeting a customer's expectations, the representative's FIRST responsibility would be to

    A. tell the customer of the organization's inability to comply
    B. shape the customer's expectations to match what the organization is capable of doing for him/her
    C. encourage the customer to believe that the organization can do as he/she asks
    D. make the sale on the organization's product

20._____

21. The following is an example of a *bonus benefit* associated with a product or service: A customer

    A. buys a sporty sedan and finds that its tight turning ratio makes it easy to park
    B. buys bread specifically because he wants to receive a coupon for his next purchase
    C. purchases a car and discovers a strange smell in the upholstery
    D. buys a music audiotape and discovers that there are advertisements at the beginning and end of the tape

21._____

22. Approximately _____ percent of customers who voice complaints with an organization will continue to do business with the organization if the complaint is resolved promptly.

    A. 25   B. 40   C. 75   D. 95

22._____

23. Though necessary, a positive, proactive customer satisfaction policy will USUALLY be restricted by costs and

    A. volume of service problems
    B. limitations of management personnel authority
    C. unreasonable customer demands
    D. limitations of service policy

23._____

24. According to MOST customers, _____ prevents good listening on the part of a service representative when a customer is speaking.   24._____

    A. technological apparatus (e.g. voicemail)
    B. frequent interruptions by other staff or customers
    C. asking unnecessary questions
    D. background noise

25. The ability to provide the promised service or product dependably and accurately may be defined as.   25._____

    A. assurance   B. responsiveness
    C. courtesy   D. reliability

KEY (CORRECT ANSWERS)

1.	C	11.	A
2.	B	12.	D
3.	C	13.	D
4.	D	14.	C
5.	B	15.	A
6.	C	16.	B
7.	B	17.	D
8.	C	18.	B
9.	A	19.	C
10.	D	20.	B

21.	A
22.	D
23.	D
24.	B
25.	D

EXAMINATION SECTION
TEST 1

DIRECTIONS: Each question or incomplete statement is followed by several suggested answers or completions. Select the one that BEST answers the question or completes the statement. *PRINT THE LETTER OF THE CORRECT ANSWER IN THE SPACE AT THE RIGHT.*

1. An employee who is not sure how to do a job that the supervisor has just assigned should

    A. ask another employee how to do the job
    B. ask the supervisor how to do the job
    C. do some other work until the supervisor gives further instructions
    D. do the best he can

1.____

2. An employee who is asked by the supervisor to work one hour overtime cannot stay because of previous arrangements made with the family. The employee should

    A. ask another employee who does not have a family to take over
    B. explain the situation to the supervisor and ask to be excused
    C. go home, but leave a note for the supervisor explaining the reason for not being able to stay
    D. refuse, giving the excuse that time-and-a-half is not being paid for overtime

2.____

3. A department's MAIN purpose in setting up employee rules and regulations is to

    A. explain the department's work to the public
    B. give an official history of the department
    C. help in the efficient running of the department
    D. limit the number of employees who break the rules

3.____

4. The MAIN reason an employee should be polite is that

    A. he may get into trouble if he is not polite
    B. he never knows when he may be talking to an official
    C. politeness is a duty which any employee owes the public
    D. politeness will make him appear to be alert and efficient

4.____

5. Public employees would *most probably* be expected by their supervisor to do

    A. a fair day's work according to their ability
    B. more work than the employees of other supervisors
    C. more work than the supervisor really knows they can do
    D. the same amount of work that a little better than average employee can do

5.____

6. Your supervisor gives you a special job to do without saying when it must be finished and then leaves for another job location. A little before quitting time you realize that you will not be able to finish the job that day. You should

    A. ask a few of the other employees to help you finish the job
    B. go home at quitting time and finish the job the next day
    C. stay on the job till you get in touch with your supervisor by phone and get further instructions
    D. work overtime till you finish the job

6.____

7. "While on duty an employee is not permitted to smoke in public." Of the following, the   7.____
    most likely reason for such a rule is that

    A. government employees must be willing to surrender some of their personal liber-
        ties
    B. lighted cigarettes create a fire hazard
    C. nicotine in tobacco will lessen a city employee's ability to perform assigned duties
        properly
    D. smoking on duty may make an unfavorable impression on the public

8. While you are on duty someone asks you how to get somewhere. Supposing that you   8.____
    know how to get there, you should

    A. give him the necessary directions
    B. make believe you did not hear him
    C. tell him it is not your duty to give information
    D. tell him you are too busy to give the information

9. The BEST way to make sure that a piece of important mail will be received is to send it   9.____
    by

    A. first class mail   B. fourth class mail
    C. registered mail   D. special delivery

10. Letters, if they don't weigh more than an ounce, need a   10.____

    A. 37¢ stamp   B. 38¢ stamp
    C. 39¢ stamp   D. 40¢ stamp

QUESTIONS 11-15.

Answer questions 11 to 15 *ONLY* on the basis of the information given in the following paragraph.

If an employee thinks he can save money, time, or material for the city or has an idea about how
to do something better than it is being done, he should not keep it to himself. He should send
his ideas to the Employee's Suggestion Program, using the special form which is kept on hand
in all departments. An employee may send in as many ideas as he wishes. To make sure that
each idea is judged fairly, the name of the suggestor is not made known until an award is made.
The awards are certificates of merit or cash prizes ranging from $10 to $500.

11. According to the above paragraph, an employee who knows how to do a job in a better   11.____
    way should

    A. be sure it saves enough time to be worthwhile
    B. get paid the money he saves for the city
    C. keep it to himself to avoid being accused of causing a speed-up
    D. send his ideas to the Employee's Suggestion Program

12. In order to send his idea to the Employee's Suggestion Program, an employee should   12.____

    A. ask the Department of Personnel for a special form
    B. get the special form in his own department

C. mail the idea, using Special Delivery
D. send it on plain, white, letter-sized paper

13. An employee may send to the Employee's Suggestion Program   13.____

A. as many ideas as he can think of
B. no more than one idea each week
C. no more than ten ideas in a month
D. only one idea on each part of the job

14. The reason the name of an employee who makes a suggestion is not made known at   14.____
    first is to

A. give the employee a larger award
B. help the judges give more awards
C. insure fairness in judging
D. make sure no employee gets two awards

15. An employee whose suggestion receives an award may be given a   15.____

A. bonus once a year
B. cash price of up to $500
C. certificate for $10
D. salary increase of $500

QUESTIONS 16-18.

Answer questions 16 to 18 *ONLY* on the basis of the information given in the following paragraph.

According to the rules of the Department of Personnel, the work of every permanent City
employee is reviewed and rated by his supervisor at least once a year. The civil service rating
system gives the employee and his supervisor a chance to talk about the progress made during
the past year as well as about those parts of the job in which the employee needs to do better.
In order to receive a pay increase each year, the employee must have a satisfactory service rating. Service ratings also count toward an employee's final mark on a promotion examination.

16. According to the above paragraph, a permanent City employee is rated *at least* once   16.____

A. before his work is reviewed
B. every six months
C. yearly by his supervisor
D. yearly by the Department of Personnel

17. According to the above paragraph, under the rating system the supervisor and the   17.____
    employee can discuss how

A. much more work needs to be done next year
B. the employee did his work last year
C. the work can be made easier next year
D. the work of the Department can be increased

18. According to the above paragraph, a permanent City employee will NOT receive a yearly   18.____
pay increase

    A. if he received a pay increase for the year before
    B. if he used his service rating for his mark on a promotion examination
    C. if his service rating is unsatisfactory
    D. unless he got some kind of a service rating

19. "Employees on duty represent their Department to the citizens and are expected to be   19.____
neat and orderly in their dress at all times." According to this statement, neat and orderly
dress of employees while on duty is important because

    A. citizens don't care about the appearance of city employees who are off duty
    B. employees who are neat and orderly in their dress make better citizens
    C. if an employee dresses neatly while at work, he will dress neatly when away from
work
    D. people might judge a department by the appearance of its employees

20. "In the city there are 266 shoe factories which employ 10,000 workers while in all the   20.____
other cities of the state there are 62 shoe factories which employ 27,000 workers."
According to this statement, the shoe factories in the city

    A. are larger than the shoe factories in any other city in the state
    B. employ more workers than all the other shoe factories in the state
    C. make cheaper shoes than the shoe factories in other cities of the state
    D. are greater in number than the shoe factories in all the other cities of the state

21. "All mail matter up to and including eight ounces in weight which is not classified as first   21.____
or second class mail is third class mail. If a package weighs more than eight ounces, it is
put into the fourth class and sent as parcel-post mail." According to this statement, mail
weighing eight ounces or less may be

    A. classified as parcel-post mail
    B. first, second, or third class mail
    C. second class mail but not third class
    D. third or fourth class mail

QUESTIONS 22-24.

Answer questions 22 to 24 ONLY on the basis of the information given in the following paragraph.

Keeping the City of New York operating day and night requires the services of more than
200,000 civil service workers-roughly the number of people who live in Syracuse. This huge
army of specialists work at more than 2,000 different jobs. The City's civil service workers are
able to do everything that needs doing to keep the City running. Their only purpose is the well-
being, comfort and safety of the citizens of New York.

22. Of the following titles, the one that most nearly gives the meaning of the above para-   22.____
graph is:

    A. "Civil Service in Syracuse"
    B. "Everyone Works"

C.   "Job Variety"
D.   "Serving New York City"

23.   According to the above paragraph, in order to keep New York City operating 24 hours a   23.____
day

A.   half of the civil service workers work days and half work nights
B.   more than 200,000 civil service workers are needed on the day shift
C.   the City needs about as many civil service workers as there are people in Syra-
cuse
D.   the services of some people who live in Syracuse is required

24.   According to the above paragraph, it is MOST reasonable to assume that in New York   24.____
City's civil service

A.   a worker can do any job that needs doing
B.   each worker works at a different job
C.   some workers work at more than one job
D.   some workers work at the same jobs

QUESTIONS 25-28.

Answer questions 25 to 28 ONLY on the basis of the information given in the following paragraph.

The National and City flags are displayed daily from those public buildings which are equipped
with vertical or horizontal flag staffs. Where a building has only one flag staff, only the National
flag is displayed. When the National flag is to be raised at the same time as other flags, the
National flag shall be raised about 6 feet in advance of the other flags; if the flags are raised
separately, the National flag shall always be raised first. When more than one flag is flown on
horizontal staffs, the National flag shall be flown so that it is to the extreme left as the observer
faces the flag.
When more than one flag is displayed, they should all by the same size. Under no circumstances should the National flag be smaller in size than any other flag in a combination display.
The standard size for flags flown from City buildings is 5' x 8'.

25.   From the above paragraph, a REASONABLE conclusion about flag staffs on public build-   25.____
ings is that a public building

A.   might have no flag staff at all
B.   needs two flag staffs
C.   should have at least one flag staff
D.   usually has a horizontal and a vertical flag staff

26.   According to the above paragraph, a public building that has only one flag staff should   26.____
raise the National flag

A.   and no other flag
B.   at sunrise
C.   first and then the City flag
D.   six feet in advance of any other flag

27. According to the above paragraph, the order, from left to right, in which the National flag   27._____
flying from one of four horizontal staffs appear to a person who is facing the flag staffs is:

    A.   Flag 1, flag 2, flag 3, National flag
    B.   National flag, flag 1, flag 2, flag 3
    C.   Flag 1, flag 2, National flag, flag 3
    D.   Flag 1, National flag, flag 2, flag 3

28. According to the above paragraph, a combination display of flags on a City building   28._____
would *usually* have

    A.   a 6' x 10' National flag
    B.   all flags 5' x 8' size
    C.   all other flags smaller than the National flag
    D.   5' x 8' National and City flags and smaller sized other flags

QUESTIONS 29-30.

Answer questions 29 to 30 *ONLY* on the basis of the information given in the following paragraph.

Supplies are to be ordered from the stock room once a week. The standard requisition form, Form SP 21, is to be used for ordering all supplies. The form is prepared in triplicate, one white original and two green copies. The white and one green copy are sent to the stock room, and the remaining green copy is to be kept by the orderer until the supplies are received.

29. According to the above paragraph, there is a limit on the   29._____

    A.   amount of supplies that may be ordered
    B.   day on which supplies may be ordered
    C.   different kinds of supplies that may be ordered
    D.   number of times supplies may be ordered in one year

30. According to the above paragraph, when the standard requisition form for supplies is,   30._____
prepared

    A.   a total of four requisition blanks is used
    B.   a white form is the original
    C.   each copy is printed in two colors
    D.   one copy is kept by the stock clerk

QUESTIONS 31-55.

Each of questions 31 to 55 consists of a word in capital letters followed by four suggested meanings of the word. For each question, choose the word or phrase which means *most nearly* the SAME as the word in capital letters.

31. ABOLISH   31._____

    A.   count up   B.   do away with
    C.   give more   D.   pay double for

32. ABUSE   32.____

    A.   accept   B.   mistreat
    C.   respect   D.   touch

33. ACCURATE   33.____

    A.   correct   B.   lost
    C.   neat   D.   secret

34. ASSISTANCE   34.____

    A.   attendance   B.   belief
    C.   help   D.   reward

35. CAUTIOUS   35.____

    A.   brave   B.   careful
    C.   greedy   D.   hopeful

36. COURTEOUS   36.____

    A.   better   B.   easy
    C.   polite   D.   religious

37. CRITICIZE   37.____

    A.   admit   B.   blame
    C.   check on   D.   make dirty

38. DIFFICULT   38.____

    A.   capable   B.   dangerous
    C.   dull   D.   hard

39. ENCOURAGE   39.____

    A.   aim at   B.   beg for
    C.   cheer on   D.   free from

40. EXTENT   40.____

    A.   age   B.   size
    C.   truth   D.   wildness

41. EXTRAVAGANT   41.____

    A.   empty   B.   helpful
    C.   over   D.   wasteful

42. FALSE   42.____

    A.   absent   B.   colored
    C.   not enough   D.   wrong

43. INDICATE   43.____

    A.   point out   B.   show up
    C.   shrink from   D.   take to

44. NEGLECT   44.____

    A. disregard   B. flatten
    C. likeness   D. thoughtfulness

45. PENALIZE   45.____

    A. make   B. notice
    C. pay   D. punish

46. POSTPONED   46.____

    A. put off   B. repeated
    C. taught   D. went to

47. PUNCTUAL   47.____

    A. bursting   B. catching
    C. make a hole in   D. on time

48. RARE   48.____

    A. large   B. ride up
    C. unusual   D. young

49. RELY   49.____

    A. depend   B. do again
    C. use   D. wait for

50. REVEAL   50.____

    A. leave   B. renew
    C. soften   D. tell

51. SERIOUS   51.____

    A. important   B. order
    C. sharp   D. tight

52. TRIVIAL   52.____

    A. alive   B. empty
    C. petty   D. troublesome

53. VENTILATE   53.____

    A. air out   B. darken
    C. last   D. take a chance

54. VOLUNTARY   54.____

    A. common   B. paid
    C. sharing   D. willing

55. WHOLESOME   55.____

    A. cheap   B. healthful
    C. hot   D. together

56. An employee earns $96 a day and works 5 days a week. He will earn $4,320 in _____ weeks.   56.____

    A. 5   B. 7   C. 8   D. 9

57. In a certain bureau the entire staff consists of 1 senior supervisor, 2 supervisors, 6 assistant supervisors and 54 associate workers. The percent of the staff who are NOT associate workers is *most nearly*   57.____

    A. 14   B. 21   C. 27   D. 32

58. In a certain bureau, five employees each earn $2,000 a month, another three employees each earn $2,400 a month and another two employees each earn $8,200 a month. The monthly payroll for those employees is   58.____

    A. 27,200   B. 27,600   C. 33,600   D. 36,000

59. An employee contributes 5% of his salary to the pension fund. If his salary is $2,400 a month, the amount of his contribution to the pension fund in a year is   59.____

    A. 960   B. 1,440   C. 1,920   D. 2,400

60. The amount of square feet in an area that is 50 feet long and 30 feet wide is   60.____

    A. 80   B. 150   C. 800   D. 1,500

61. An injured person who is unconscious should NOT be given a liquid to drink *mainly* because   61.____

    A. cold liquid may be harmful
    B. he may choke on it
    C. he may not like the liquid
    D. his unconsciousness may be due to too much liquid

62. The MOST important reason for putting a bandage on a cut is to   62.____

    A. help prevent germs from getting into the cut
    B. hide the ugly scar
    C. keep the blood pressure down
    D. keep the skin warm

63. In first aid for an injured person, the MAIN purpose of a tourniquet is to   63.____

    A. prevent infection
    B. restore circulation
    C. support a broken bone
    D. stop severe bleeding

64. Artificial respiration is given in first aid *mainly* to   64.____

    A. force air into the lungs
    B. force blood circulation by even pressure
    C. keep the injured person awake
    D. prevent shock by keeping the victim's body in motion

65. The aromatic spirits of ammonia in a first aid kit should be used to 65.____

    A. clean a dirty wound
    B. deaden pain
    C. revive a person who has fainted
    D. warm a person who is chilled

QUESTIONS 66-70.

Read the chart below showing the absences in Unit A for the period November 1 through November 15; then answer questions 66 to 70 according to the information given.

ABSENCE RECORD-UNIT A
November 1-15

Date:	1	2	3	4	5	6	7	8	9	10	11	12	13	14	15
Employee															
Ames	X	S	H					X			H			X	X
Bloom	X		H				X	X	S	S	H	S	S		X
Deegan	X	J	H	J	J	J	X	X			H				X
Howard	X		H					X			H			X	X
Jergens	X	M	H	M	M	M		X			H			X	X
Lange	X		H			S	X	X							X
Morton	X						X	X	V	V	H				X
O'Shea	X		H			0		X			H	X		X	X

Code for Types of Absence
X-Saturday or Sunday
H-Legal Holiday
P-Leave without pay
M-Military leave
J-Jury duty
V-Vacation
S-Sick leave
O-Other leave or absence

Note: If there is no entry against an employee's name under a date, the employee worked on that date.

66. According to the above chart, NO employee in Unit A was absent on 66.____

    A. leave without pay
    B. military leave
    C. other leave of absence
    D. vacation

67. According to the above chart, all but one of the employees in Unit A were present on the 67.____

    A. 3rd   B. 5th   C. 9th   D. 13th

68. According to the above chart, the *only* employees who worked on a legal holiday when   68._____
the other employees were absent are

    A. Deegan and Morton   B. Howard and O'Shea
    C. Lange and Morton   D. Morton and O'Shea

69. According to the above chart, the employee who was absent *only* on a day that was   69._____
either a Saturday, Sunday or legal holiday was

    A. Bloom   B. Howard   C. Morton   D. O'Shea

70. The employee who had more absences than anyone else are   70._____

    A. Bloom and Deegan
    B. Bloom, Deegan, and Jergens
    C. Deegan and Jergens
    D. Deegan, Jergens, and O'Shea

KEY (CORRECT ANSWERS)

#		#		#		#		#	
1.	B	16.	C	31.	B	46.	A	61.	B
2.	B	17.	B	32.	B	47.	D	62.	A
3.	C	18.	C	33.	A	48.	C	63.	D
4.	C	19.	D	34.	C	49.	A	64.	A
5.	A	20.	D	35.	B	50.	D	65.	C
6.	B	21.	B	36.	C	51.	A	66.	A
7.	D	22.	D	37.	B	52.	C	67.	D
8.	A	23.	C	38.	D	53.	A	68.	C
9.	C	24.	D	39.	C	54.	D	69.	B
10.	C	25.	A	40.	B	55.	B	70.	B
11.	D	26.	A	41.	D	56.	D		
12.	B	27.	B	42.	D	57.	A		
13.	A	28.	B	43.	A	58.	C		
14.	C	29.	D	44.	A	59.	B		
15.	B	30.	B	45.	D	60.	D		

TEST 2

DIRECTIONS: Each question consists of a statement. You are to indicate whether the statement is TRUE (T) or FALSE (F). *PRINT THE LETTER OF THE CORRECT ANSWER IN THE SPACE AT THE RIGHT.*

QUESTIONS 1-4.

Read the paragraph below about "shock" and then answer questions 1 to 4 according to the information given in the paragraph.

SHOCK

'While not found in all injuries, shock is present in all serious injuries caused by accidents. During shock, the normal activities of the body slow down. This partly explains why one of the signs of shock is a pale, cold skin, since insufficient blood goes to the body parts during shock.

1. If the injury caused by an accident is serious, shock is sure to be present.   1._____

2. In shock, the heart beats faster than normal.   2._____

3. The face of a person suffering from shock is usually red and flushed.   3._____

4. Not enough blood goes to different parts of the body during shock.   4._____

QUESTIONS 5-8.

Read the paragraph below about carbon monoxide gas and then answer questions 5 to 8 according to the information given in this paragraph.

CARBON MONOXIDE GAS

Carbon monoxide is a deadly gas from the effects of which no one is immune. Any person's strength will be cut down considerably by breathing this gas, even though he does not take in enough to overcome him. Wearing a handkerchief tied around the nose and mouth offers some protection against the irritating fumes of ordinary smoke, but many people have died convinced that a handkerchief will stop carbon monoxide. Any person entering a room filled with this deadly gas should wear a mask equipped with an air hose, or even better, an oxygen breathing apparatus.

5. Some people get no ill effects from carbon monoxide gas until they are overcome.   5._____

6. A person can die from breathing carbon monoxide gas.   6._____

7. A handkerchief around the mouth and nose gives some protection against the effects of ordinary smoke.   7._____

8. It is better for a person entering a room filled with carbon monixide to wear a mask equipped with an air hose than an oxygen breathing apparatus.   8._____

QUESTIONS 9-17.

Read the paragraph below about moving an office and then answer questions 9 to 17 according to the information given in the paragraph.

MOVING AN OFFICE

An office with all its equipment is sometimes moved during working hours. This is a difficult task, and must be done in an orderly manner to avoid confusion. The operation should be planned in such a way as not to interrupt the progress of work usually done in the office and to make possible the accurate placement of the furniture and records in the new location. If the office moves to a place inside the same building, the desks and files are moved with all their contents. If the movement is to another building, the contents of each desk and file are placed in boxes. Each box is marked with a letter showing the particular section in the new quarters to which it is to be moved. Also marked on each box is the number of the desk or file on which the box is to be placed. Each piece of equipment must have a numbered tag. The number of each piece of equipment is put in soft chalk on the floor in the new office to show the proper location, and several floor plans are made to show where each piece of equipment goes. When the moving is done someone is stationed at each of the several exits of the old office to see that each box or piece of equipment has its destination clearly marked on it. At the new office someone stands at each of the several entrances with a copy of the floor plan, and directs the placing of the furniture and equipment according to the floor plan. No one should interfere at this point with the arrangements shown on the plan. Improvements in arrangement can be considered and made at a later date.

9.   It is a hard job to move an office from one place to another during working hours.   9.____

10. Confusion CANNOT be avoided if an office is moved during working hours.   10.____

11. The work usually done in an office must be stopped for the day when the office is moved   11.____
     during working hours.

12. If an office is moved from one floor to another in the same building, the contents of a   12.____
     desk are taken out and put into boxes for moving.

13. If boxes are used to hold material from desks when moving an office, the box is num-   13.____
     bered the same as the desk on which it is to be put.

14. Letters are marked in soft chalk on the floor at new quarters to show where the desks   14.____
     should go when moved.

15. When the moving begins, a person is put at each exit of the old office to check that each   15.____
     box and piece of equipment has clearly marked on it where it is to go.

16. A person stationed at each entrance of the new quarters to direct the placing of the furni-   16.____
     ture and equipment has a copy of the floor plan of the new quarters.

17. If, while the furniture is being moved into the new office, a person helping at a doorway   17.____
     gets an idea of a better way to arrange the furniture, he should change the planned
     arrangement and make a record of the change.

QUESTIONS 18-25.

Read the paragraph below about polishing brass fixtures and then answer questions 18 to 25 according to the information given in this paragraph.

POLISHING BRASS FIXTURES

Uncoated brass should be polished in the usual way using brass polish. Special attention need be given only to brass fixtures coated with lacquer. The surface of these fixtures will not endure abrasive cleaners or polishes and should be cleaned regularly with mild soap and water. Lacquer seldom fails to properly protect the surface of brass for the period guaranteed by the manufacturer. But, if the attendant finds darkening or corrosion, or any other symptom of failure of the lacquer, he should notify his foreman. If the guarantee period has not expired, the foreman will have the article returned to the manufacturer. If the guarantee period is over, it is necessary to first remove the old lacquer, refinish and then relacquer the fixture at the agency's shop. It is emphasized that all brass polish contains some abrasive. For this reason, no brass polish should be used on lacquered brass.

18. All brass fixtures should be cleaned in a special way.   18.____

19. A mild brass polish is good for cleaning brass fixtures coated with clear lacquer.   19.____

20. Lacquer coating on brass fixtures usually protects the surfaces for the period of the man-   20.____
ufacturer's guarantee.

21. If an attendant finds corrosion in any lacquered brass article, he should relacquer the   21.____
article.

22. The attendant should notify his foreman of failure of lacquer on a brass fixture only if the   22.____
period of guarantee has expired.

23. The brass fixtures relacquered at the agency's shops are those on which the manufac-   23.____
turer's guarantee has expired.

24. Before a brass fixture Is relacquered, the old lacquer should be taken off.   24.____

25. Brass polish should NOT be used on lacquered surfaces because it contains acid.   25.____

QUESTIONS 26-50.

Questions 26 to 50 relate to word meaning.

26. "The foreman had received a few requests." In this sentence, the word 'requests' means   26.____
nearly the SAME as 'complaints.'

27. "The procedure for doing the work was modified." In this sentence, the word 'modified'   27.____
means *nearly* the SAME as 'discovered.'

28. "He stressed the importance of doing the job right ." In this sentence, the word 'stressed'   28.____
means *nearly* the SAME as 'discovered.'

29. "He worked with rapid movements." In this sentence, the word 'rapid' means *nearly* the   29.____
SAME as 'slow.'

30. "The man resumed his work when the foreman came in." In this sentence, the word   30.____
'resumed' means *nearly* the SAME as 'stopped.'

31. "The interior door would not open." In this sentence, the word 'interior' means *nearly* the SAME as 'inside.' 31._____

32. "He extended his arm." In this sentence, the word 'extended' means *nearly* the SAME as 'stretched out.' 32._____

33. "He answered promptly." In this sentence, the word 'promptly' means *nearly* the SAME as 'quickly.' 33._____

34. "He punctured a piece of rubber." In this sentence, the word 'punctured' means *nearly* the SAME as 'bought.' 34._____

35. "A few men were assisting the attendant." In this sentence, the word 'assisting' means *nearly* the SAME as 'helping.' 35._____

36. "He opposed the idea of using a vacuum cleaner for this job." In this sentence, the word 'opposed' means *nearly* the SAME as 'suggested.' 36._____

37. "Four employees were selected." In this sentence, the word 'selected' means *nearly* the SAME as 'chosen.' 37._____

38. "This man is constantly supervised." In this sentence, the word 'constantly' means *nearly* the SAME as 'rarely.' 38._____

39. "One part of soap to two parts of water is sufficient." In this sentence, the word 'sufficient' means *nearly* the SAME as 'enough.' 39._____

40. "The fire protection system was inadequate." In this sentence, the word 'inadequate' means *nearly* the SAME as 'enough.' 40._____

41. "The nozzle of the hose was clogged." In this sentence, the word 'clogged' means *nearly* the SAME as 'brass.' 41._____

42. "He resembles the man who worked here before." In this sentence, the word 'resembles,' means *nearly* the SAME as 'replaces.' 42._____

43. "They eliminated a number of items." In this sentence, the word 'eliminated' means *nearly* the SAME as 'bought.' 43._____

44. "He is a dependable worker." In this sentence, the word 'dependable' means *nearly* the SAME as 'poor.' 44._____

45. "Some wood finishes color the wood and conceal the natural grain." In this sentence, the word 'conceal' means *nearly* the SAME as 'hide.' 45._____

46. "Paint that is chalking sometimes retains its protective value." In this sentence, the word 'retains' means *nearly* the SAME as 'keeps.' 46._____

47. "Wood and trash had accumulated." In this sentence, the word 'accumulated' means *nearly* the SAME as 'piled up.' 47._____

48. An 'inflammable' liquid is one that is easily set on fire. 48._____

49. "The amounts were then compared." In this sentence, the word 'compared' means *nearly* the SAME as 'added.'   49.____

50. "The boy had fallen into a shallow pool." In this sentence, the work 'shallow' means *nearly* the SAME as 'deep.'   50.____

KEY (CORRECT ANSWERS)

1.	T	11.	F	21.	F	31.	T	41.	F
2.	F	12.	F	22.	F	32.	T	42.	F
3.	F	13.	T	23.	T	33.	T	43.	F
4.	T	14.	F	24.	T	34.	F	44.	F
5.	F	15.	T	25.	F	35.	T	45.	T
6.	T	16.	T	26.	F	36.	F	46.	T
7.	T	17.	F	27.	T	37.	T	47.	T
8.	F	18.	F	28.	F	38.	F	48.	T
9.	T	19.	F	29.	F	39.	T	49.	F
10.	F	20.	T	30.	F	40.	F	50.	F

EXAMINATION SECTION
TEST 1

DIRECTIONS: Each question or incomplete statement is followed by several suggested answers or completions. Select the one that BEST answers the question or completes the statement. *PRINT THE LETTER OF THE CORRECT ANSWER IN THE SPACE AT THE RIGHT.*

1. If you can't come to work in the morning because you do not feel well, you should   1._____

    A. call your supervisor and let him know that you are sick
    B. try to get someone else to take your place
    C. have your doctor call your office as proof that you are sick
    D. come to work anyway so that you won't lose your job

2. Many machines have certain safety devices for the operators.   2._____
   The MOST important reason for having these safety devices is to

    A. increase the amount of work that the machines can do
    B. permit repairs to be made on the machines without shutting them down
    C. help prevent accidents to people who use the machines
    D. reduce the cost of electric power needed to run the machines

3. While working on the job, you accidentally break a window pane. No one is around, and   3._____
   you are able to clean up the broken pieces of glass.
   It would then be BEST for you to

    A. leave a note near the window that a new glass has to be put in because it was accidentally broken
    B. forget about the whole thing because the window was not broken on purpose
    C. write a report to your supervisor telling him that you saw a broken window pane that has to be fixed
    D. tell your supervisor that you accidentally broke the window pane while working

4. There is a two-light fixture in the room where you are working. One of the light bulbs goes   4._____
   out , and you need more light to work by.
   You should

    A. change the fuse in the fuse box
    B. have a new bulb put in
    C. call for an electrician and stop work until he comes
    D. find out what is causing the short circuit

5. The BEST way to remove some small pieces of broken glass from a floor is to   5._____

    A. use a brush and dust pan
    B. pick up the pieces carefully with your hands
    C. use a wet mop and a wringer
    D. sweep the pieces into the corner of the room

6. When you are not sure about some instructions that your supervisor has given you on how to do a certain job, it would be BEST for you to

    A. start doing the work and stop when you come to the part that you do not understand
    B. ask the supervisor to go over the instructions which are not clear to you
    C. do the job immediately from beginning to the end, leaving out the part that you are not sure of
    D. wait until the supervisor leaves and then ask a more experienced worker to explain the job to you

6.____

7. When an employee first comes on the job, he is given a period of training by his supervisor.
The MAIN reason for this training period is to

    A. make sure that the employee will learn to do his work correctly and safely
    B. give the employee a chance to show the supervisor that he can learn quickly
    C. allow the supervisor and the employee a chance to become friendly with each other
    D. find out which employees will make good supervisors later on

7.____

8. After you open a sealed box of supplies, you find that the box is not full and that some of the supplies are missing.
You should

    A. use fewer supplies than you intended to
    B. seal the box and take it back to the storeroom
    C. get signed statements from other employees that when you opened the box, it was not full
    D. tell your supervisor about it

8.____

9. Suppose that after you have been on the job a few months, your supervisor shows you some small mistakes you are making in your work.
You should

    A. tell your supervisor that these mistakes don't keep you from finishing your work
    B. ask your supervisor how you can avoid these mistakes
    C. try to show your supervisor that your way of doing the work is just as good as his way of doing it
    D. check with the other workers to find out if your supervisor is also finding fault with them

9.____

10. If your supervisor gives you an order to do a special job which you do not like to do, you should

    A. take a long time to do the job so that you won't get this job again
    B. do the job the best way you know how even though you don't like it
    C. make believe that you didn't hear your supervisor and do your regular work
    D. say nothing but tell another employee that the supervisor wants him to do this special job

10.____

11. If two employees who are working together on a job do not agree on how to do the job, it would be BEST

    A. for each worker to do the job in his own way until it is finished
    B. to put off doing the job until both workers agree to do it the same way
    C. to ask the supervisor to decide on the way the job is to be done
    D. for each worker to ask for a transfer to another assignment because they can't get along with each other

11.____

12. Suppose that in order to finish your work, you have to lift a heavy box off the floor onto an empty desk.
You should

    A. leave the box where it is and tell your supervisor that you have finished your work
    B. lift the box by yourself very quickly so that your supervisor will see that you are a strong, willing worker
    C. ask another employee to give you a hand to lift the box off the floor
    D. complain to your supervisor that he should check a job before giving you such a tough assignment

12.____

13. Bulletin boards for the posting of official notices are usually put up near the place where employees check in and out each day.
For an employee to spend a few minutes each day to read the new notices is

    A. *good;* these notices give him information about the Department and his own work
    B. *bad;* all important information is given to employees by their supervisors
    C. *good;* this is a way to "take a break" during the day
    D. *bad;* the notices can't help him in his work

13.____

14. Suppose that your supervisor gives you a job to do and tells you that he wants you to finish it in three hours.
If you finish the work at the end of 2 hours, you should

    A. wait until the three hours are up and then tell your supervisor that you are finished
    B. go to your supervisor and tell him that you finished a half-hour ahead of time
    C. spend the next half-hour getting ready for the next job you think your supervisor may give you
    D. take a half-hour rest period because good work deserves a reward

14.____

15. Which one of the following is it LEAST important to include in an accident report?

    A. Name and address of the injured person
    B. Date, time, and place where the accident happened
    C. Name and address of the injured person's family doctor
    D. An explanation of how the accident happened

15.____

16. If, near the end of the day, you realize that you made a mistake in your work and you can't do the work over, you should

    A. forget about it because there is only a small chance that the mistake can be traced back to you
    B. wait a few days and take the blame for the mistake if it is caught
    C. ask the other employees to keep the mistake a secret so that no one can be blamed
    D. tell your supervisor about the mistake right away

16.____

17. Employees should wipe up water spilled on floors immediately.
The BEST reason for this is that water on a floor

A. is a sign that employees are sloppy
B. makes for a slippery condition that could cause an accident
C. will eat into the wax protecting the floor
D. is against health regulations

18. Another worker, who is a good friend of yours, leaves work an hour before quitting time to take care of a personal matter. When you leave later, you find that your friend did not sign out on the timesheet.
For you to sign out for your friend would be

A. *good,* because he will do the same for you some day when you want to leave early
B. *bad,* because other employees will also want you to do the same favor for them on other days
C. *good,* because the timesheet should not have any empty spaces on it
D. *bad,* because timesheets are official records which employees should keep honestly and accurately

19. While you are working, a person asks you how to get to an office which you know is one floor above you in the building where you work.
It would be BEST for you to tell this person that

A. you can't answer any questions because you have to finish your work
B. he should go back to the lobby and check the list of offices
C. the office he is looking for is on the next floor
D. he should call the office he is looking for to get exact instructions on how to get there

20. While you are at work, you find a sealed brown envelope under a desk. The envelope is marked *Personal - Hand Delivery* and is addressed to an official who has an office in the building where you are working.
You should

A. drop the envelope into the nearest mailbox so that it can be delivered the next day
B. look up the telephone number of the official and call him up to tell him what you have found
C. put the envelope in your pocket and come in early the next day to deliver it personally to the official
D. give the envelope to your supervisor right away and tell him where you found it

21. A messenger delivered 32 letters on Monday, 47 on Tuesday, 29 on Wednesday, 36 on Thursday, and 41 on Friday.
How many letters did he deliver altogether?

A. 157   B. 185   C. 218   D. 229

22. Mr. White paid 4% sales tax on a $95 television set.
The amount of sales tax that he paid was

A. $9.50   B. $4.00   C. $3.80   D. $.95

23. How many square feet are there in a room which is 25 feet long and 35 feet wide? _____ square feet.   23.____
  A. 600   B. 750   C. 875   D. 925

24. How much would it cost to send a 34 pound package by parcel post if the postage is $1.60 for the first 20 pounds and 7 for each additional pound?   24.____
  A. $2.34   B. $2.58   C. $2.66   D. $2.80

25. Adding together 1/2, 3/4, and 1/8, the total is   25.____
  A. 1 1/4   B. 1 1/2   C. 1 3/8   D. 1 3/4

26. If a piece of wood 40 inches long is cut into two pieces so that the larger piece is three times as long as the, smaller piece, the smaller piece is _____ inches.   26.____
  A. 4   B. 5   C. 8   D. 10

27. Two friends, Smith and Jones, together spend $1,800 to buy a car. If Smith put up twice as much money as Jones, then Jones' share of the cost of the car was   27.____
  A. $300   B. $600   C. $900   D. $1,200

28. In a certain agency, two-thirds of the employees are clerks and the remainder are typists. If there are 180 clerks, then the number of typists in this agency is   28.____
  A. 270   B. 90   C. 240   D. 60

Questions 29-35.

DIRECTIONS: Answer Questions 29 through 35 ONLY according to the information given in the chart below.

EMPLOYEE RECORD

Name of Employee	Where Assigned	Number of Days Absent Vacation	Sick Leave	Yearly Salary
Carey	Laundry	18	4	$18,650
Hayes	Mortuary	24	8	$17,930
Irwin	Buildings	20	17	$18,290
King	Supply	12	10	$17,930
Lane	Mortuary	17	8	$17,750
Martin	Buildings	13	12	$17,750
Prince	Buildings	5	7	$17,750
Quinn	Supply	19	0	$17,250
Sands	Buildings	23	10	$18,470
Victor	Laundry	21	2	$18,150

29. The *only* employee who was NOT absent because of sickness is   29.____

    A. Hayes   B. Lane   C. Victor   D. Quinn

30. The employee with the HIGHEST salary is   30.____

    A. Carey   B. Irwin   C. Sands   D. Victor

31. The employee with the LOWEST salary is assigned to the _____ Bureau.   31.____

    A. Laundry   B. Mortuary   C. Building   D. Supply

32. Which one of these was absent or on vacation more than 20 days?   32.____

    A. Irwin   B. Lane   C. Quinn   D. Victor

33. The number of employees whose salary is LESS than $18,100 a year is   33.____

    A. 4   B. 5   C. 6   D. 7

34. MOST employees are assigned to   34.____

    A. Laundry   B. Mortuary   C. Buildings   D. Supply

35. From the chart, you can figure out for each employee   35.____

    A. how long he has worked in his present assignment
    B. how many days vacation he has left
    C. how many times he has been late
    D. how much he earns a month

KEY (CORRECT ANSWERS)

1.	A		16.	D
2.	C		17.	B
3.	D		18.	D
4.	B		19.	C
5.	A		20.	D
6.	B		21.	B
7.	A		22.	C
8.	D		23.	C
9.	B		24.	B
10.	B		25.	C
11.	C		26.	D
12.	C		27.	B
13.	A		28.	B
14.	B		29.	D
15.	C		30.	A

31.	D
32.	D
33.	C
34.	C
35.	D

TEST 2

DIRECTIONS: Each question or incomplete statement is followed by several suggested answers or completions. Select the one that BEST answers the question or completes the statement. *PRINT THE LETTER OF THE CORRECT ANSWER IN THE SPACE AT THE RIGHT.*

Questions 1-5.

DIRECTIONS: Answer Questions 1 to 5 ONLY according to the information given in the following passage.

EMPLOYEE LEAVE REGULATIONS

Peter Smith, as a full-time permanent City employee under the Career and Salary Plan, earns an "annual leave allowance" This consists of a certain number of days off a year with pay and may be used for vacation, personal business, and for observing religious holidays. As a newly appointed employee, during his first eight years of City service, he will earn an "annual leave allowance" of twenty days off a year (an average of 1 2/3 days off a month). After he has finished eight full years of working for the City, he will begin earning an additional five days off a year. His "annual leave allowance," therefore, will then be twenty-five days a year and will remain at this amount for seven full years. He will begin earning an additional two days off a year after he has completed a total of fifteen years of City employment. Therefore, in his sixteenth year of working for the City, Mr. Smith will be earning twenty-seven days off a year as his "annual leave allowance" (an average of 2 1/4 days off a month).

A "sick leave allowance" of one day a month is also given to Mr. Smith, but it can be used only in case of actual illness. When Mr. Smith returns to work after using "sick leave allowance," he must have a doctor's note if the absence is for a total of more than three days, but he may also be required to show a doctor's note for absences of one, two, or three days.

1. According to the above passage, Mr. Smith's *annual leave allowance* consists of a certain number of days off a year which he   1.____

    A. does not get paid for
    B. gets paid for at time and a half
    C. may use for personal business
    D. may not use for observing religious holidays

2. According to the above passage, after Mr. Smith has been working for the City for nine years, his *annual leave allowance* will be _____ days a year.   2.____

    A. 20   B. 25   C. 27   D. 37

3. According to the above passage, Mr. Smith will begin earning an average of 2 1/4 days off a month as his *annual leave allowance* after he has worked for the City for _____ full years.   3.____

    A. 7   B. 8   C. 15   D. 17

4. According to the above passage, Mr. Smith is given a *sick leave allowance* of   4.____

    A. 1 day every 2 months   B. 1 day per month
    C. 1 2/3 days per month   D. 2 1/4 days a month

5. According to the above passage, when he uses *sick leave allowance,* Mr. Smith may be   5.____
    required to show a doctor's note

    A. even if his absence is for only 1 day
    B. only if his absence is for more than 2 days
    C. only if his absence is for more than 3 days
    D. only if his absence is for 3 days or more

Questions 6-9.

DIRECTIONS: Answer Questions 6 to 9 ONLY according to the information given in the follow-
               ing passag

MOPPING FLOORS

When mopping hardened cement floors, either painted or unpainted, a soap and water mixture should be used. This should be made by dissolving 1/2 a cup of soft soap in a pail of hot
water. It is not desirable, however, under any circumstances, to use a soap and water mixture
on cement floors that are not hardened. For mopping this type of floor, it is recommended that
the cleaning agent be made up of two ounces of laundry soda mixed in a pail of water.

Soaps are not generally used on hard tile floors because slippery films may build up on the
floor. It is generally recommended that these floors be mopped using a pail of hot water in which
has been mixed two ounces of washing powder for each gallon of water. The floors should then
be rinsed thoroughly.

After the mopping is finished, proper care should be taken of the mop. This is done by first
cleaning the mop in clear, warm water. Then, it should be wrung out, after which the strands of
the mop should be untangled. Finally, the mop should be hung by its handle to dry.

6. According to the above passage, you should NEVER use a soap and water mixture when   6.____
    mopping _____ floors.

    A. hardened cement   B. painted
    C. unhardened cement   D. unpainted

7. According to the above passage, using laundry soda mixed in a pail of water as a clean-   7.____
    ing agent is recommended for

    A. all floors
    B. all floors except hard tile floors
    C. some cement floors
    D. lineoleum floor coverings only

8. According to the above passage, the generally recommended mixture for mopping hard   8.____
    tile floors is

    A. 1/2 a cup of soft soap for each gallon of hot water
    B. 1/2 a cup of soft soap in a pail of hot water
    C. 2 ounces of washing powder in a pail of hot water
    D. 2 ounces of washing powder for each gallon of hot water

9. According to the above passage, the proper care of a mop after it is used includes   9.____

    A. cleaning it in clear cold water and hanging it by its handle to dry
    B. wringing it out, untangling and drying it
    C. untangling its strands before wringing it out
    D. untangling its strands while cleaning it in clear water

Questions 10-13.

DIRECTIONS: Answer Questions 10 to 13 ONLY according to the information given in the following passage.

HANDLING HOSPITAL LAUNDRY

In a hospital, care must be taken when handling laundry in order to reduce the chance of germs spreading. There is always the possibility that dirty laundry will be carrying dangerous germs. To avoid catching germs when they are working with dirty laundry, laundry workers should be sure that any cuts or wounds they have are bandaged before they touch the dirty laundry. They should also be careful when handling this laundry not to rub their eyes, nose, or mout. Just like all other hospital workers, laundry workers should also protect themselves against germs by washing and rinsing their hands thoroughly before eating meals and before leaving work at the end of the day.

To be sure that germs from dirty laundry do not pass onto clean laundry and thereby increase the danger to patients, clean and dirty laundry should not be handled near each other or by the same person. Special care also has to be taken with laundry that comes from a patient who has a dangerous, highly contagious disease so that as few people as possible come in direct contact with this laundry. Laundry from this patient, therefore, should be kept separate from other dirty laundry at all times.

10. According to the above passage, when working with dirty laundry, laundry workers   10.____
    should

    A. destroy laundry carrying dangerous germs
    B. have any cuts bandaged before touching the dirty laundry
    C. never touch the dirty laundry directly
    D. rub their eyes, nose, and mouth to protect them from germs

11. According to the above passage, all hospital workers should wash their hands thoroughly   11.____

    A. after eating meals to remove any trace of food from their hands
    B. at every opportunity to show good example to the patients
    C. before eating meals to protect themselves against germs
    D. before starting work in the morning to feel fresh and ready to do a good day's work

12. According to the above passage, the danger to patients will increase   12.____

    A. unless a worker handles dirty and clean laundry at the same time
    B. unless clean and dirty laundry are handled near each other
    C. when clean laundry is ironed frequently
    D. when germs pass from dirty laundry to clean laundry

13. According to the above passage, laundry from a patient with a dangerous, highly conta-   13.___
gious disease should be

    A. given special care so that as few people as possible come in direct contact with it
    B. handled in the same way as any other dirty laundry
    C. washed by hand
    D. separated from the other dirty laundry just before it is washed

Questions 14-17.

DIRECTIONS: Answer Questions 14 to 17 ONLY according to the information given in the following passage.

EMPLOYEE SUGGESTIONS

To increase the effectiveness of the New York City governments the City asks its employees to offer suggestions when they feel an improvement could be made in some government
operation. The Employees' Suggestions Program was started to encourage City employees to
do this. Through this Program, which is only for City employees, cash awards may be given to
those whose suggestions are submitted and approve Suggestions are looked for not only from
supervisors but from all City employees as any City employee may get an idea which might be
approved and contribute greatly to the solution of some problem of City government.

Therefore, all suggestions for improvement are welcome, whether they be suggestions on
how to improve working conditions, or on how to increase the speed with which work is done, or
on how to reduce or eliminate such things as waste, time losses, accidents, or fire hazards.
There are, however, a few types of suggestions for which cash awards can not be given. An
example of this type would be a suggestion to increase salaries or a suggestion to change the
regulations about annual leave or about sick leave. The number of suggestions sent in has
increased sharply during the past few years. It is hoped that it will keep increasing in the future
in order to meet the City's needs for more ideas for improved ways of doing things.

14. According to the above passage, the main reason why the City asks its employees for   14.___
suggestions about government operations is to

    A. increase the effectiveness of the City government
    B. show that the Employees' Suggestion Program is working well
    C. show that everybody helps run the City government
    D. have the employee win a prize

15. According to the above passage, the Employees' Suggestion Program can approve   15.___
awards only for those suggestions that come from

    A. City employees
    B. City employees who are supervisors
    C. City employees who are not supervisors
    D. experienced employees of the City

16. According to the above passage, a cash award can not be given through the Employees'   16.____
Suggestion Program for a suggestion about

     A.   getting work done faster
     B.   helping prevent accidents on the job
     C.   increasing the amount of annual leave for City employees
     D.   reducing the chance of fire where City employees work

17. According to the above passage, the suggestions sent in during the past few years have   17.____

     A.   all been approved
     B.   generally been well written
     C.   been mostly about reducing or eliminating waste
     D.   been greater in number than before

Questions 18-21.

DIRECTIONS: Answer Questions 18 to 21 ONLY according to the information given in the following passage.

ACCIDENT PREVENTION

Many accidents and injuries can be prevented if employees learn to be more careful. The wearing of shoes with thin or badly worn soles or open toes can easily lead to foot injuries from tacks, nails, and chair and desk legs. Loose or torn clothing should not be worn near moving machinery. This is especially true of neckties which can very easily become caught in the machine. You should not place objects so that they block or partly block hallways, corridors, or other passageways. Even when they are stored in the proper place, tools, supplies, and equipment should be carefully placed or piled so as not to fall, nor have anything stick out from a pile. Before cabinets, lockers, or ladders are moved, the tops should be cleared of anything which might injure someone or fall of If necessary, use a dolly to move these or other bulky objects.

Despite all efforts to avoid accidents and injuries, however, some will happen. If an employee is injured, no matter how small the injury, he should report it to his supervisor and have the injury treated. A small cut that is not attended to can easily become infected and can cause more trouble than some injuries which at first seem more serious. It never pays to take chances.

18. According to the above passage, the one statement that is NOT true is that   18.____

     A.   by being more careful, employees can reduce the number of accidents that happen
     B.   women should wear shoes with open toes for comfort when working
     C.   supplies should be piled so that nothing is sticking out from the pile
     D.   if an employee sprains his wrist at work, he should tell his supervisor about it

19. According to the above passage, you should NOT wear loose clothing when you are   19.____

     A.   in a corridor   B.   storing tools
     C.   opening cabinets   D.   near moving machinery

20. According to the above passage, before moving a ladder, you should

    A. test all the rungs
    B. get a dolly to carry the ladder at all times
    C. remove everything from the top of the ladder which might fall off
    D. remove your necktie

20.____

21. According to the above passage, an employee who gets a slight cut should

    A. have it treated to help prevent infection
    B. know that a slight cut becomes more easily infected than a big cut
    C. pay no attention to it as it can't become serious
    D. realize that it is more serious than any other type of injury

21.____

Questions 22-24.

DIRECTIONS: Answer Questions 22 to 24 ONLY according to the information given in the following passage.

GOOD EMPLOYEE PRACTICES

As a City employee, you will be expected to take an interest in your work and perform the duties of your job to the best of your ability and in a spirit of cooperation. Nothing shows an interest in your work more than coming to work on time, not only at the start of the day but also when returning from lunch. If it is necessary for you to keep a personal appointment at lunch hour which might cause a delay in getting back to work on time, you should explain the situation to your supervisor and get his approval to come back a little late before you leave for lunch.

You should do everything that is asked of you willingly and consider important even the small jobs that your supervisor gives you. Although these jobs may seem unimportant, if you forget to do them or if you don't do them right, trouble may develop later.

Getting along well with your fellow workers will add much to the enjoyment of your work. You should respect your fellow workers and try to see their side when a disagreement arises. The better you get along with your fellow workers and your supervisor, the better you will like your job and the better you will be able to do it.

22. According to the above passage, in your job as a City employee, you are expected to

    A. show a willingness to cooperate on the job
    B. get your supervisor's approval before keeping any personal appointments at lunch hour
    C. avoid doing small jobs that seem unimportant
    D. do the easier jobs at the start of the day and the more difficult ones later on

22.____

23. According to the above passage, getting to work on time shows that you

    A. need the job
    B. have an interest in your work
    C. get along well with your fellow workers
    D. like your supervisor

23.____

24. According to the above passage, the one of the following statements that is NOT true is   24.____

    A. if you do a small job wrong, trouble may develop
    B. you should respect your fellow workers
    C. if you disagree with a fellow worker, you should try to see his side of the story
    D. the less you get along with your supervisor, the better you will be able to do your job

Questions 25-35.   <u>VOCABULARY</u>

25. The porter cleaned the VACANT room.   25.____
In this sentence, the word VACANT means nearly the same as

    A. empty   B. large   C. main   D. crowded

26. The supervisor gave a BRIEF report to his men.   26.____
In this sentence, the word BRIEF means nearly the same as

    A. long   B. safety   C. complete   D. short

27. The supervisor told him to CONNECT the two pieces.   27.____
In this sentence, the word CONNECT means nearly the same as

    A. join   B. .paint   C. return   D. weigh

28. Standing on the top of a ladder is RISKY.   28.____
In this sentence, the word RISKY means nearly the same as

    A. dangerous   B. sensible   C. safe   D. foolish

29. He RAISED the cover of the machine.   29.____
In this sentence, the word RAISED means nearly the same as

    A. broke   B. lifted   C. lost   D. found

30. The form used for reporting the finished work was REVISED.   30.____
In this sentence, the word REVISED means nearly the same as

    A. printed   B. ordered   C. dropped   D. changed

31. He did his work RAPIDLY.   31.____
In this sentence, the word RAPIDLY means nearly the same as

    A. carefully   B. quickly   C. slowly   D. quietly

32. The worker was OCCASIONALLY late   32.____
In this sentence, the word OCCASIONALLY means nearly the same as

    A. sometimes   B. often   C. never   D. always

33. He SELECTED the best tool for the job.   33.____
In this sentence, the word SELECTED means nearly the same as

    A. bought   B. picked   C. lost   D. broke

34. He needed ASSISTANCE to lift the package.
In this sentence, the word ASSISTANCE means nearly the same as

   A. strength   B. time   C. help   D. instructions

34.____

35. The tools were ISSUED by the supervisor.
In this sentence, the word ISSUED means nearly the same as

   A. collected   B. cleaned up
   C. given out   D. examined

35.____

KEY (CORRECT ANSWERS)

1. C		16. C	
2. B		17. D	
3. C		18. B	
4. B		19. D	
5. A		20. C	
6. C		21. A	
7. C		22. A	
8. D		23. B	
9. B		24. D	
10. B		25. A	
11. C		26. D	
12. D		27. A	
13. A		28. A	
14. A		29. B	
15. A		30. D	

31. B
32. A
33. B
34. C
35. C

EXAMINATION SECTION
TEST 1

DIRECTIONS: Each question or incomplete statement is followed by several suggested answers or completions. Select the one that BEST answers the question or completes the statement. *PRINT THE LETTER OF THE CORRECT ANSWER IN THE SPACE AT THE RIGHT.*

Questions 1-22.

DIRECTIONS: Read through each group of words. Indicate in the space at the right the letter of the misspelled word.

1.	A. miniature		B. recession		1._____
	C. accommodate		D. supress		
2.	A. mortgage		B. illogical		2._____
	C. fasinate		D. pronounce		
3.	A. calendar		B. heros		3._____
	C. ecstasy		D. librarian		
4.	A. initiative		B. extraordinary		4._____
	C. villian		D. exaggerate		
5.	A. absence		B. sense		5._____
	C. dosn't		D. height		
6.	A. curiosity		B. ninety		6._____
	C. truely		D. grammar		
7.	A. amateur		B. definate		7._____
	C. meant		D. changeable		
8.	A. excellent		B. studioes		8._____
	C. achievement		D. weird		
9.	A. goverment		B. description		9._____
	C. sergeant		D. desirable		
10.	A. proceed		B. anxious		10._____
	C. neice		D. precede		
11.	A. environment		B. omitted		11._____
	C. apparant		D. misconstrue		
12.	A. comparative		B. hindrance		12._____
	C. benefited		D. unamimous		
13.	A. embarrass		B. recommend		13._____
	C. desciple		D. argument		
14.	A. sophomore		B. superintendent		14._____
	C. concievable		D. disastrous		

15. A. agressive   B. questionnaire   15.____
    C. occurred   D. rhythm

16. A. peaceable   B. conscientious   16.____
    C. redicule   D. deterrent

17. A. mischievious   B. writing   17.____
    C. competition   D. athletics

18. A. auxiliary   B. synonymous   18.____
    C. maneuver   D. repitition

19. A. existence   B. optomistic   19.____
    C. acquitted   D. tragedy

20. A. hypocrisy   B. parrallel   20.____
    C. exhilaration   D. prevalent

21. A. convalesence   B. infallible   21.____
    C. destitute   D. grotesque

22. A. magnanimity   B. asassination   22.____
    C. incorrigible   D. pestilence

Questions 23-40.

DIRECTIONS: In Questions 23 through 40, one sentence fragment contains an error in punctuation or capitalization. Indicate the letter of the INCORRECT sentence fragment and place it in space at the right.

23. A. Despite a year's work   23.____
    B. in a well-equipped laboratory,
    C. my Uncle failed to complete his research;
    D. now he will never graduate.

24. A. Gene, if you are going to sleep   24.____
    B. all afternoon I will enter
    C. that ladies' golf tournament
    D. sponsored by the Chamber of Commerce.

25. A. Seeing the cat slink toward the barn,   25.____
    B. the farmer's wife jumped off the
    C. ladder picked up a broom, and began
    D. shouting at the top of her voice.

26. A. Extending over southeast Idaho and   26.____
    B. northwest Wyoming, the Tetons
    C. are noted for their height; however the
    D. highest peak is actually under 14,000 feet.

27. A. "Sarah, can you recall the name
    B. of the English queen
    C. who supposedly said, 'We are not
    D. amused?'"   27._____

28. A. My aunt's graduation present to me
    B. cost, I imagine more than she could
    C. actually afford. It's a
    D. Swiss watch with numerous features.   28._____

29. A. On the left are examples of buildings
    B. from the Classical Period; two temples
    C. one of which was dedicated to Zeus; the
    D. Agora, a marketplace; and a large arch.   29._____

30. A. Tired of sonic booms, the people who
    B. live near Springfield's Municipal Airport
    C. formed an anti noise organization
    D. with the amusing name of Sound Off.   30._____

31. A. "Joe, Mrs. Sweeney said, "your family
    B. arrives Sunday. Since you'll be in
    C. the Labor Day parade, we could ask Mr.
    D. Krohn, who has a big car, to meet them."   31._____

32. A. The plumber emerged from the basement and
    B. said, "Mr. Cohen I found the trouble in
    C. your water heater. Could you move those
    D. Schwinn bikes out of my way?"   32._____

33. A. The President walked slowly to the
    B. podium, bowed to Edward Everett Hale
    C. the other speaker, and began his formal address:
    D. "Fourscore and seven years ago...."   33._____

34. A. Mr. Fontana, I hope, will arrive before
    B. the beginning of the ceremonies; however,
    C. if his plane is delayed, I have a substitute
    D. speaker who can be here at a moments' notice.   34._____

35. A. Gladys wedding dress, a satin creation,
    B. lay crumpled on the floor; her veil,
    C. torn and streaked, lay nearby. "Jilted!"
    D. shrieked Gladys. She was clearly annoyed.   35._____

36. A. Although it is poor grammar, the word
    B. hopefully has become television's newest
    C. pet expression; I hope (to use the correct
    D. form) that it will soon pass from favor.   36._____

37. A.
    B.
    C.
    D.

                                 Plaza Apartment Hotel   37.___
                                 103 Tower road
                                 Hampstead, Iowa 52025
                                 March 13, 2008

38. A. Circulation Department   38.___
    B. British History Illustrated
    C. 3000 Walnut Street
    D. Boulder Colorado 80302

39. A. Dear Sirs: 39.___
    B.   Last spring I ordered a subscription to your
    C. magazine. I had read and enjoyed the May
    D. issue containing the article titled "kings."

40. A.   I have not however, received a   40.___
    B. single issue. Will you check this?
    C. Sincerely,
    D. Maria Herrera

Questions 41-70.

DIRECTIONS: Questions 41 through 70 represent common grammatical concerns: subject-verb agreement, appropriate use of pronouns, and appropriate use of verbs. Read each sentence and indicate the letter of the grammatically CORRECT answer in the space at the right.

41. THE REIVERS, one of William Faulkner's last works, _____ made into a movie starring 41.___
Steve McQueen.

    A. has been   B. have been
    C. are being   D. were

42. He _____ on the ground, his eyes fastened on an ant slowly pushing a morsel of food 42.___
toward the ant hill.

    A. layed   B. laid   C. had laid   D. lay

43. Nobody in the tri-cities _____ to admit that a flood could be disastrous. 43.___

    A. are willing   B. have been willing
    C. is willing   D. were willing

44. "_____," the senator asked, "have you convinced to run against the incumbent?" 44.___

    A. Who   B. Whom   C. Whomever   D. Whomsoever

45. Of all the psychology courses that I took, Statistics 101 _____ the most demanding. 45.___

    A. was   B. are   C. is   D. were

46. Neither the conductor nor the orchestra members _____ the music to be applauded so enthusiastically.   46.____

    A. were expecting   B. was expecting
    C. is expected   D. has been expecting

47. The requirements for admission to the Lettermen's Club _____ posted outside the athletic director's office for months.   47.____

    A. was   B. was being
    C. has been   D. have been

48. Please give me a list of the people _____ to compete in the kayak race.   48.____

    A. whom you think have planned
    B. who you think has planned
    C. who you think is planning
    D. who you think are planning

49. I saw Eloise and Abelard earlier today; _____ were riding around in a fancy 1956 MG.   49.____

    A. she and him   B. her and him
    C. she and he   D. her and he

50. If you _____ the trunk in the attic, I'll unpack it later today.   50.____

    A. can sit   B. are able to sit
    C. can set   D. have sat

51. _____ all of the flour been used, or may I borrow three cups?   51.____

    A. Have   B. Has   C. Is   D. Could

52. In exasperation, the cycle shop's owner suggested that _____ there too long.   52.____

    A. us boys were   B. we boys were
    C. us boys had been   D. we boys had been

53. Idleness as well as money _____ the root of all evil.   53.____

    A. have been   B. were to have been
    C. is   D. are

54. Only the string players from the quartet – Gregory, Isaac, _____ - remained after the concert to answer questions.   54.____

    A. him, and I   B. he, and I
    C. him, and me   D. he, and me

55. Of all the antiques that _____ for sale, Gertrude chose to buy a stupid glass thimble.   55.____

    A. was   B. is
    C. would have   D. were

56. The detective snapped, "Don't confuse me with theories about _____ you believe committed the crime!"   56.____

    A. who   B. whom   C. whomever   D. which

57. _____ when we first called, we might have avoided our present predicament.   57.____

   A. The plumber's coming
   B. If the plumber would have come
   C. If the plumber had come
   D. If the plumber was to have come

58. We thought the sun _____ in the north until we discovered that our compass was defec-   58.____
   tive.

   A. had rose   B. had risen
   C. had rised   D. had raised

59. Each play of Shakespeare's _____ more than _____ share of memorable characters.   59.____

   A. contain; its   B. contains; its
   C. contains; it's   D. contain; their

60. Our English teacher suggested to _____ seniors that either Tolstoy or Dickens _____   60.____
   the outstanding novelist of the nineteenth century.

   A. we; was considered   B. we; were considered
   C. us; was considered   D. us; were considered

61. Sherlock Holmes, together with his great friend and companion Dr. Watson, _____ to   61.____
   aid the woman _____ had stumbled into the room.

   A. has agreed; who   B. have agreed; whom
   C. has agreed; whom   D. have agreed; who

62. Several of the deer _____ when they spotted my backpack _____ open in the   62.____
   meadow.

   A. was frightened; laying   B. were frightened; lying
   C. were frightened; laying   D. was frightened; lying

63. After the Scholarship Committee announces _____ selection, hysterics often _____.   63.____

   A. it's; occur   B. its; occur
   C. their; occur   D. their; occurs

64. I _____ the key on the table last night so you and _____ could find it.   64.____

   A. layed; her   B. lay; she
   C. laid; she   D. laid; her

65. Some of the antelope _____ wandered away from the meadow where the rancher   65.____
   _____ the block of salt.

   A. has; sat   B. has; set
   C. have; had set   D. has; sets

66. Macaroni and cheese _____ best to us (that is, to Andy and _____) when Mother adds   66.____
   extra cheddar cheese.

   A. tastes; I   B. tastes; me
   C. taste; me   D. taste; I

67. Frank said, "It must have been _____ called the phone company."   67.____

    A. she who   B. she whom
    C. her who   D. her whom

68. The herd _____ moving restlessly at every bolt of lightning; it was either Ted or _____   68.____
who saw the beginning of the stampede.

    A. was; me   B. were; I
    C. was; I   D. have been; me

69. The foreman _____ his lateness by saying that his alarm clock _____ until six minutes   69.____
before eight.

    A. explains; had not rang
    B. explained; has not rung
    C. has explained; rung
    D. explained; hadn't rung

70. Of all the coaches, Ms. Cox is the only one who _____ that Sherry dives more grace-   70.____
fully than _____.

    A. is always saying; I
    B. is always saying; me
    C. are always saying; I
    D. were always saying; me

Questions 71-90.

DIRECTIONS: Choose the word in Questions 71 through 90 that is MOST opposite in meaning to the italicized word.

71. *fact*   71.____

    A. statistic   B. statement
    C. incredible   D. conjecture

72. *stiff*   72.____

    A. fastidious   B. babble
    C. supple   D. apprehensive

73. *blunt*   73.____

    A. concise   B. tactful
    C. artistic   D. humble

74. *foreign*   74.____

    A. pertinent   B. comely
    C. strange   D. scrupulous

75. *anger*   75.____

    A. infer   B. pacify   C. taint   D. revile

76. *frank*   76.____

    A. earnest   B. reticent   C. post   D. expensive

77. *secure*   77.____

    A. precarious   B. acquire   C. moderate   D. frenzied

78. *petty*   78.____

    A. harmonious   B. careful   C. forthright   D. momentous

79. *concede*   79.____

    A. dispute   B. reciprocate
    C. subvert   D. propagate

80. *benefit*   80.____

    A. liquidation   B. bazaar
    C. detriment   D. profit

81. *capricious*   81.____

    A. preposterous   B. constant
    C. diabolical   D. careless

82. *boisterous*   82.____

    A. devious   B. valiant   C. girlish   D. taciturn

83. *harmony*   83.____

    A. congruence   B. discord   C. chagrin   D. melody

84. *laudable*   84.____

    A. auspicious   B. despicable
    C. acclaimed   D. doubtful

85. *adherent*   85.____

    A. partisan   B. stoic   C. renegade   D. recluse

86. *exuberant*   86.____

    A. frail   B. corpulent   C. austere   D. bigot

87. *spurn*   87.____

    A. accede   B. flail
    C. efface   D. annihilate

88. *spontaneous*   88.____

    A. hapless   B. corrosive
    C. intentional   D. willful

89. *disparage*   89.____

    A. abolish   B. exude   C. incriminate   D. extol

90. *timorous*   90.____

    A. succinct   B. chaste
    C. audacious   D. insouciant

KEY (CORRECT ANSWERS)

1.	D	21.	A	41.	A	61.	A	81.	B
2.	C	22.	B	42.	D	62.	B	82.	D
3.	B	23.	C	43.	C	63.	B	83.	B
4.	C	24.	B	44.	B	64.	C	84.	B
5.	C	25.	C	45.	A	65.	C	85.	C
6.	C	26.	C	46.	A	66.	B	86.	C
7.	B	27.	D	47.	D	67.	A	87.	A
8.	B	28.	B	48.	A	68.	C	88.	C
9.	A	29.	B	49.	C	69.	D	89.	D
10.	C	30.	C	50.	C	70.	A	90.	C
11.	C	31.	A	51.	B	71.	D		
12.	D	32.	B	52.	D	72.	C		
13.	C	33.	B	53.	C	73.	B		
14.	C	34.	D	54.	B	74.	A		
15.	A	35.	A	55.	D	75.	B		
16.	C	36.	B	56.	B	76.	B		
17.	A	37.	B	57.	C	77.	A		
18.	D	38.	D	58.	B	78.	D		
19.	B	39.	D	59.	B	79.	A		
20.	B	40.	A	60.	C	80.	C		

LOGICAL REASONING
EVALUATING CONCLUSIONS IN LIGHT OF KNOWN FACTS

EXAMINATION SECTION
TEST 1

DIRECTIONS: For the following questions, select the letter before the statement below which BEST expresses the relationship between the facts and the conclusion. Mark your answer:
- A. The facts prove the conclusion; or
- B. The facts disprove the conclusion; or
- C. The facts neither prove nor disprove the conclusion.

PRINT THE LETTER OF THE CORRECT ANSWER IN THE SPACE AT THE RIGHT.

1. FACTS: Andy types half as fast as Bill. Bill types twice as slow as Charlie. Bill types 60 words a minute.

   CONCLUSION: Charlie types 30 words a minute.

   1._____

2. FACTS: If Albert gets traded to the Cubs, Chris will have to be traded to the Padres. Albert will avoid being traded only if he hits a home run in his turn at bat. If Chris goes to the Padres, Dave will be traded to the Dodgers. Albert strikes out in this crucial at-bat.

   CONCLUSION: Dave gets traded to the Dodgers.

   2._____

3. FACTS: All beads are forms of jewelry. All jewelry is expensive. Everyone loves expensive beads.

   CONCLUSION: All beads are expensive.

   3._____

4. FACTS: No shrimp are mussels. Mussels are bivalves. All mussels have shells.

   CONCLUSION: Therefore, no shrimp have shells.

   4._____

5. FACTS: On their latest diet, Abby, Bea, Celia, and Donna lost a combined total of 260 pounds. Abby lost twice as much as Celia. Celia lost half as much as the woman who lost the most. Donna lost 80 pounds.

   CONCLUSION: Abby lost 100 pounds; Bea, 30; Celia, 50; and Donna, 80.

   5._____

6. FACTS: Ann's office is two floors above Brenda's. Brenda's office is one floor below the only woman in the building whose birthday is today. Sally's office is on the third floor. Ann's office is on the fourth floor.

   CONCLUSION: Today is Ann's birthday.

   6._____

7. FACTS: Douglas Ave. is perpendicular to Bates St. Bates St. is parallel to Adams Ave. Douglas Ave. is parallel to Charles St. Evans Ave. is parallel to the streets that are perpendicular to Bates St.

   CONCLUSION: Evans Ave. is perpendicular to Douglas Ave.

   7._____

8. FACTS: There's one out, and Bill is the runner on third base. If Arnie hits the ball hard, Bill will run, but so slowly that he will be out at home plate. The team captain, on second base, will not run unless Arnie hits the ball hard. The captain runs.

   CONCLUSION: Bill is safe.

   8.____

9. FACTS: Some members of this genus are members of that species. All members of that species are butterflies. Some butterflies are different from others.

   CONCLUSION: Some members of this genus are butterflies.

   9.____

10. FACTS: Some woodwinds are clarinets. Flutes are not clarinets. All clarinets are beautiful things.

    CONCLUSION: Therefore, all beautiful things are woodwinds.

    10.____

11. FACTS: Using a grid exactly like the one below, Joe Genius filled in the numbers 1 through 9 in the boxes. Each horizontal, vertical, and diagonal row added up to 15. A different number went in each box.

    11.____

    CONCLUSION: The number Joe put in the middle box was 6.

12. FACTS: Max, Nick, Pete, and Ollie all bought different colored suits: grey, green, blue, and brown, but not necessarily respectively. Max paid less for his green suit than Nick paid for his suit. Ollie paid twice what Pete paid. Pete paid the same as the man who bought the grey suit. Ollie bought the brown suit.

    CONCLUSION: Ollie paid the most.

    12.____

13. FACTS: Four people (Alice, Bob, Carol, and Dave) are sitting at a square table, discussing their favorite sports. Bob sits directly across from the jogger. Carol sits to the right of the basketball player. Alice sits across from Dave. The golfer sits to the left of the tennis player. A man sits on Dave's right.

    CONCLUSION: Dave plays golf.

    13.____

14. FACTS: An employer decided to offer a job to everyone who scored higher than 50 on an exam. Alice scored 20. Betty scored lower than Carol, but more than twice as high as Alice.

    CONCLUSION: Of the three women, only Carol was offered the job.

    14.____

15. FACTS: If Camille's squirrel has rabies and the squirrel bites Casey's cat, the squirrel will have to be caught and the cat will get rabies. If the cat has had rabies shots within the last two years, the cat will not get rabies. Casey's cat did not get rabies.

    CONCLUSION: Casey's cat has had rabies shots within the last two years.

    15.____

16. FACTS: Sally will file a grievance only if Bill fires her. If Laura tells Frank the whole story, Frank will tell it to Bill. If Bill hears the whole story, he will not fire Sally. Laura tells Fred the whole story.

    CONCLUSION: Sally files a grievance.

    16.____

17. FACTS: If Alice leaves work early, Barb has to work late, and Barb wants to go to the game tonight. The singing of the National Anthem always precedes the game. Carl calls Alice and asks her out to dinner. Due to a thunderstorm, the singing of the National Anthem gets delayed. If Alice goes out to dinner with Carl, she will have to leave work early so she can go home and turn off her crockpot. Alice accepts Carl's invitation.

    CONCLUSION: Barb misses the first inning of the game.

    17.____

18. FACTS: Earl thinks of any whole number from 1 through 10. Because she is using the most efficient system, Eva absolutely guarantees Earl that she can correctly guess the number he's thinking of in five questions or less. Eva asks Earl a series of *yes/no* questions and guesses the number in five questions or less every time. Earl and Eva agree to play the game again in the exact same way, except that he will think of a whole number from 1 through 6.

    CONCLUSION: Using the same system, four is the absolute highest number of *yes/no* questions that Eva will need to ask in order to guess the number that Earl is thinking of this time.

    18.____

19. FACTS: Lois will cook dinner today only if Ted, Robbie, and Jennifer are all home by 6 P.M. Robbie will come home by 6 P.M. only if band practice ends early. If Ted plays Softball after work, he will take Jennifer with him, and they will not be home by 6 P.M. Band practice ends early today.

    CONCLUSION: Lois cooks dinner today.

    19.____

20. FACTS: Three card players each start with $10. Each round they play has two losers and one winner. The losers in each round have to give the winner $2 apiece. Chuck wins the first and third rounds; Bruce wins the second. At the end of the third round, Artie proposes that they change the rules so that the losers each have to give the winner half their accumulated money. They agree, play one more round, and Artie wins it.

    CONCLUSION: At the end of the fourth round, Chuck has less money than Artie.

    20.____

21. FACTS: No part-time workers at this plant get paid vacations. All cleaners at this plant are part-time workers. Joe gets a paid vacation.

    CONCLUSION: All cleaners at this plant get paid vacations.

    21.____

22. FACTS: If Myles breaks the lamp, Lucy will scream. If Tom finds Rachel spraying Windex into the cat's dish, he'll scream. If Geoffrey doesn't hear from the French soon, he'll scream. Tom screams.

    22.____

CONCLUSION: Myles broke the lamp.

23. FACTS: If Tina goes to the store, Ike will go with her. If Ike goes to the store, he will buy doughnuts. If Dick cleans the house, Sally will go to the store. If Sally goes to the store, Tina will go with her. Dick cleans the house.

    23.____

    CONCLUSION: Ike buys doughnuts.

24. FACTS: If Joe passes the test, Jill won't apply for the job. If Jill applies for the job, she'll get it. If Jill doesn't apply for the job, Jeanne will be annoyed. Joe passes the test.

    24.____

    CONCLUSION: Jeanne gets annoyed.

25. FACTS: Mary, Debbie, May, and Joan are the only people waiting for the photocopier to be fixed. When it's fixed, Debbie has to use it first because she's doing work for the boss. Joan has to use it right after the person who's been waiting the longest. The person who has the most work to copy gets to use the machine second. May has been waiting the longest. The person who has been waiting longest is not the person who has the most work to copy.

    25.____

    CONCLUSION: Joan gets to use the photocopier third.

KEY (CORRECT ANSWERS)

1.	B		11.	B
2.	A		12.	A
3.	A		13.	A
4.	C		14.	C
5.	C		15.	C
6.	B		16.	C
7.	B		17.	C
8.	B		18.	A
9.	A		19.	C
10.	C		20.	A

21.	B
22.	C
23.	A
24.	A
25.	B

SOLUTIONS

1. **CORRECT ANSWER: B**
This is an easy problem if you read it carefully. The third sentence says that Bill types 60 words a minute; the second sentence says that Bill types twice as slow as Charlie. If Bill types twice as slow as Charlie, then Charlie types twice as fast as Bill, or 2 x 60. This means that Charlie types 120 words a minute, not 30 words a minute. These two sentences alone are all you need to disprove the conclusion; the first sentence is just a decoy. If you had *fallen for it* and misread the paragraph, you would most likely have chosen A. You probably would have skimmed the second sentence and assumed that it said *twice as <u>fast</u>,* just because the first sentence said *half as fast.*

2. **CORRECT ANSWER: A**
This question may look more difficult than it is because the facts are thrown together haphazardly. Many of these logic questions present the *facts* in a very strange fashion. No one would ever talk like this in real life - at least not if they wanted to be understood. The point, of course, is to see how well you can sift through these things, avoid the pitfalls, and find the *truth* of the matter. If you approach a question carefully and attack it systematically, you will usually find that it is not really all that difficult. In this case, by studying the facts, you can see that Albert gets traded. He needs a home run to avoid being traded (sentence 2), but he strikes out in his at-bat (sentence 4). You can assume that this is the at-bat that determines his future because of the way the fourth sentence is worded. It uses the words, *this crucial at-bat.* Knowing the sad truth that he's been traded, you can then trace the chain of events: Chris goes to the Padres (sentence 1), which means that Dave goes to the Dodgers (sentence 3). So the conclusion is, indeed, proved by the facts given to us.

3. **CORRECT ANSWER: A**
This is a classic form of logic problem, and, like question 2, it doesn't correspond to reality. We all know perfectly well that some beads are cheap, but that has NO bearing on this problem. You often have to let go of your common sense and experience when doing problems like these. Just stick to the facts as they are stated in the problem. The first two sentences are given as facts, and they are enough to prove the conclusion that *all beads are expensive.* In any problem where you are told that a given fact is all-inclusive, such as that *all A are B,* you can just substitute A for B in any other factual sentence in the problem. What is true of B is true of A. Therefore, when you come across another all-inclusive *truth,* such as *all B are C,* you know that *all A are C* must be true too.
Here are two examples. Although only one corresponds to reality as we know it, they both follow the logic formula we've outlined above, and so both are *true* according to logic.

> All dogs (A) are mammals (B).
> All mammals (B) have backbones (C).
> All dogs (A) have backbones (C).
>
> All apples (A) are bananas (B).
> All bananas (B) have yellow skins (C).
> All apples (A) have yellow skins (C).

Note that this does not work in reverse. All bananas aren't necessarily apples, all things with yellow skins aren't necessarily bananas or apples, and all mammals aren't necessarily dogs. Don't worry if this is confusing to you. The key here is to know the formula and not think about it too much in terms of reality.

In this problem, the *A* is the beads, the *B* is the jewelry, and the *C* is expensive.

4.   CORRECT ANSWER: C
This looks a lot like the previous question, but, in fact, the sentences show no relationship between shrimp and shells. You can eliminate the second sentence because it has nothing at all to do with the conclusion. Of the two remaining sentences, one says that mussels have shells, the other says that no shrimp are mussels. This doesn't tell us that <u>no shrimp have shells</u> because it is not really telling us anything about how these two animals compare with each other on this issue. It's as if we said, *all boys like sports* and *no boys are girls.* These statements don't tell us whether girls like sports. They tell us that boys and girls are different, but we don't know how different they are. Are they completely different, or do they have things in common? Is liking sports one of the ways they differ or one of the ways they are alike?

For this reason, there is also nothing in the question to show that shrimp <u>do have shells.</u> Here we have another case where common sense can get you into trouble. You may want to choose answer B, simply because you know that the conclusion is false. But you are <u>not</u> being asked whether the conclusion is true or false; you are being asked whether it is <u>proved</u> true or false <u>by the facts as given.</u> If sentence 3 had said, *only mussels have shells,* then the facts would prove the conclusion, even if that doesn't correspond to reality. But as it is, the facts neither prove nor disprove the conclusion.

5.   CORRECT ANSWER: C
This is a tricky one. You may have added all the pounds in the conclusion, and been relieved to find that they totaled the 260 pounds mentioned in the first sentence. You would have been tricked into picking A because the numbers checked out. But it doesn't matter that the numbers match because the problem here is to decide whether the facts <u>prove</u> that those are the exact number of pounds <u>each woman</u> lost. And the facts show that, without knowing Bea's weight loss, we're sure of only one figure - Donna's 80-pound weight loss. This is shown below:

NAME	AMOUNT LOST
Abby	2 x Celia
Bea	?
Celia	1/2 of Abby
Donna	80

You may have tried to work the problem by assuming that Donna's 80 pounds was the highest amount lost because that clue is contained in the problem. If Donna's 80 pounds were the greatest weight loss, Celia would have lost 40 pounds because sentence 3 says that Celia lost half of the greatest amount lost. But this creates a problem because it would mean that Abby also lost 80. Sentence 2 says Abby lost twice what Celia lost. And Abby COULDN'T have lost 80 pounds because that would mean that two women (Abby and Donna) lost the most. This is impossible because sentence 3 says Celia lost half as much as the woman (not women) who lost the most. So the greatest amount lost must have been more than 80 pounds, and Abby must have been the one who lost it. All we know, then, is the following: Donna lost 80 pounds, the greatest amount lost was more than 80 pounds, Celia's amount was half the greatest amount, and Abby lost more than 80 pounds. As long as all these conditions are met, Bea's loss might be any amount that makes up the difference between 260 and the others' total weight loss. For example, the losses could have been:

Abby	84		Abby	90		Abby	94
Bea	54	OR	Bea	45	OR	Bea	39
Celia	42		Celia	45		Celia	47
Donna	80		Donna	80		Donna	80
	260			260			260

Or many other possible combinations. The facts simply don't give us enough information to either prove or disprove that the amounts given in the conclusion are the actual amounts each woman lost. That's why the correct answer is C.

6. CORRECT ANSWER: B

To see why B is the correct answer, it is helpful to draw a diagram of the floors. We know that Ann is on Four (sentence 4) and that Sally is on Three (sentence 3). If Ann is two floors above Brenda (sentence 1), Brenda must be on Two. Now we can draw:

Ann - - - - - - - - - - - - - (4)
Sally - - - - - - - - - - - - (3)
Brenda - - - - - - - - - - - (2)

So, if Brenda is one floor below the birthday-girl (sentence 2), today must be Sally's birthday, not Ann's.

7. CORRECT ANSWER: B

Here, you need to know what perpendicular and parallel mean. If you do, a simple diagram should show you that the facts disprove the conclusion. Perpendicular streets are those at right angles to one another, like the two lines in a plus sign (+). Parallel streets are those that run in the same direction, never touching - like the two l's in the word all. The first three facts tell us that the streets look like this:

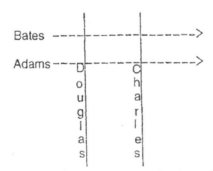

If Evans is parallel to the streets that are perpendicular to Bates (sentence 4), then Evans itself must be perpendicular to Bates. The completed diagram now looks like this:

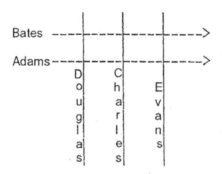

This diagram graphically shows that Evans is NOT perpendicular to Douglas, but parallel to it. The facts, then, disprove the conclusion.

8. CORRECT ANSWER: B

If you start from the last fact given in this problem and work backwards, you will be able to find the cause of each event. This will enable you to either prove or disprove the conclusion. In this case, since the last fact says that the captain ran, that must have been because Arnie hit the ball hard (sentence 3). Even though Arnie hit the ball hard, Bill is out because Bill is so slow that he will be out at home plate (sentence 2). This disproves the conclusion, which says he is safe.

9. CORRECT ANSWER: A

This is an easy problem if you translate the facts into a picture. First of all, ignore sentence 3, which has nothing to do with the problem. Now, draw a circle to represent all the members of this genus (sentence 1). Next, draw a smaller circle to represent the members of that species (sentence 1). You may know that a species is a subgroup of a genus, just as *semi-precious* is a subgroup of gems, or hardwoods is a subgroup of trees. For this reason, the *species* circle should be contained entirely within the *genus* circle. The problem doesn't tell you this about genus and species, but you don't need to know it to answer the question correctly. You could simply place the smaller circle partially in and partially out of the larger circle. No matter which way you portray the relationship, some members of the genus will belong to that species. You can see this in the diagrams below. Since all members of that species are butterflies (sentence 2), the *species* circle also represents butterflies.

Not all members of this genus are butterflies; this is demonstrated by the fact that there is plenty of room inside the *genus* circle for other, non-butterfly critters. But the picture clearly shows that some members of the genus are butterflies, as the conclusion states.

10. **CORRECT ANSWER: C**
    The facts prove only that some woodwinds (those that are clarinets) are beautiful things; they do not prove that all beautiful things are woodwinds. If you draw circles to represent *beautiful things* and *clarinets,* the latter would have to be a smaller circle inside the former, since all clarinets are beautiful things (sentence 3).

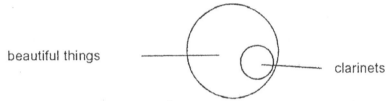

But where does the *woodwind* circle go? All the facts tell us is that some of its members are clarinets. We don't know whether it's bigger, smaller, or the same size as the circle of *beautiful things.* It could look like the following:

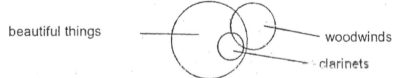

That way, there could be plenty of beautiful things that are not woodwinds, some beautiful things that are woodwinds and clarinets, and some woodwinds that are beautiful things but not clarinets. And the conclusion would be false.
OR, the *woodwinds* circle could be identical to the *beautiful things* circle:

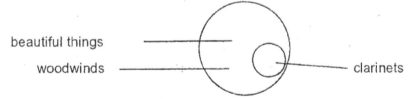

making the conclusion true.
You may have circled answer B, simply because the conclusion is obviously a false statement. But remember, the question is not whether the conclusion is true or false; it's whether it is proved or disproved by the facts given. In this case, it is neither proved nor disproved by the facts. Sentence 2, incidentally, is irrelevant, since the rest of the problem has nothing to do with flutes.

11. CORRECT ANSWER: B

You could use a trial-and-error approach to this problem, but it would be very time-con-suming. As you worked with this problem, you may have realized that, since the num-ber in the middle box gets added to every other number, you can solve the problem more easily by putting 6 into the diagram and adding the larger numbers to it to see if it's workable. After placing 6 in the center, you can see there is nowhere to put 9. The horizontal, vertical, and diagonal rows must add up to 15, but wherever you try to put 9, you will have a row that adds up to more than 15. Since 9 + 6 = 15 and 0 is not one of the options, there is no number that can be put in the third box in the row.

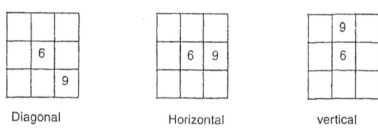

Diagonal   Horizontal   vertical

So, 6 cannot be the number in the middle box; it's too big. The facts disprove the con-clusion.

12. CORRECT ANSWER: A

The first sentence in this problem says that these men bought various colored suits, but not necessarily <u>respectively</u>. This means that the first man (Max) didn't necessarily buy the first color suit (grey), the second man (Nick) didn't necessarily buy the second color suit (green), and so on. <u>Respectively</u> means *in the same order*.

At first glance, this problem looks impossible, but it can be simplified by drawing a chart to show what we *know* about each person:

NAME	PAID	FOR THIS COLOR SUIT
Max	less than Nick	green
Nick	same as Pete	grey (not green, brown or blue)
Pete	same as Nick	blue (not grey, green or brown)
Ollie	2x Nick; 2x Pete	brown

Sentence 2 says Max's suit is green, and sentence 5 says Ollie's is brown, but how do we know Pete's is blue? Well, sentence 4 indicates that someone other than Pete bought the grey one. That means Nick got the grey one. Since the grey, green, and brown suits are all accounted for, the blue one must be Pete's.

Now, all we need to know is who paid the most! Ollie paid twice what Pete paid (sentence 3). This means that he also paid twice what Nick paid because Pete paid the same as the man who bought the grey suit (sentence 4) - and Nick bought the grey suit. So the high-est-payer can't be Nick or Pete; it must either be Ollie or Max. But sentence 2 says Max paid <u>less</u> than Nick. So the highest-payer must be Ollie, as proved by the facts given.

13. CORRECT ANSWER: A

The man sitting on Dave's right (sentence 6) has to be Bob because he's the only other man in the group. Alice sits across from Dave (sentence 4). This means that Carol must be sitting across from Bob. From this information, you can draw a diagram of the table and the people seated at it:

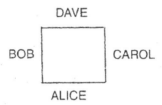

Now all you need to know is whether Dave plays golf. It may help keep everything straight if you put the name of the sport next to the name of the proper person as you figure out each one. Here, we have abbreviated each sport using a lower-case initial (j for jogging, g for golf, and so on). Since Carol sits to the right of the basketball player (sentence 3), Alice must play basketball. (Remember, it's not Carol's right; it's the basketball player's right. This confuses some people.) Since Bob sits across from the jogger (sentence 2), Carol must jog. After adding this information, your diagram would look like this:

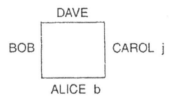

At this point, all you need to know is: Does Bob golf and Dave play tennis, or is it the other way around? A quick trial-and-error produces the answer. Sentence 5 says the golfer sits to the left of the tennis player. If Dave played tennis, would this be true? No. So, it must be Bob who's the tennis player, and Dave who's the golfer. The conclusion is thus proved by the facts. If you have spatial problems, you might want to twist the diagram around to see this more clearly.

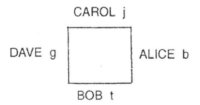

14. CORRECT ANSWER: C

To visualize this problem it is helpful to draw a small chart, showing what we know about each woman's score.

NAME	SCORE
Carol	higher than Betty

Betty	higher than 40 (according to sentence 3 she scored more than twice as high as Alice
Alice	20

From this chart, we can see that Carol's score could have been <u>any</u> number higher than 41. It could have been 50, or 65, or 92–in which case she would have scored high enough to be hired. But it also could have been 42, or 43, or 47–in which case she would not have scored high enough. So, we can't prove that Carol was offered the job, but we can't prove that she wasn't either. In addition, we can't prove that Carol was the only one who was offered the job. We know Alice didn't get an offer (with a score of 20), but we don't know about Betty. She could have gotten anything above 40. So, the facts here neither prove nor disprove the conclusion.

15. CORRECT ANSWER: C
This is a sneaky little question. If you read it quickly, you might have thought it was easy. The cat didn't get rabies (sentence 3), so the cat had had its rabies shots within the last two years (sentence 2). But perhaps the cat didn't get rabies because the squirrel never bit it, or perhaps the squirrel never had rabies to begin with. The first sentence says, *If Camille's squirrel has rabies"* and *(if) the squirrel bites Casey's cat...the cat will get rabies.* (The second if is implied by the structure of the sentence.) Nothing in this paragraph ever tells us that the squirrel had rabies or that the squirrel bit the cat. As we said - sneaky. Since you don't know why the cat didn't get rabies, you can't prove that it was spared because it had had its shots, and you can't disprove it either. Therefore, C is the only possible answer.

16. CORRECT ANSWER: C
This is another sneaky question. (The exams haven't used this kind of trick lately, but we wanted to give you practice – just in case.) If you didn't read the problem carefully, you might have chosen B. You would have thought that Laura told Frank (sentence 4), who told Bill (sentence 2), who chose not to fire Sally (sentence 3). Since Sally didn't get fired, she didn't file a grievance (sentence 1). The only problem is that Laura told <u>Fred</u>, not Frank, and we have no way of knowing how Fred fits into this crew. He could have told Frank, thereby setting in motion the cycle above and preventing Sally from getting fired. In that case, the conclusion would be false. Or he could have not told any-one, Sally would have gotten fired, she would have filed a grievance, and the conclusion would have been true. You just don't know, so C is the only option.

17. CORRECT ANSWER: C
Obviously, if the *pre-game* song gets delayed, the game will also be delayed, but we don't know for how long. We also don't know how late Barb had to work. (We know that she <u>did</u> have to work late, because of sentences 1, 5, and 6.) For all we know, the game may have been delayed for an hour due to the storm, and Barb may have had to work only a half hour later than usual–thereby not missing any of the game at all. In questions of this type, it is always good to work backwards from the conclusion and try to see if there is a cause of that conclusion contained in the facts. In this case, although we can find a cause for Barb's having to work late (Alice's acceptance of Carl's invitation), we can find nothing that would <u>necessarily</u> cause Barb to miss the first inning of the game.

18. CORRECT ANSWER: A

The conclusion seems likely because it only takes Eva five tries to guess a number from 1 through 10. The most efficient way to guess is to eliminate half of all possible numbers with each guess. When the number is from 1 through 10, the first question should be, *Is the number you're thinking of 6 or more?* The answer to that question, whether it's yes or no, will eliminate five numbers - half of all the numbers Earl could possibly be thinking of. Let's say Earl said yes. The second question would be, *Is it 8 or more?* That answer will eliminate two or three of the five remaining possible numbers. No matter what range of numbers Earl wants to use, whether it be 1 through 50, 1 through 100, or whatever, Eva could use this method until she narrows the answers down to one possible number. (We can assume that she uses this method because sentence 2 says she is using the most efficient method.)

For the range 1 through 6, then, you can see that four is the highest number of guesses she will need using this system. The most she can be sure of eliminating with one guess is 3 numbers. *(Is the number you're thinking of 4 or more?)* At that point, she <u>may</u> need as many as three more guesses to eliminate the two remaining wrong numbers one by one and then to *guess* the right number. Since this is four guesses, the facts prove the conclusion.

19. CORRECT ANSWER: C

Here is a case in which it is clear that certain facts are missing. You know from sentences 4 and 2 that Robbie is home in time for Lois to make dinner, but what about Ted and Jennifer? Nowhere in the facts does it say whether or not Ted played softball after work. Since sentence 1 says Lois will cook only if <u>all</u> <u>three</u> are home by 6 P.M., we simply don't have enough information to either prove or disprove the conclusion.

20. CORRECT ANSWER: A

Unless you are excellent in math, just about the only way to figure this one out is to set up a grid showing the amount of money each player has after each round. After setting up such a grid, the answer can be found quite easily.

		ARTIE $10	BRUCE $10	CHUCK $10
AFTER ROUND	#1	$8	$8	$14
	#2	$6	$12	$12
	#3	$4	$10	$16
	#4	$17	$5	$8

Chuck won the first round (sentence 4). Since everyone started with $10 (sentence 1), you can see that after Round #1, each loser would be out $2 (sentences 2 and 3), bringing their totals down to $8 each. Chuck, on the other hand, would be up to $14, having collected $2 from each of the two losers. The second line of the grid shows the situation after Round #2, which was won by Bruce (sentence 4). The third line shows the situation after Round #3, when Chuck is way ahead (sentence 4). Likewise, the fourth line shows the situation after Round #4, when the rules had been changed and Artie won (sentences 5 and 6). Since each of the other two had to give him half their money (sentence 5), he collected $5 from Bruce and $8 from Chuck. His total of $17 was $9 more than

Chuck had at that point. So, the conclusion that Artie ended up with more money than Chuck is proven by the facts given.

21. CORRECT ANSWER: B

The facts prove just the opposite of the conclusion. If <u>all</u> cleaners work part-time (sentence 2), and <u>no</u> part-timers get paid vacations (sentence 1), then <u>no</u> cleaners can get paid vacations. Where *facts* are given in the form, *No A are B, and all C are A,* you can simply substitute C for A, and that will prove that no C are B. (This is much like question 3, except the first fact is all-exclusive rather than all-inclusive. It excludes rather than includes all of something. See the explanation to question 3, if this is not clear.) In this case, *A* is the part-timers, *B* represents recipients of paid vacations, and *C* is cleaners. The facts disprove the conclusion. Since we don't know what Joe's occupation is, sentence 3 is irrelevant to this problem.

22. CORRECT ANSWER: C

In this case, no amount of *following the trail* of facts will lead you to the conclusion given because there is no trail. No fact implies, or leads to, any other; they are simply a collection of statements with no relationship to one another. The facts neither prove nor disprove the conclusion.

23. CORRECT ANSWER: A

Unlike question 22, this question lends itself to *following the trail* of facts. As we've noticed earlier, a good place to begin the trail is with the last fact. It follows from sentence 5 (Dick cleans the house) that Sally goes to the store (sentence 3), which means that Tina also goes to the store (sentence 4). This, in turn, means that Ike goes (sentence 1), and buys the doughnuts (sentence 2). The facts here prove the conclusion.

24. CORRECT ANSWER: A

To decide whether the facts prove the conclusion, you must understand what each fact means. The fact that Joe passed the test (sentence 4) means that Jill didn't apply for the job (sentence 1). Knowing this, all you have to do is reread sentence 3 to see that Jeanne does, indeed, get annoyed. Sentence 2 is not needed to solve this problem, although it may explain why Jeanne got annoyed.

25. CORRECT ANSWER: B

It is helpful to make a list of who's using the machine when, and to fill in the facts you're given. Then you can gradually deduce more information, until you can see whether the conclusion is proved, disproved, or neither. Sentence 2 says Debbie goes first, so your list, at the start, would look something like this:

First - Debbie
Second - ?
Third - ?
Last - ?

It is clear from sentences 3 and 5 that Joan immediately follows May. This also means that Joan cannot be second, May cannot be last, and Mary cannot be third. You may then wish to enter the possibilities to your list:

First - Debbie
Second - May or Mary

Third - May or Joan
Last - Joan or Mary

Now, all we need to know is: Does May go second? If so, the conclusion is proved by the facts; if not, it's disproved. We know from sentence 4 that the person with the most work goes second. That person can't be May, however, because May has been waiting longest (sentence 5), and the longest-waiter is not the person with the most work (sentence 6). So, Debbie is first, Mary is second, May is third, Joan is fourth, and the conclusion is disproved.

First - Debbie
Second - Mary
Third - May
Last - Joan

EXAMINATION SECTION
TEST 1

DIRECTIONS: Each question or incomplete statement is followed by several suggested answers or completions. Select the one that BEST answers the question or completes the statement. *PRINT THE LETTER OF THE CORRECT ANSWER IN THE SPACE AT THE RIGHT.*

Questions 1-7.

DIRECTIONS: Questions 1 through 7 are to be answered based on the following set of facts.

The four towns of Alpha, Beta, Gamma, and Delta lie in a straight line from left to right, but not necessarily in that order. Each town has a different maximum speed limit, and each maximum speed limit ends in 0 or 5. Delta lies to the east of Beta. Alpha lies east of Beta, but west of Delta. The distance between Beta and Alpha equals the distance between Alpha and Delta. Alpha and Gamma are adjacent towns. Gamma and Delta are 50 miles apart. The distance between Alpha and Gamma is less than 10 miles.

Concerning the maximum speed limits, Beta's is one-third that of Alpha's, Delta's is higher than Alpha's by 10 m.p.h., and Gamma has the highest. No town's maximum speed limit exceeds 80 m.p.h. nor is less than 20 m.p.h.

1. Which of the following is the CORRECT order of towns from west to east?   1.____

    A.   Beta, Delta, Gamma, Alpha   B.   Beta, Alpha, Gamma, Delta
    C.   Delta, Alpha, Gamma, Beta   D.   Gamma, Alpha, Beta, Delta
    E.   Delta, Gamma, Alpha, Beta

2. What is Gamma's MAXIMUM speed limit in m.p.h.?   2.____

    A.   65   B.   70   C.   Over 70
    D.   60   E.   Under 60

3. What is the ratio of Beta's MAXIMUM speed limit to that of Delta?   3.____

    A.   4:15   B.   1:3   C.   1:4   D.   3:5   E.   2:7

4. Suppose that next year Beta's maximum speed limit is tripled, and Alpha's is reduced by 5 m.p.h.   4.____
    What would be the CORRECT order of towns from lowest to highest maximum speed limit?

    A.   Delta, Alpha, Beta, Gamma   B.   Beta, Delta, Alpha, Gamma
    C.   Alpha, Delta, Beta, Gamma   D.   Alpha, Beta, Delta, Gamma
    E.   Beta, Alpha, Gamma, Delta

5. What is the distance, in miles, between Delta and Alpha?   5.____

    A.   Between 50 and 55 inclusive   B.   Under 50
    C.   Over 55 but under 65   D.   Over 50 but under 60
    E.   Over 60

6. The distance between Beta and Delta must be less than _____ miles.   6.___

    A. 50   B. 65   C. 75   D. 90   E. 120

7. For which towns can the EXACT maximum speed limit be determined?   7.___

    A. Alpha and Gamma   B. Alpha, Beta, and Delta
    C. Beta, Delta, and Gamma   D. Beta and Gamma
    E. All four towns

Questions 8-14.

DIRECTIONS: Questions 8 through 14 are to be answered based upon the following set of facts.

   Johnny Quicksale sells three types of books: biographical, novels, and statistical. Each type of book comes in three different versions: condensed, regular, and expanded. For each type of book, the order of cost from least expensive to most expensive is condensed, regular, and expanded. Each type has a different price, and the pricing between books is somewhat involved. Condensed statistical books cost more than both regular novels and regular biographies, but less than expanded novels. Expanded biographies cost less than regular novels, but more than condensed novels. Condensed biographies are the cheapest. Expanded statistical books are not the most expensive. The price for each condensed and regular book is a multiple of $5, whereas the price of each expanded book is a multiple of $25. Each book sells for less than $95. A regular statistical book costs less than $45.

8. The CORRECT sequence of the first three books (in increasing price) starting from the cheapest is: 8.___

    A. Condensed biography, regular biography, consensed novel
    B. Condensed novel, condensed biography, condensed statistical
    C. Condensed statistical, condensed novel, condensed biography
    D. Condensed novel, condensed biography, regular novel
    E. Condensed biography, condensed novel, regular biography

9. How many books cost over $10?   9.___

    A. 3   B. 4 or 5   C. 6   D. 7 or 8   E. all 9

10. If just the expanded versions were listed in correct order from the most expensive to the cheapest, that order would be: 10.___

    A. Novel, statistical, biography
    B. Statistical, biography, novel
    C. Biography, novel, statistical
    D. Statistical, novel, biography
    E. Biography, statistical, novel

11. How many books cost under $30?   11.___

    A. 2   B. 3   C. 4   D. 5   E. 6 or more

12. For which type(s) of books are the prices arranged so that the regular version could be the average in price of the prices of the condensed and expanded versions?   12.____

    A. Only novels
    B. Only biographies
    C. Only statistical
    D. Exactly 2 types
    E. All 3 types

13. For which type(s) of books are the prices arranged so that the condensed version costs MORE than the expanded version?   13.____

    A. All 3 types
    B. Exactly 2 types
    C. Only biographies
    D. Only novels
    E. None

14. Suppose that next year the cost of the condensed statistical book doubled, but all other prices remained the same.   14.____
Which statement(s) is(are) CORRECT?
    I. The condensed statistical book would be the most expensive.
    II. The price of the condensed statistical book would equal the price of the expanded novel book.
    III. The price of the condensed statistical book would exceed that of the expanded statistical book.
The CORRECT answer is:

    A. I *only*
    B. II *only*
    C. III *only*
    D. None of the above
    E. Exactly 2 of the above

Questions 15-22.

DIRECTIONS: Questions 15 through 22 are to be answered on the basis of the following set of facts.

    Ann, Beth, Carol, Diane, and Eve have entered a local beauty contest in which Mr. Brown, Mr. Smith, and Mr. Jones are the judges. The point system to be used is 0, 1, 2, 3, and 4, where 4 is the highest. Each judge will rank each applicant exactly once, and no judges may assign the same ranking to two or more applicants. The girl with the highest total wins the contest. Brown and Jones both ranked Diane the same, and this ranking matched the score that Smith gave to Carol. Smith's ranking for Ann was exactly double Jones' ranking for Ann, but less than the score Brown assigned to Ann. Brown ranked Eve higher than Ann. Carol accumulated the same number of points as Ann. Carol and Ann were the only applicants who received three different rankings from the three judges.

15. Who won the contest?   15.____

    A. Ann   B. Beth   C. Carol   D. Diane   E. Eve

16. If the rules were adjusted so that for each applicant only the best two rankings given by the three judges would count, who would have the HIGHEST total?   16.____

    A. Ann   B. Beth   C. Carol   D. Diane   E. Eve

17. What is the complete list of applicants who did NOT receive any 0 rating?   17.____

    A. Ann, Carol, Diane   B. Ann, Beth, Eve
    C. Beth, Carol, Eve   D. Ann, Diane, Eve
    E. Beth, Carol, Diane

18. Who came in second place?   18.____

    A. Ann   B. Beth   C. Carol   D. Diane   E. Eve

19. Which judge(s) scored Diane the LOWEST?   19.____

    A. Only Brown   B. Only Jones
    C. Only Smith   D. Exactly 2 of them
    E. All 3 judges

20. Which judge(s) scored Ann the HIGHEST?   20.____

    A. Only Brown   B. Only Jones
    C. Only Smith   D. Exactly 2 of them
    E. None of them

21. How many applicants earned the HIGHEST ranking at least once?   21.____

    A. All 5   B. 4   C. 3   D. 2   E. 1

22. Which is(are) correct?   22.____
    I. Ann's total + Diane's total = Carol's total
    II. Beth's total + Diane's total = Ann's total
    III. Carol's total + Diane's total = Beth's total
The CORRECT answer is:

    A. I only   B. II only   C. III only
    D. All of them   E. None of them

Questions 23-25.

DIRECTIONS: Questions 23 through 25 are based on the following paragraph.

There are 200 correctional facilities nationwide. Exactly 75% of all inmates with the disease AIDS are housed in correctional facilities in just three states: New Jersey, New York, and Pennsylvania. Also, 4% of the entire nation's correctional institutions have 72% of all the inmate AIDS cases; 50% of all such institutions are totally free of the disease.

23. How many AIDS-infected inmates are housed outside the states of New York, New Jersey, and Pennsylvania?   23.____

    A. 8   B. 25   C. 50   D. 75   E. 100

24. If one could find a total of 216 inmates with AIDS in just eight institutions, then the LEAST number of AIDS-infected inmates nationwide would be   24.____

    A. 240   B. 270   C. 300   D. 330   E. 360

25. It is a certainty that exactly _____ correctional facilities combined would contribute 28%   25.____
of the total number of inmates with AIDS, where none of these institutions are disease-
free.

   A. 46   B. 50   C. 72   D. 92   E. 100

KEY (CORRECT ANSWERS)

1.	B		11.	C
2.	C		12.	B
3.	E		13.	E
4.	D		14.	C
5.	D		15.	E
6.	E		16.	E
7.	D		17.	B
8.	E		18.	B
9.	D		19.	D
10.	A		20.	E

21.	D
22.	C
23.	C
24.	C
25.	D

SOLUTIONS TO PROBLEMS

For Questions 1 through 7, the order of towns from west to east are: Beta, Alpha, Gamma, Delta, and would be arranged mileage wise as:

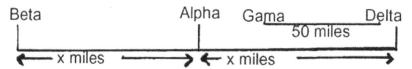

The present maximum speed limits are:

Beta = 20 m.p.h.   Alpha = 60 m.p.h.
Delta = 70 m.p.h.   Gamma = 75 m.p.h. or 80 m.p.h.

For Questions 8 through 14, the correct sequence in order of increasing price would be:

Condensed biography, condensed novel, regular biography, expanded biography, regular novel, condensed statistical, regular statistical, expanded statistical, expanded novel.

There are three possible sets of solutions for the prices:

1st solution:	$5,	$10,	$15,	$25,	$30,	$35,	$40,	$50,	$75
2nd solution:	$5,	$10,	$20,	$25,	$30,	$35,	$40,	$50,	$75
3rd solution:	$5,	$15,	$20,	$25,	$30,	$35,	$40,	$50,	$75

Note that the differences occurred only in the lowest three prices.

For Questions 15 through 22, the scoring by each judge and for each applicant appears as:

	Ann	Beth	Carol	Diane	Eve
Brown	3	1	2	0	4
Jones	1	3	4	0	2
Smith	2	3	0	1	4

23. 100% - 75% = 25% of AIDS-infected inmates are located outside the 3 states of New York, New Jersey, and Pennsylvania. (25%)(200) = 50. (Ans. C)

24. Eight institutions could represent the 4% of the entire nation's correctional facilities which have 72% of all inmate AIDS cases (200 times 4% =8). If 216 represents 72% of all such infected inmates, then the total number of AIDS-infected inmates is 216 ÷ 72% = 300. (Ans. C)

25. 100% - 4% - 50% = 46%, which could contribute 28% of the total number of inmates with AIDS. This 46% figure would represent the fraction of institutions outside the 4% and outside the 50% (which have no such cases). (46%)(200) = 92. (Ans. D)

CLERICAL ABILITIES

EXAMINATION SECTION
TEST 1

DIRECTIONS: Each question or incomplete statement is followed by several suggested answers or completions. Select the one that BEST answers the question or completes the statement. *PRINT THE LETTER OF THE CORRECT ANSWER IN THE SPACE AT THE RIGHT.*

Questions 1-4.

DIRECTIONS: Questions 1 through 4 are to be answered on the basis of the information given below.

The most commonly used filing system and the one that is easiest to learn is alphabetical filing. This involves putting records in an A to Z order, according to the letters of the alphabet. The name of a person is filed by using the following order: first, the surname or last name; second, the first name; third, the middle name or middle initial. For example, *Henry C. Young* is filed under *Y* and thereafter under *Young, Henry C.* The name of a company is filed in the same way. For example, *Long Cabinet Co.* is filed under *L*, while *John T. Long Cabinet Co.* is filed under *L* and thereafter under *Long., John T. Cabinet Co.*

1. The one of the following which lists the names of persons in the CORRECT alphabetical order is:

    A. Mary Carrie, Helen Carrol, James Carson, John Carter
    B. James Carson, Mary Carrie, John Carter, Helen Carrol
    C. Helen Carrol, James Carson, John Carter, Mary Carrie
    D. John Carter, Helen Carrol, Mary Carrie, James Carson

1.____

2. The one of the following which lists the names of persons in the CORRECT alphabetical order is:

    A. Jones, John C.; Jones, John A.; Jones, John P.; Jones, John K.
    B. Jones, John P.; Jones, John K.; Jones, John C.; Jones, John A.
    C. Jones, John A.; Jones, John C.; Jones, John K.; Jones, John P.
    D. Jones, John K.; Jones, John C.; Jones, John A.; Jones, John P.

2.____

3. The one of the following which lists the names of the companies in the CORRECT alphabetical order is:

    A. Blane Co., Blake Co., Block Co., Blear Co.
    B. Blake Co., Blane Co., Blear Co., Block Co.
    C. Block Co., Blear Co., Blane Co., Blake Co.
    D. Blear Co., Blake Co., Blane Co., Block Co.

3.____

4. You are to return to the file an index card on *Barry C. Wayne Materials and Supplies Co.* Of the following, the CORRECT alphabetical group that you should return the index card to is

    A. A to G   B. H to M   C. N to S   D. T to Z

4.____

Questions 5-10.

DIRECTIONS: In each of Questions 5 through 10, the names of four people are given. For each question, choose as your answer the one of the four names given which should be filed FIRST according to the usual system of alphabetical filing of names, as described in the following paragraph.

In filing names, you must start with the last name. Names are filed in order of the first letter of the last name, then the second letter, etc. Therefore, BAILY would be filed before BROWN, which would be filed before COLT. A name with fewer letters of the same type comes first; i.e., Smith before Smithe. If the last names are the same, the names are filed alphabetically by the first name. If the first name is an initial, a name with an initial would come before a first name that starts with the same letter as the initial. Therefore, I. BROWN would come before IRA BROWN. Finally, if both last name and first name are the same, the name would be filed alphabetically by the middle name, once again an initial coming before a middle name which starts with the same letter as the initial. If there is no middle name at all, the name would come before those with middle initials or names.

Sample Question: A. Lester Daniels
B. William Dancer
C. Nathan Danzig
D. Dan Lester

The last names beginning with D are filed before the last name beginning with L. Since DANIELS, DANCER, and DANZIG all begin with the same three letters, you must look at the fourth letter of the last name to determine which name should be filed first. C comes before I or Z in the alphabet, so DANCER is filed before DANIELS or DANZIG. Therefore, the answer to the above sample question is B.

5. A. Scott Biala
    B. Mary Byala
    C. Martin Baylor
    D. Francis Bauer

    5._____

6. A. Howard J. Black
    B. Howard Black
    C. J. Howard Black
    D. John H. Black

    6._____

7. A. Theodora Garth Kingston
    B. Theadore Barth Kingston
    C. Thomas Kingston
    D. Thomas T. Kingston

    7._____

8. A. Paulette Mary Huerta
    B. Paul M. Huerta
    C. Paulette L. Huerta
    D. Peter A. Huerta

    8._____

9. A. Martha Hunt Morgan
    B. Martin Hunt Morgan
    C. Mary H. Morgan
    D. Martine H. Morgan

9._____

10. A. James T. Meerschaum
    B. James M. Mershum
    C. James F. Mearshaum
    D. James N. Meshum

10._____

Questions 11-14.

DIRECTIONS: Questions 11 through 14 are to be answered SOLELY on the basis of the following information.

You are required to file various documents in file drawers which are labeled according to
the following pattern:

DOCUMENTS

MEMOS		LETTERS	
File	Subject	File	Subject
84PM1 - (A-L)		84PC1 - (A-L)	
84PM2 - (M-Z)		84PC2 - (M-Z)	

REPORTS		INQUIRIES	
File Subject		File	Subject
84PR1 - (A-L)		84PQ1 - (A-L)	
84PR2 - (M-Z)		84PQ2 - (M-Z)	

11. A letter dealing with a burglary should be filed in the drawer labeled

11._____

    A. 84PM1   B. 84PC1   C. 84PR1   D. 84PQ2

12. A report on Statistics should be found in the drawer labeled

12._____

    A. 84PM1   B. 84PC2   C. 84PR2   D. 84PQ2

13. An inquiry is received about parade permit procedures. It should be filed in the drawer
labeled

13._____

    A. 84PM2   B. 84PC1   C. 84PR1   D. 84PQ2

14. A police officer has a question about a robbery report you filed.
You should pull this file from the drawer labeled

14._____

    A. 84PM1   B. 84PM2   C. 84PR1   D. 84PR2

Questions 15-22.

DIRECTIONS: Each of Questions 15 through 22 consists of four or six numbered names. For
each question, choose the option (A, B, C, or D) which indicates the order in
which the names should be filed in accordance with the following filing instructions:
- File alphabetically according to last name, then first name, then middle initial.
- File according to each successive letter within a name.

- When comparing two names in which, the letters in the longer name are identical to the corresponding letters in the shorter name, the shorter name is filed first.
- When the last names are the same, initials are always filed before names beginning with the same letter.

15.   I.   Ralph Robinson
        II. Alfred Ross
        III. Luis Robles
        IV. James Roberts
The CORRECT filing sequence for the above names should be

   A. IV, II, I, III   B. I, IV, III, II
   C. III, IV, I, II   D. IV, I, III, II

15.____

16.   I.   Irwin Goodwin
        II. Inez Gonzalez
        III. Irene Goodman
        IV. Ira S. Goodwin
        V. Ruth I. Goldstein
        VI. M.B. Goodman
The CORRECT filing sequence for the above names should be

   A. V, II, I, IV, III, VI   B. V, II, VI, III, IV, I
   C. V, II, III, VI, IV, I   D. V, II, III, VI, I, IV

16.____

17.   I.   George Allan
        II. Gregory Allen
        III. Gary Allen
        IV. George Allen
The CORRECT filing sequence for the above names should be

   A. IV, III, I, II   B. I, IV, II, III
   C. III, IV, I, II   D. I, III, IV, II

17.____

18.   I.   Simon Kauffman
        II. Leo Kaufman
        III. Robert Kaufmann
        IV. Paul Kauffmann
The CORRECT filing sequence for the above names should be

   A. I, IV, II, III   B. II, IV, III, I
   C. III, II, IV, I   D. I, II, III, IV

18.____

19.   I.   Roberta Williams
        II. Robin Wilson
        III. Roberta Wilson
        IV. Robin Williams
The CORRECT filing sequence for the above names should be

   A. III, II, IV, I   B. I, IV, III, II
   C. I, II, III, IV   D. III, I, II, IV

19.____

20.   I.   Lawrence Shultz   20.____
        II.   Albert Schultz
        III. Theodore Schwartz
        IV.   Thomas Schwarz
        V.   Alvin Schultz
        VI.   Leonard Shultz
    The CORRECT filing sequence for the above names should be

    A. II, V, III, IV, I, VI   B. IV, III, V, I, II, VI
    C. II, V, I, VI, III, IV   D. I, VI, II, V, III, IV

21.   I.   McArdle   21.____
        II.   Mayer
        III. Maletz
        IV.   McNiff
        V.   Meyer
        VI.   MacMahon
    The CORRECT filing sequence for the above names should be

    A. I, IV, VI, III, II, V   B. II, I, IV, VI, III, V
    C. VI, III, II, I, IV, V   D. VI, III, II, V, I, IV

22.   I.   Jack E. Johnson   22.____
        II.   R.H. Jackson
        III. Bertha Jackson
        IV.   J.T. Johnson
        V.   Ann Johns
        VI.   John Jacobs
    The CORRECT filing sequence for the above names should be

    A. II, III, VI, V, IV, I   B. III, II, VI, V, IV, I
    C. VI, II, III, I, V, IV   D. III, II, VI, IV, V, I

Questions 23-30.

DIRECTIONS: The code table below shows 10 letters with matching numbers. For each ques-
              tion, there are three sets of letters. Each set of letters is followed by a set of
              numbers which may or may not match their correct letter according to the code
              table. For each question, check all three sets of letters and numbers and mark
              your answer:
              A.   if no pairs are correctly matched
              B.   if only one pair is correctly matched
              C.   if only two pairs are correctly matched
              D.   if all three pairs are correctly matched

CODE TABLE

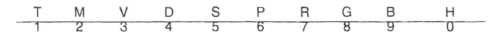

T	M	V	D	S	P	R	G	B	H
1	2	3	4	5	6	7	8	9	0

Sample Question: TMVDSP - 123456
                          RGBHTM - 789011
                          DSPRGB - 256789

In the sample question above, the first set of numbers correctly matches its set of letters. But the second and third pairs contain mistakes. In the second pair, M is incorrectly matched with number 1. According to the code table, letter M should be correctly matched with number 2. In the third pair, the letter D is incorrectly matched with number 2. According to the code table, letter D should be correctly matched with number 4. Since only one of the pairs is correctly matched, the answer to this sample question is B.

23.   RSBMRM 759262   23._____
       GDSRVH 845730
       VDBRTM 349713

24.   TGVSDR 183247   24._____
       SMHRDP 520647
       TRMHSR 172057

25.   DSPRGM 456782   25._____
       MVDBHT 234902
       HPMDBT 062491

26.   BVPTRD 936184   26._____
       GDPHMB 807029
       GMRHMV 827032

27.   MGVRSH 283750   27._____
       TRDMBS 174295
       SPRMGV 567283

28.   SGBSDM 489542   28._____
       MGHPTM 290612
       MPBMHT 269301

29.   TDPBHM 146902   29._____
       VPBMRS 369275
       GDMBHM 842902

30.   MVPTBV 236194   30._____
       PDRTMB 647128
       BGTMSM 981232

KEY (CORRECT ANSWERS)

1.	A	11.	B	21.	C
2.	C	12.	C	22.	B
3.	B	13.	D	23.	B
4.	D	14.	D	24.	B
5.	D	15.	D	25.	C
6.	B	16.	C	26.	A
7.	B	17.	D	27.	D
8.	B	18.	A	28.	A
9.	A	19.	B	29.	D
10.	C	20.	A	30.	A

———

TEST 2

DIRECTIONS: Each question or incomplete statement is followed by several suggested answers or completions. Select the one that BEST answers the question or completes the statement. *PRINT THE LETTER OF THE CORRECT ANSWER IN THE SPACE AT THE RIGHT.*

Questions 1-10.

DIRECTIONS: Questions 1 through 10 each consists of two columns, each containing four lines of names, numbers and/or addresses. For each question, compare the lines in Column I with the lines in Column II to see if they match exactly, and mark your answer A, B, C, or D, according to the following instructions:
- A. all four lines match exactly
- B. only three lines match exactly
- C. only two lines match exactly
- D. only one line matches exactly

	COLUMN I	COLUMN II	
1.	I. Earl Hodgson II. 1409870 III. Shore Ave. IV. Macon Rd.	Earl Hodgson 1408970 Schore Ave. Macon Rd.	1.____
2.	I. 9671485 II. 470 Astor Court III. Halprin, Phillip IV. Frank D. Poliseo	9671485 470 Astor Court Halperin, Phillip Frank D. Poliseo	2.____
3.	I. Tandem Associates II. 144-17 Northern Blvd. III. Alberta Forchi IV. Kings Park, NY 10751	Tandom Associates 144-17 Northern Blvd. Albert Forchi Kings Point, NY 10751	3.____
4.	I. Bertha C. McCormack II. Clayton, MO. III. 976-4242 IV. New City, NY 10951	Bertha C. McCormack Clayton, MO. 976-4242 New City, NY 10951	4.____
5.	I. George C. Morill II. Columbia, SC 29201 III. Louis Ingham IV. 3406 Forest Ave.	George C. Morrill Columbia, SD 29201 Louis Ingham 3406 Forest Ave.	5.____
6.	I. 506 S. Elliott Pl. II. Herbert Hall III. 4712 Rockaway Pkway IV. 169 E. 7 St.	506 S. Elliott Pl. Hurbert Hall 4712 Rockaway Pkway 169 E. 7 St.	6.____

	COLUMN I	COLUMN II	

7.
I. 345 Park Ave.   345 Park Pl.   7.____
II. Colman Oven Corp.   Coleman Oven Corp.
III. Robert Conte   Robert Conti
IV. 6179846   6179846

8.
I. Grigori Schierber   Grigori Schierber   8.____
II. Des Moines, Iowa   Des Moines, Iowa
III. Gouverneur Hospital   Gouverneur Hospital
IV. 91-35 Cresskill Pl.   91-35 Cresskill Pl.

9.
I. Jeffery Janssen   Jeffrey Janssen   9.____
II. 8041071   8041071
III. 40 Rockefeller Plaza   40 Rockafeller Plaza
IV. 407 6 St.   406 7 St.

10.
I. 5971996   5871996   10.____
II. 3113 Knickerbocker Ave.   3113 Knickerbocker Ave.
III. 8434 Boston Post Rd.   8424 Boston Post Rd.
IV. Penn Station   Penn Station

Questions 11-14.

DIRECTIONS: Questions 11 through 14 are to be answered by looking at the four groups of names and addresses listed below (I, II, III, and IV) and then finding out the number of groups that have their corresponding numbered lines exactly the same.

GROUP I
Line 1. Richmond General Hospital
Line 2. Geriatric Clinic
Line 3. 3975 Paerdegat St.
Line 4 Loudonville, New York 11538

GROUP II
Richman General Hospital
Geriatric Clinic
3975 Peardegat St.
Londonville, New York 11538

GROUP III
Line 1. Richmond General Hospital
Line 2. Geriatric Clinic
Line 3. 3795 Paerdegat St.
Line 4. Loudonville, New York 11358

GROUP IV
Richmend General Hospital
Geriatric Clinic
3975 Paerdegat St.
Loudonville, New York 11538

11. In how many groups is line one exactly the same?   11.____
   A. Two   B. Three   C. Four   D. None

12. In how many groups is line two exactly the same?   12.____
   A. Two   B. Three   C. Four   D. None

13. In how many groups is line three exactly the same?   13.____
   A. Two   B. Three   C. Four   D. None

14. In how many groups is line four exactly the same?   14._____

    A. Two   B. Three   C. Four   D. None

Questions 15-18.

DIRECTIONS: Each of Questions 15 through 18 has two lists of names and addresses. Each list contains three sets of names and addresses. Check each of the three sets in the list on the right to see if they are the same as the corresponding set in the list on the left. Mark your answers:

    A. if none of the sets in the right list are the same as those in the left list
    B. if only one of the sets in the right list is the same as those in the left list
    C. if only two of the sets in the right list are the same as those in the left list
    D. if all three sets in the right list are the same as those in the left list

15.

Mary T. Berlinger	Mary T. Berlinger
2351 Hampton St.	2351 Hampton St.
Monsey, N.Y. 20117	Monsey, N.Y. 20117
Eduardo Benes	Eduardo Benes
473 Kingston Avenue	473 Kingston Avenue
Central Islip, N.Y. 11734	Central Islip, N.Y. 11734
Alan Carrington Fuchs	Alan Carrington Fuchs
17 Gnarled Hollow Road	17 Gnarled Hollow Road
Los Angeles, CA 91635	Los Angeles, CA 91685

15._____

16.

David John Jacobson	David John Jacobson
178 35 St. Apt. 4C	178 53 St. Apt. 4C
New York, N.Y. 00927	New York, N.Y. 00927
Ann-Marie Calonella	Ann-Marie Calonella
7243 South Ridge Blvd.	7243 South Ridge Blvd.
Bakersfield, CA 96714	Bakersfield, CA 96714
Pauline M. Thompson	Pauline M. Thomson
872 Linden Ave.	872 Linden Ave.
Houston, Texas 70321	Houston, Texas 70321

16._____

17.

Chester LeRoy Masterton	Chester LeRoy Masterson
152 Lacy Rd.	152 Lacy Rd.
Kankakee, III. 54532	Kankakee, III. 54532
William Maloney	William Maloney
S. LaCrosse Pla.	S. LaCross Pla.
Wausau, Wisconsin 52146	Wausau, Wisconsin 52146
Cynthia V. Barnes	Cynthia V. Barnes
16 Pines Rd.	16 Pines Rd.
Greenpoint, Miss. 20376	Greenpoint, Miss. 20376

17._____

18. Marcel Jean Frontenac   Marcel Jean Frontenac   18.____
    8 Burton On The Water   6 Burton On The Water
    Calender, Me. 01471   Calender, Me. 01471

    J. Scott Marsden   J. Scott Marsden
    174 S. Tipton St.   174 Tipton St.
    Cleveland, Ohio   Cleveland, Ohio

    Lawrence T. Haney   Lawrence T. Haney
    171 McDonough St.   171 McDonough St.
    Decatur, Ga. 31304   Decatur, Ga. 31304

Questions 19-26.

DIRECTIONS: Each of Questions 19 through 26 has two lists of numbers. Each list contains three sets of numbers. Check each of the three sets in the list on the right to see if they are the same as the corresponding set in the list on the left. Mark your answers:
  A. if none of the sets in the right list are the same as those in the left list
  B. if only one of the sets in the right list is the same as those in the left list
  C. if only two of the sets in the right list are the same as those in the left list
  D. if all three sets in the right list are the same as those in the left list

19. 7354183476   7354983476   19.____
  4474747744   4474747774
  57914302311   57914302311

20. 7143592185   7143892185   20.____
  8344517699   8344518699
  9178531263   9178531263

21. 2572114731   257214731   21.____
  8806835476   8806835476
  8255831246   8255831246

22. 331476853821   331476858621   22.____
  6976658532996   6976655832996
  3766042113715   3766042113745

23. 8806663315   8806663315   23.____
  74477138449   74477138449
  211756663666   211756663666

24. 990006966996   99000696996   24.____
  53022219743   53022219843
  4171171117717   4171171177717

25. 24400222433004   24400222433004   25.____
  5300030055000355   5300030055500355
  20000075532002022   20000075532002022

26. 611166640660001116
    711130011700110733
    26666446664476518

    61116664066001116
    711130011700110733
    26666446664476518

26.____

Questions 27-30.

DIRECTIONS: Questions 27 through 30 are to be answered by picking the answer which is in the correct numerical order, from the lowest number to the highest number, in each question.

27. A. 44533, 44518, 44516, 44547
    B. 44516, 44518, 44533, 44547
    C. 44547, 44533, 44518, 44516
    D. 44518, 44516, 44547, 44533

27.____

28. A. 95587, 95593, 95601, 95620
    B. 95601, 95620, 95587, 95593
    C. 95593, 95587, 95601, 95620
    D. 95620, 95601, 95593, 95587

28.____

29. A. 232212, 232208, 232232, 232223
    B. 232208, 232223, 232212, 232232
    C. 232208, 232212, 232223, 232232
    D. 232223, 232232, 232208, 232212

29.____

30. A. 113419, 113521, 113462, 113588
    B. 113588, 113462, 113521, 113419
    C. 113521, 113588, 113419, 113462
    D. 113419, 113462, 113521, 113588

30.____

KEY (CORRECT ANSWERS)

1.	C	11.	A	21.	C
2.	B	12.	C	22.	A
3.	D	13.	A	23.	D
4.	A	14.	A	24.	A
5.	C	15.	C	25.	C
6.	B	16.	B	26.	C
7.	D	17.	B	27.	B
8.	A	18.	B	28.	A
9.	D	19.	B	29.	C
10.	C	20.	B	30.	D

READING COMPREHENSION
UNDERSTANDING AND INTERPRETING WRITTEN MATERIAL
EXAMINATION SECTION
TEST 1

DIRECTIONS: Each question or incomplete statement is followed by several suggested answers or completions. Select the one that BEST answers the question or completes the statement. *PRINT THE LETTER OF THE CORRECT ANSWER IN THE SPACE AT THE RIGHT.*

Questions 1-3.

DIRECTIONS: Questions 1 through 3 are to be answered SOLELY on the basis of the following statement.

The equipment in a mailroom may include a mail metering machine. This machine simultaneously stamps, postmarks, seals, and counts letters as fast as the operator can feed them. It can also print the proper postage directly on a gummed strip to be affixed to bulky items. It is equipped with a meter which is removed from the machine and sent to the postmaster to be set for a given number of stampings of any denomination. The setting of the meter must be paid for in advance. One of the advantages of metered mail is that it bypasses the cancellation operation and thereby facilitates handling by the post office. Mail metering also makes the pilfering of stamps impossible, but does not prevent the passage of personal mail in company envelopes through the meters unless there is established a rigid control or censorship over outgoing mail.

1. According to this statement, the postmaster

    A. is responsible for training new clerks in the use of mail metering machines
    B. usually recommends that both large and small firms adopt the use of mail metering machines
    C. is responsible for setting the meter to print a fixed number of stampings
    D. examines the mail metering machine to see that they are properly installed in the mailroom

1.____

2. According to this statement, the use of mail metering machines

    A. requires the employment of more clerks in a mailroom than does the use of postage stamps
    B. interferes with the handling of large quantities of outgoing mail
    C. does not prevent employees from sending their personal letters at company expense
    D. usually involves smaller expenditures for mailroom equipment than does the use of postage stamps

2.____

3. On the basis of this statement, it is MOST accurate to state that

    A. mail metering machines are often used for opening envelopes
    B. postage stamps are generally used when bulky packages are to be mailed
    C. the use of metered mail tends to interfere with rapid mail handling by the post office
    D. mail metering machines can seal and count letters at the same time

3.____

Questions 4-5.

DIRECTIONS: Questions 4 and 5 are to be answered SOLELY on the basis of the following
statement.

Forms are printed sheets of paper on which information is to be entered. While what is
printed on the form is most important, the kind of paper used in making the form is also
important. The kind of paper should be selected with regard to the use to which the form will
be subjected. Printing a form on an unnecessarily expensive grade of papers is wasteful. On
the other hand, using too cheap or flimsy a form can materially interfere with satisfactory performance of the work the form is being planned to do. Thus, a form printed on both sides normally requires a heavier paper than a form printed only on one side. Forms to be used as
permanent records, or which are expected to have a very long life in files, requires a quality of
paper which will not disintegrate or discolor with age. A form which will go through a great
deal of handling requires a strong, tough paper, while thinness is a necessary qualification
where the making of several copies of a form will be required.

4.   According to this statement, the type of paper used for making forms
     4._____

    A.   should be chosen in accordance with the use to which the form will be put
    B.   should be chosen before the type of printing to be used has been decided upon
    C.   is as important as the information which is printed on it
    D.   should be strong enough to be used for any purpose

5.   According to this statement, forms that are
     5._____

    A.   printed on both sides are usually economical and desirable
    B.   to be filed permanently should not deteriorate as time goes on
    C.   expected to last for a long time should be handled carefully
    D.   to be filed should not be printed on inexpensive paper

Questions 6-8.

DIRECTIONS: Questions 6 through 8 are to be answered SOLELY on the basis of the following paragraph.

The increase in the number of public documents in the last two centuries closely
matches the increase in population in the United States. The great number of public documents has become a serious threat to their usefulness. It is necessary to have programs
which will reduce the number of public documents that are kept and which will, at the same
time, assure keeping those that have value. Such programs need a great deal of thought to
have any success.

6.   According to the above paragraph, public documents may be LESS useful if
     6._____

    A.   the files are open to the public
    B.   the record room is too small
    C.   the copying machine is operated only during normal working hours
    D.   too many records are being kept

7. According to the above paragraph, the growth of the population in the United States has matched the growth in the quantity of public documents for a period of MOST NEARLY _____ years.

    A. 50   B. 100   C. 200   D. 300

7._____

8. According to the above paragraph, the increased number of public documents has made it necessary to

    A. find out which public documents are worth keeping
    B. reduce the great number of public documents by decreasing government services
    C. eliminate the copying of all original public documents
    D. avoid all new copying devices

8._____

Questions 9-10.

DIRECTIONS: Questions 9 and 10 are to be answered SOLELY on the basis of the following paragraph.

    The work goals of an agency can best be reached if the employees understand and agree with these goals. One way to gain such understanding and agreement is for management to encourage and seriously consider suggestions from employees in the setting of agency goals.

9. On the basis of the above paragraph, the BEST way to achieve the work goals of an agency is to

    A. make certain that employees work as hard as possible
    B. study the organizational structure of the agency
    C. encourage employees to think seriously about the agency's problems
    D. stimulate employee understanding of the work goals

9._____

10. On the basis of the above paragraph, understanding and agreement with agency goals can be gained by

    A. allowing the employees to set agency goals
    B. reaching agency goals quickly
    C. legislative review of agency operations
    D. employee participation in setting agency goals

10._____

Questions 11-13.

DIRECTIONS: Questions 11 through 13 are to be answered SOLELY on the basis of the following paragraph.

    In order to organize records properly, it is necessary to start from their very beginning and trace each copy of the record to find out how it is used, how long it is used, and what may finally be done with it. Although several copies of the record are made, one copy should be marked as the copy of record. This is the formal legal copy, held to meet the requirements of the law. The other copies may be retained for brief periods for reference purposes, but these copies should not be kept after their usefulness as reference ends. There is another reason for tracing records through the office and that is to determine how long it takes the copy of record to reach the central file. The copy of record must not be kept longer than necessary by the section of the office which has prepared it, but should be sent to the central file as soon as possible so that it can be available to the various sections of the office. The central file can make the copy of record available to the various sections of the office at an early date only if it arrives at the central file as quickly as possible. Just as soon as its immediate or active service period is ended, the copy of record should be removed from the central file and put into the inactive file in the office to be stored for whatever length of time may be necessary to meet legal requirements, and then destroyed.

11. According to the above paragraph, a reason for tracing records through an office is to   11._____

    A. determine how long the central file must keep the records
    B. organize records properly
    C. find out how many copies of each record are required
    D. identify the copy of record

12. According to the above paragraph, in order for the central file to have the copy of record available as soon as possible for the various sections of the office, it is MOST important that the   12._____

    A. copy of record to be sent to the central file meets the requirements of the law
    B. copy of record is not kept in the inactive file too long
    C. section preparing the copy of record does not unduly delay in sending it to the central file
    D. central file does not keep the copy of record beyond its active service period

13. According to the above paragraph, the length of time a copy of a record is kept in the inactive file of an office depends CHIEFLY on the   13._____

    A. requirements of the law
    B. length of time that is required to trace the copy of record through the office
    C. use that is made of the copy of record
    D. length of the period that the copy of record is used for reference purposes

Questions 14-16.

DIRECTIONS: Questions 14 through 16 are to be answered SOLELY on the basis of the following paragraph.

The office was once considered as nothing more than a focal point of internal and external correspondence. It was capable only of dispatching a few letters upon occasion and of preparing records of little practical value. Under such a concept, the vitality of the office force was impaired. Initiative became stagnant, and the lot of the office worker was not likely to be a happy one. However, under the new concept of office management, the possibilities of waste and mismanagement in office operation are now fully recognized, as are the possibilities for the modern office to assist in the direction and control of business operations. Fortunately, the modern concept of the office as a centralized service-rendering unit is gaining ever greater acceptance in today's complex business world, for without the modern office, the production wheels do not turn and the distribution of goods and services is not possible.

14. According to the above paragraph, the fundamental difference between the old and the new concept of the office is the change in the

14._____

    A. accepted functions of the office
    B. content and the value of the records kept
    C. office methods and systems
    D. vitality and morale of the office force

15. According to the above paragraph, an office operated today under the old concept of the office MOST likely would

15._____

    A. make older workers happy in their jobs
    B. be part of an old thriving business concern
    C. have a passive role in the conduct of a business enterprise
    D. attract workers who do not believe in modern methods

16. Of the following, the MOST important implication of the above paragraph is that a present-day business organization cannot function effectively without the

16._____

    A. use of modern office equipment
    B. participation and cooperation of the office
    C. continued modernization of office procedures
    D. employment of office workers with skill and initiative

Questions 17-20.

DIRECTIONS: Questions 17 through 20 are to be answered SOLELY on the basis of the following paragraph.

A report is frequently ineffective because the person writing it is not fully acquainted with all the necessary details before he actually starts to construct the report. All details pertaining to the subject should be known before the report is started. If the essential facts are not known, they should be investigated. It is wise to have essential facts written down rather than to depend too much on memory, especially if the facts pertain to such matters as amounts, dates, names of persons, or other specific data. When the necessary information has been gathered, the general plan and content of the report should be thought out before the writing is actually begun. A person with little or no experience in writing reports may find that it is wise to make a brief outline. Persons with more experience should not need a written outline, but they should make mental notes of the steps they are to follow. If writing reports without dictation is a regular part of an office worker's duties, he should set aside a certain time during the day when he is least likely to be interrupted. That may be difficult, but in most offices there are certain times in the day when the callers, telephone calls, and other interruptions are not numerous. During those times, it is best to write reports that need undivided concentration. Reports that are written amid a series of interruptions may be poorly done.

17. Before starting to write an effective report, it is necessary to

17._____

    A. memorize all specific information
    B. disregard ambiguous data
    C. know all pertinent information
    D. develop a general plan

18. Reports dealing with complex and difficult material should be

    A. prepared and written by the supervisor of the unit
    B. written when there is the least chance of interruption
    C. prepared and written as part of regular office routine
    D. outlined and then dictated

18.____

19. According to the paragraph, employees with no prior familiarity in writing reports may find it helpful to

    A. prepare a brief outline
    B. mentally prepare a synopsis of the report's content
    C. have a fellow employee help in writing the report
    D. consult previous reports

19.____

20. In writing a report, needed information which is unclear should be

    A. disregarded
    B. memorized
    C. investigated
    D. gathered

20.____

Questions 21-25.

DIRECTIONS: Questions 21 through 25 are to be answered SOLELY on the basis of the following passage.

Positive discipline minimizes the amount of personal supervision required and aids in the maintenance of standards. When a new employee has been properly introduced and carefully instructed, when he has come to know the supervisor and has confidence in the supervisor's ability to take care of him, when he willingly cooperates with the supervisor, that employee has been under positive discipline and can be put on his own to produce the quantity and quality of work desired. Negative discipline, the fear of transfer to a less desirable location, for example, to a limited extent may restrain certain individuals from overt violation of rules and regulations governing attendance and conduct which in governmental agencies are usually on at least an agency-wide basis. Negative discipline may prompt employees to perform according to certain rules to avoid a penalty such as, for example, docking for tardiness.

21. According to the above passage, it is reasonable to assume that in the area of discipline, the first-line supervisor in a governmental agency has GREATER scope for action in

    A. *positive* discipline, because negative discipline is largely taken care of by agency rules and regulations
    B. *negative* discipline, because rules and procedures are already fixed and the supervisor can rely on them
    C. *positive* discipline, because the supervisor is in a position to recommend transfers
    D. *negative* discipline, because positive discipline is reserved for people on a higher supervisory level

21.____

22. In order to maintain positive discipline of employees under his supervision, it is MOST important for a supervisor to

    A. assure each employee that he has nothing to worry about
    B. insist at the outset on complete cooperation from employees

22.____

C. be sure that each employee is well trained in his job
D. inform new employees of the penalties for not meeting standards

23. According to the above passage, a feature of negative discipline is that it   23.____

A. may lower employee morale
B. may restrain employees from disobeying the rules
C. censures equal treatment of employees
D. tends to create standards for quality of work

24. A REASONABLE conclusion based on the above passage is that positive discipline ben-   24.____
efits a supervisor because

A. he can turn over orientation and supervision of a new employee to one of his sub-
ordinates
B. subordinates learn to cooperate with one another when working on an assignment
C. it is easier to administer
D. it cuts down, in the long run, on the amount of time the supervisor needs to spend
on direct supervision

25. Based on the above passage, it is REASONABLE to assume, that an important differ-   25.____
ence between positive discipline and negative discipline is that positive discipline

A. is concerned with the quality of work and negative discipline with the quantity of
work
B. leads to a more desirable basis for motivation of the employee
C. is more likely to be concerned with agency rules and regulations
D. uses fear while negative discipline uses penalties to prod employees to adequate
performance

KEY (CORRECT ANSWERS)

1.	C	11.	B
2.	C	12.	C
3.	D	13.	A
4.	A	14.	A
5.	B	15.	C
6.	D	16.	B
7.	C	17.	C
8.	A	18.	B
9.	D	19.	A
10.	D	20.	B

21.	A
22.	C
23.	B
24.	D
25.	B

TEST 2

DIRECTIONS: Questions 1 through 6 are to be answered SOLELY on the basis of the following passage.

Inherent in all organized endeavors is the need to resolve the individual differences
involved in conflict. Conflict may be either a positive or negative factor since it may lead to
creativity, innovation and progress on the one hand, or it may result, on the other hand, in a
deterioration or even destruction of the organization. Thus, some forms of conflict are desirable, whereas others are undesirable and ethically wrong.

There are three management strategies which deal with interpersonal conflict. In the
divide-and-rule strategy, management attempts to maintain control by limiting the conflict to
those directly involved and preventing their disagreement from spreading to the larger group.
The *suppression-of-differences strategy* entails ignoring conflicts or pretending they are irrelevant. In the *working-through-differences strategy,* management actively attempts to solve or
resolve intergroup or interpersonal conflicts. Of the three strategies, only the last directly
attacks and has the potential for eliminating the causes of conflict. An essential part of this
strategy, however, is its employment by a committed and relatively mature management
team.

1.   According to the above passage, the *divide-and-rule strategy tor* dealing with conflict is   1._____
     the attempt to

     A.   involve other people in the conflict
     B.   restrict the conflict to those participating in it
     C.   divide the conflict into positive and negative factors
     D.   divide the conflict into a number of smaller ones

2.   The word *conflict* is used in relation to both positive and negative factors in this passage.   2._____
     Which one of the following words is MOST likely to describe the activity which the word
     conflict, in the sense of the passage, implies?

     A.   Competition   B.   Confusion
     C.   Cooperation   D.   Aggression

3.   According to the above passage, which one of the following characteristics is shared by   3._____
     both the *suppression-of-differences strategy* and the *divide-and-rule strategy*?

     A.   Pretending that conflicts are irrelevant
     B.   Preventing conflicts from spreading to the group situation
     C.   Failure to directly attack the causes of conflict
     D.   Actively attempting to resolve interpersonal conflict

4.   According to the above passage, the successful resolution of interpersonal conflict   4._____
     requires

     A.   allowing the group to mediate conflicts between two individuals
     B.   division of the conflict into positive and negative factors
     C.   involvement of a committed, mature management team
     D.   ignoring minor conflicts until they threaten the organization

5. Which can be MOST reasonably inferred from the above passage? Conflict between two   5.____
individuals is LEAST likely to continue when management uses

    A. the *working-through differences strategy*
    B. the *suppression-of differences strategy*
    C. the *divide-and-rule strategy*
    D. a combination of all three strategies

6. According to the above passage, a DESIRABLE result of conflict in an organization is   6.____
when conflict

    A. exposes production problems in the organization
    B. can be easily ignored by management
    C. results in advancement of more efficient managers
    D. leads to development of new methods

Questions 7-13.

DIRECTIONS: Questions 7 through 13 are to be answered SOLELY on the basis of the passage below.

    Modern management places great emphasis on the concept of communication. The communication process consists of the steps through which an idea or concept passes from its inception by one person, the sender, until it is acted upon by another person, the receiver. Through an understanding of these steps and some of the possible barriers that may occur, more effective communication may be achieved. The first step in the communication process is ideation by the sender. This is the formation of the intended content of the message he wants to transmit. In the next step, encoding, the sender organizes his ideas into a series of symbols designed to communicate his message to his intended receiver. He selects suitable words or phrases that can be understood by the receiver, and he also selects the appropriate media to be used—for example, memorandum, conference, etc. The third step is transmission of the encoded message through selected channels in the organizational structure. In the fourth step, the receiver enters the process by tuning in to receive the message. If the receiver does not function, however, the message is lost. For example, if the message is oral, the receiver must be a good listener. The fifth step is decoding of the message by the receiver, as for example, by changing words into ideas. At this step, the decoded message may not be the same idea that the sender originally encoded because the sender and receiver have different perceptions regarding the meaning of certain words. Finally, the receiver acts or responds. He may file the information, ask for more information, or take other action. There can be no assurance, however, that communication has taken place unless there is some type of feedback to the sender in the form of an acknowledgement that the message was received.

7. According to the above passage, *ideation* is the process by which the   7.____

    A. sender develops the intended content of the message
    B. sender organizes his ideas into a series of symbols
    C. receiver tunes in to receive the message
    D. receiver decodes the message

8. In the last sentence of the passage, the word *feedback* refers to the process by which the 　8.＿＿＿＿
sender is assured that the

  A. receiver filed the information
  B. receiver's perception is the same as his own
  C. message was received
  D. message was properly interpreted

9. Which one of the following BEST shows the order of the steps in the communication pro- 　9.＿＿＿＿
cess as described in the passage?

  A. 1 - ideation　　　　2 - encoding
   3 - decoding　　　　4 - transmission
   5 - receiving　　　　6 - action
   7 - feedback to the sender

  B. 1 - ideation　　　　2 - encoding
   3 - transmission　　4 - decoding
   5 - receiving　　　　6 - action
   7 - feedback to the sender

  C. 1 - ideation　　　　2 - decoding
   3 - transmission　　4 - receiving
   5 - encoding　　　　6 - action
   7 - feedback to the　sender

  D. 1 - ideation　　　　2 - encoding
   3 - transmission　　4 - receiving
   5 - decoding　　　　6 - action
   7 - feedback to the sender

10. Which one of the following BEST expresses the main theme of the passage? 　10.＿＿＿＿

  A. Different individuals have the same perceptions regarding the meaning of words.
  B. An understanding of the steps in the communication process may achieve better
   communication.
  C. Receivers play a passive role in the communication process.
  D. Senders should not communicate with receivers who transmit feedback.

11. The above passage implies that a receiver does NOT function properly when he 　11.＿＿＿＿

  A. transmits feedback　　　　　　B. files the information
  C. is a poor listener　　　　　　　D. asks for more information

12. Which one of the following, according to the above passage, is included in the SECOND 　12.＿＿＿＿
step of the communication process?

  A. Selecting the appropriate media to be used in transmission
  B. Formulation of the intended content of the message
  C. Using appropriate media to respond to the receiver's feedback
  D. Transmitting the message through selected channels in the organization

13. The above passage implies that the *decoding process* is MOST NEARLY the reverse of 　13.＿＿＿＿
the ＿＿＿＿＿ process.

  A. transmission　　　　　　　　B. receiving
  C. feedback　　　　　　　　　　D. encoding

Questions 14-19.

DIRECTIONS: Questions 14 through 19 are to be answered SOLELY on the basis of the following passage.

It is often said that no system will work if the people who carry it out do not want it to work. In too many cases, a departmental reorganization that seemed technically sound and economically practical has proved to be a failure because the planners neglected to take the human factor into account. The truth is that employees are likely to feel threatened when they learn that a major change is in the wind. It does not matter whether or not the change actually poses a threat to an employee; the fact that he believes it does or fears it might is enough to make him feel insecure. Among the dangers he fears, the foremost is the possibility that his job may cease to exist and that he may be laid off or shunted into a less skilled position at lower pay. Even if he knows that his own job category is secure, however, he is likely to fear losing some of the important intangible advantages of his present position—for instance, he may fear that he will be separated from his present companions and thrust in with a group of strangers, or that he will find himself in a lower position on the organizational ladder if a new position is created above his.

It is important that management recognize these natural fears and take them into account in planning any kind of major change. While there is no cut-and-dried formula for preventing employee resistance, there are several steps that can be taken to reduce employees' fears and gain their cooperation. First, unwarranted fears can be dispelled if employees are kept informed of the planning from the start and if they know exactly what to expect. Next, assurance on matters such as retraining, transfers, and placement help should be given as soon as it is clear what direction the reorganization will take. Finally, employees' participation in the planning should be actively sought. There is a great psychological difference between feeling that a change is being forced upon one from the outside, and feeling that one is an insider who is helping to bring about a change.

14. According to the above passage, employees who are not in real danger of losing their jobs because of a proposed reorganization

    A. will be eager to assist in the reorganization
    B. will pay little attention to the reorganization
    C. should not be taken into account in planning the reorganization
    D. are nonetheless likely to feel threatened by the reorganization

14.____

15. The passage mentions the *intangible advantages* of a position.
Which of the following BEST describes the kind of advantages alluded to in the passage?

    A. Benefits such as paid holidays and vacations
    B. Satisfaction of human needs for things like friendship and status
    C. Qualities such as leadership and responsibility
    D. A work environment that meets satisfactory standards of health and safety

15.____

16. According to the passage, an employee's fear that a reorganization may separate him from his present companions is a (n)

    A. childish and immature reaction to change
    B. unrealistic feeling since this is not going to happen

16.____

C. possible reaction that the planners should be aware of
D. incentive to employees to participate in the planning

17. On the basis of the above passage, it would be DESIRABLE, when planning a departmental reorganization, to

    A. be governed by employee feelings and attitudes
    B. give some employees lower positions
    C. keep employees informed
    D. lay off those who are less skilled

17.____

18. What does the passage say can be done to help gain employees' cooperation in a reorganization?

    A. Making sure that the change is technically sound, that it is economically practical,
and that the human factor is taken into account
    B. Keeping employees fully informed, offering help in fitting them into new positions,
and seeking their participation in the planning
    C. Assuring employees that they will not be laid off, that they will not be reassigned to
a group of strangers, and that no new positions will be created on the organization
ladder
    D. Reducing employees' fears, arranging a retraining program, and providing for
transfers

18.____

19. Which of the following suggested titles would be MOST appropriate for this passage?

    A. PLANNING A DEPARTMENTAL REORGANIZATION
    B. WHY EMPLOYEES ARE AFRAID
    C. LOOKING AHEAD TO THE FUTURE
    D. PLANNING FOR CHANGE: THE HUMAN FACTOR

19.____

Questions 20-22.

DIRECTIONS: Questions 20 through 22 are to be answered SOLELY on the basis of the following passage.

The achievement of good human relations is essential if a business office is to produce
at top efficiency and is to be a pleasant place in which to work. All office workers plan an
important role in handling problems in human relations. They should, therefore, strive to
acquire the understanding, tactfulness, and awareness necessary to deal effectively with
actual office situations involving co-workers on all levels. Only in this way can they truly
become responsible, interested, cooperative, and helpful members of the staff.

20. The selection implies that the MOST important value of good human relations in an office
is to develop

    A. efficiency   B. cooperativeness
    C. tact   D. pleasantness and efficiency

20.____

21. Office workers should acquire understanding in dealing with

    A. co-workers   B. subordinates
    C. superiors   D. all members of the staff

21.____

22. The selection indicates that a highly competent secretary who is also very argumentative   22._____
    is meeting office requirements

    A. wholly   B. partly
    C. slightly   D. not at all

Questions 23-25.

DIRECTIONS: Questions 23 through 25 are to be answered SOLELY on the basis of the fol-
               lowing passage.

It is common knowledge that ability to do a particular job and performance on the job do
not always go hand in hand. Persons with great potential abilities sometimes fall down on the
job because of laziness or lack of interest in the job, while persons with mediocre talents have
often achieved excellent results through their industry and their loyalty to the interests of their
employers. It is clear; therefore, that in a balanced personnel program, measures of
employee ability need to be supplemented by measures of employee performance, for the
final test of any employee is his performance on the job.

23. The MOST accurate of the following statements, on the basis of the above paragraph, is   23._____
    that

    A. employees who lack ability are usually not industrious
    B. an employee's attitudes are more important than his abilities
    C. mediocre employees who are interested in their work are preferable to employees
        who possess great ability
    D. superior capacity for performance should be supplemented with proper attitudes

24. On the basis of the above paragraph, the employee of most value to his employer is NOT   24._____
    necessarily the one who

    A. best understands the significance of his duties
    B. achieves excellent results
    C. possesses the greatest talents
    D. produces the greatest amount of work

25. According to the above paragraph, an employee's efficiency is BEST determined by an   25._____

    A. appraisal of his interest in his work
    B. evaluation of the work performed by him
    C. appraisal of his loyalty to his employer
    D. evaluation of his potential ability to perform his work

———————

KEY (CORRECT ANSWERS)

1.	B		11.	C
2.	A		12.	A
3.	C		13.	D
4.	C		14.	D
5.	A		15.	B
6.	D		16.	C
7.	A		17.	C
8.	C		18.	B
9.	D		19.	D
10.	B		20.	D

21.	D
22.	B
23.	D
24.	C
25.	B

TEST 3

Questions 1-8.

DIRECTIONS: Questions 1 through 8 are to be answered SOLELY on the basis of the following information and directions.

Assume that you are a clerk in a city agency. Your supervisor has asked you to classify each of the accidents that happened to employees in the agency into the following five categories:

A. An accident that occurred in the period from January through June, between 9 A.M. and 12 Noon, that was the result of carelessness on the part of the injured employee, that caused the employee to lose less than seven working hours, that happened to an employee who was 40 years of age or over, and who was employed in the agency for less than three years;

B. An accident that occurred in the period from July through December, after 1 P.M., that was the result of unsafe conditions, that caused the injured employee to lose less than seven working hours, that happened to an employee who was 40 years of age or over, and who was employed in the agency for three years or more;

C. An accident that occurred in the period from January through June, after 1 P.M., that was the result of carelessness on the part of the injured employee, that caused the injured employee to lose seven or more working hours, that happened to an employee who was less than 40 years old, and who was employed in the agency for three years or more;

D. An accident that occurred in the period from July through December, between 9 A.M. and 12 Noon, that was the result of unsafe conditions, that caused the injured employee to lose seven or more working hours, that happened to an employee who was less than 40 years old, and who was employed in the agency for less than three years;

E. Accidents that cannot be classified in any of the foregoing groups. NOTE: In classifying these accidents, an employee's age and length of service are computed as of the date of accident. In all cases, it is to be assumed that each employee has been employed continuously in city service, and that each employee works seven hours a day, from 9 A.M. to 5 P.M., with lunch from 12 Noon to 1 P.M. In each question, consider only the information which will assist you in classifying the accident. Any information which is of no assistance in classifying an accident should not be considered.

1. The unsafe condition of the stairs in the building caused Miss Perkins to have an accident on October 14, 2003 at 4 P.M. When she returned to work the following day at 1 P.M., Miss Perkins said that the accident was the first one that had occurred to her in her ten years of employment with the agency. She was born on April 27, 1962.   1.____

2. On the day after she completed her six-month probationary period of employment with the agency, Miss Green, who had been considered a careful worker by her supervisor, injured her left foot in an accident caused by her own carelessness. She went home immediately after the accident, which occurred at 10 A.M., March 19, 2004, but returned to work at the regular time on the following morning. Miss Green was born July 12, 1963 in New York City.   2.____

3. The unsafe condition of a duplicating machine caused Mr. Martin to injure himself in an accident on September 8, 2006 at 2 P.M. As a result of the accident, he was unable to work the remainder of the day, but returned to his office ready for work on the following morning. Mr. Martin, who has been working for the agency since April 1, 2003, was born in St. Louis on February 1, 1968.

3.____

4. Mr. Smith was hospitalized for two weeks because of a back injury resulted from an accident on the morning of November 16, 2006. Investigation of the accident revealed that it was caused by the unsafe condition of the floor on which Mr. Smith had been walking. Mr. Smith, who is an accountant, has been anemployee of the agency since March 1, 2004, and was born in Ohio on June 10, 1968.

4.____

5. Mr. Allen cut his right hand because he was careless in operating a multilith machine. Mr. Allen, who was 33 years old when the accident took place, has been employed by the agency since August 17, 1992. The accident, which occurred on January 26, 2006, at 2 P.M., caused Mr. Allen to be absent from work for the rest of the day. He was able to return to work the next morning.

5.____

6. Mr. Rand, who is a college graduate, was born on December, 28, 1967, and has been working for the agency since January 7, 2002. On Monday, April 25, 2005, at 2 P.M., his carelessness in operating a duplicating machine caused him to have an accident and to be sent home from work immediately. Fortunately, he was able to return to work at his regular time on the following Wednesday.

6.____

7. Because he was careless in running down a flight of stairs, Mr. Brown fell, bruising his right hand. Although the accident occurred shortly after he arrived for work on the morning of May 22, 2006, he was unable to resume work until 3 P.M. that day. Mr. Brown was born on August 15, 1955, and began working for the agency on September 12, 2003, as a clerk, at a salary of $22,750 per annum.

7.____

8. On December 5, 2005, four weeks after he had begun working for the agency, the unsafe condition of an automatic stapling machine caused Mr. Thomas to injure himself in an accident. Mr. Thomas, who was born on May 19,1975, lost three working days because of the accident, which occurred at 11:45 A.M.

8.____

Questions 9-10.

DIRECTIONS: Questions 9 and 10 are to be answered SOLELY on the basis of the following paragraph.

An impending reorganization within an agency will mean loss by transfer of several professional staff members from the personnel division. The division chief is asked to designate the persons to be transferred. After reviewing the implications of this reduction of staff with his assistant, the division chief discusses the matter at a staff meeting. He adopts the recommendations of several staff members to have volunteers make up the required reduction.

9. The decision to permit personnel to volunteer for transfer is   9.____

    A. *poor;* it is not likely that the members of a division are of equal value to the division chief
    B. *good;* dissatisfied members will probably be more productive elsewhere
    C. *poor;* the division chief has abdicated his responsibility to carry out the order given to him
    D. *good;* morale among remaining staff is likely to improve in a more cohesive framework

10. Suppose that one of the volunteers is a recently appointed employee who has completed   10.____
his probationary period acceptably, but whose attitude toward division operations and agency administration tends to be rather negative and sometimes even abrasive. Because of his lack of commitment to the division, his transfer is recommended. If the transfer is approved, the division chief should, prior to the transfer,

    A. discuss with the staff the importance of commitment to the work of the agency and its relationship with job satisfaction
    B. refrain from any discussion of attitude with the employee
    C. discuss with the employee his concern about the employee's attitude
    D. avoid mention of attitude in the evaluation appraisal prepared for the receiving division chief

Questions 11-16.

DIRECTIONS: Questions 11 through 16 are to be answered SOLELY on the basis of the following paragraph.

    Methods of administration of office activities, much of which consists of providing information and *know-how* needed to coordinate both activities within that particular office and other offices, have been among the last to come under the spotlight of management analysis. Progress has been rapid during the past decade, however, and is now accelerating at such a pace that an *information revolution* in office management appears to be in the making. Although triggered by technological breakthroughs in electronic computers and other giant steps in mechanization, this information revolution must be attributed to underlying forces, such as the increased complexity of both governmental and private enterprise, and ever-keener competition. Size, diversification, specialization of function, and decentralization are among the forces which make coordination of activities both more imperative and more difficult. Increased competition, both domestic and international, leaves little margin for error in managerial decisions. Several developments during recent years indicate an evolving pattern. In 1960, the American Management Association expanded the scope of its activities and changed the name of its Office Management Division to Administrative Services Division. Also in 1960, the magazine *Office Management* merged with the magazine *American Business,* and this new publication was named *Administrative Management.*

11. A REASONABLE inference that can be made from the information in the above paragraph is that an important role of the office manager today is to

    A. work toward specialization of functions performed by his subordinates
    B. inform and train subordinates regarding any new developments in computer technology and mechanization
    C. assist the professional management analysts with the management analysis work in the organization
    D. supply information that can be used to help coordinate and manage the other activities of the organization

11.____

12. An IMPORTANT reason for the *information revolution* that has been taking place in office management is the

    A. advance made in management analysis in the past decade
    B. technological breakthrough in electronic computers and mechanization
    C. more competitive and complicated nature of private business and government
    D. increased efficiency of office management techniques in the past ten years

12.____

13. According to the above paragraph, specialization of function in an organization is MOST likely to result in

    A. the elimination of errors in managerial decisions
    B. greater need to coordinate activities
    C. more competition with other organizations, both domestic and international
    D. a need for office managers with greater flexibility

13.____

14. The word *evolving,* as used in the third from last sentence in the above paragraph, means MOST NEARLY

    A. developing by gradual changes
    B. passing on to others
    C. occurring periodically
    D. breaking up into separate, constituent parts

14.____

15. Of the following, the MOST reasonable implication of the changes in names mentioned in the last part of the above paragraph is that these groups are attempting to

    A. professionalize the field of office management and the title of Office Manager
    B. combine two publications into one because of the increased costs of labor and materials
    C. adjust to the fact that the field of office management is broadening
    D. appeal to the top managerial people rather than the office management people in business and government

15.____

16. According to the above paragraph, intense competition among domestic and international enterprises makes it MOST important for an organization's managerial staff to

    A. coordinate and administer office activities with other activities in the organization
    B. make as few errors in decision-making as possible
    C. concentrate on decentralization and reduction of size of the individual divisions of the organization
    D. restrict decision-making only to top management officials

16.____

Questions 17-21.

DIRECTIONS: Questions 17 through 21 are to be answered SOLELY on the basis of the following passage.

For some office workers, it is useful to be familiar with the four main classes of domestic mail; for others, it is essential. Each class has a different rate of postage, and some have requirements concerning wrapping, sealing, or special information to be placed on the package. First class mail, the class which may not be opened for postal inspection, includes letters, postcards, business reply cards, and other kinds of written matter. There are different rates for some of the kinds of cards which can be sent by first class mail. The maximum weight for an item sent by first class mail is 70 pounds. An item which is not letter size should be marked *First Class* on all sides. Although office workers most often come into contact with first class mail, they may find it helpful to know something about the other classes. Second class mail is generally used for mailing newspapers and magazines. Publishers of these articles must meet certain U.S. Postal Service requirements in order to obtain a permit to use second class mailing rates. Third class mail, which must weigh less than 1 pound, includes printed materials and merchandise parcels. There are two rate structures for this class - a single piece rate and a bulk rate. Fourth class mail, also known as parcel post, includes packages weighing from one to 40 pounds. For more information about these classes of mail and the actual mailing rates, contact your local post office.

17.   According to this passage, first class mail is the *only* class which   17.____

    A.   has a limit on the maximum weight of an item
    B.   has different rates for items within the class
    C.   may not be opened for postal inspection
    D.   should be used by office workers

18.   According to this passage, the one of the following items which may CORRECTLY be   18.____
sent by fourth class mail is a

    A.   magazine weighing one-half pound
    B.   package weighing one-half pound
    C.   package weighing two pounds
    D.   postcard

19.   According to this passage, there are different postage rates for   19.____

    A.   a newspaper sent by second class mail and a magazine sent by second class mail
    B.   each of the classes of mail
    C.   each pound of fourth class mail
    D.   printed material sent by third class mail and merchandise parcels sent by third class mail

20.   In order to send a newspaper by second class mail, a publisher MUST   20.____

    A.   have met certain postal requirements and obtained a permit
    B.   indicate whether he wants to use the single piece or the bulk rate
    C.   make certain that the newspaper weighs less than one pound
    D.   mark the newspaper *Second Class* on the top and bottom of the wrapper

21. Of the following types of information, the one which is NOT mentioned in the passage is   21._____
the

  A. class of mail to which parcel post belongs
  B. kinds of items which can be sent by each class of mail
  C. maximum weight for an item sent by fourth class mail
  D. postage rate for each of the four classes of mail

Questions 22-25.

DIRECTIONS: Questions 22 through 25 are to be answered SOLELY on the basis of the following paragraph.

A standard comprises characteristics attached to an aspect of a process or product by
which it can be evaluated. Standardization is the development and adoption of standards.
When they are formulated, standards are not usually the product of a single person, but represent the thoughts and ideas of a group, leavened with the knowledge and information which
are currently available. Standards which do not meet certain basic requirements become a
hindrance rather than an aid to progress. Standards must not only be correct, accurate, and
precise in requiring no more and no less than what is needed for satisfactory results, but they
must also be workable in the sense that their usefulness is not nullified by external conditions.
Standards should also be acceptable to the people who use them. If they are not acceptable,
they cannot be considered to be satisfactory, although they may possess all the other essential characteristics.

22. According to the above paragraph, a processing standard that requires the use of mate-   22._____
rials that cannot be procured is MOST likely to be

  A. incomplete   B. unworkable
  C. inaccurate   D. unacceptable

23. According to the above paragraph, the construction of standards to which the perfor-   23._____
mance of job duties should conform is MOST often

  A. the work of the people responsible for seeing that the duties are properly per-
     formed
  B. accomplished by the person who is best informed about the functions involved
  C. the responsibility of the people who are to apply them
  D. attributable to the efforts of various informed persons

24. According to the above paragraph, when standards call for finer tolerances than those   24._____
essential to the conduct of successful production operations, the effect of the standards
on the improvement of production operations is

  A. negative   B. negligible
  C. nullified   D. beneficial

25. The one of the following which is the MOST suitable title for the above paragraph is   25._____

  A. THE EVALUATION OF FORMULATED STANDARDS
  B. THE ATTRIBUTES OF SATISFACTORY STANDARDS
  C. THE ADOPTION OF ACCEPTABLE STANDARDS
  D. THE USE OF PROCESS OR PRODUCT STANDARDS

KEY (CORRECT ANSWERS)

1.	B	11.	D
2.	A	12.	C
3.	E	13.	B
4.	D	14.	A
5.	E	15.	C
6.	C	16.	B
7.	A	17.	C
8.	D	18.	C
9.	A	19.	B
10.	C	20.	A

21.	D
22.	C
23.	D
24.	A
25.	B

READING COMPREHENSION
UNDERSTANDING AND INTERPRETING WRITTEN MATERIAL
EXAMINATION SECTION
TEST 1

DIRECTIONS: All questions are to be answered *SOLELY* on the basis of the information contained in the passage. Each question or incomplete statement is followed by several suggested answers or completions. Select the one that *BEST* answers the question or completes the statement. *PRINT THE LETTER OF THE CORRECT ANSWER IN THE SPACE AT THE RIGHT.*

Questions 1-3.

The equipment in a mail room may include a mail-metering machine. This machine simultaneously stamps, postmarks, seals, and counts letters as fast as the operator can feed them. It can also print the proper postage directly on a gummed strip to be affixed to bulky items. It is equipped with a meter which is removed from the machine and sent to the postmaster to be set for a given number of stampings of any denomination. The setting of the meter must be paid for in advance. One of the advantages of metered mail is that it bypasses the cancellation operation and, thereby, facilitates handling by the post office. Mail metering also makes the pilfering of stamps impossible, but does not prevent the passage of personal mail in company envelopes through the meters unless there is established a rigid control or censorship over outgoing mail.

1. According to this statement, the postmaster   1.____

   A. is responsible for training new clerks in the use of mail-metering machines
   B. usually recommends that both large and small firms adopt the use of mail metering machines
   C. is responsible for setting the meter to print a fixed number of stampings
   D. examines the mail-metering machines to see that they are properly installed in the mail room

2. According to this statement, the use of mail-metering machines   2.____

   A. requires the employment of more clerks in a mail room than does the use of postage stamps
   B. interferes with the handling of large quantities of out-going mail
   C. does not prevent employees from sending their personal letters at company expense
   D. usually involves smaller expenditures for mail-room equipment than does the use of postage stamps

3. On the basis of this statement, it is MOST accurate to state that   3.____

   A. mail-metering machines are often used for opening envelopes
   B. postage stamps are generally used when bulky packages are to be mailed
   C. the use of metered mail tends to interfere with rapid mail handling by the post office
   D. mail-metering machines can seal and count letters at the same time

Questions 4-8.

It is the Housing Administration's policy that all tenants, whether new or transferring from one housing development to another, shall be required to pay a standard security deposit of one month's rent based on the rent at the time of admission. There are, however, certain exceptions to this policy. Employees of the Administration shall not be required to pay a security deposit if they secure an apartment in an Administration development. Where the payment of a full security deposit may present a hardship to a tenant, the development's manager may allow a tenant to move into an apartment upon payment of only part of the security deposit. In such cases, however, the tenant must agree to gradually pay the balance of the deposit. If a tenant transfers from one apartment to another within the same project, the security deposit originally paid by the tenant for his former apartment will be acceptable for his new apartment, even if the rent in the new apartment is greater than the rent in the former one. Finally, tenants who receive public assistance need not pay a security deposit before moving into an apartment if the appropriate agency states, in writing, that it will pay the deposit. However, it is the responsibility of the development's manager to make certain that payment shall be received within one month of the date that the tenant moves into the apartment.

4. According to the above passage, when a tenant transfers from one apartment to another in the same development, the Housing Administration will

    4.____

    A. *accept* the tenant's old security deposit as the security deposit for his new apartment regardless of the new apartment's rent
    B. *refund* the tenant's old security deposit and not requires him to pay a new deposit
    C. *keep* the tenant's old security deposit and require him to pay a new deposit
    D. *require* the tenant to pay a new security deposit based on the difference between his old rent and his new rent

5. On the basis of the above passage, it is INCORRECT to state that a tenant who receives public assistance may move into an Administration development if

    5.____

    A. he pays the appropriate security deposit
    B. the appropriate agency gives a written indication that it will pay the security deposit before the tenant moves in
    C. the appropriate agency states, by telephone, that it will pay the security deposit
    D. he appropriate agency writes the manager to indicate that the security deposit will be paid within one month but not less than two weeks from the date the tenant moves into the apartment

6. On the basis of the above passage, a tenant who transfers from an apartment In one development to an apartment in a different development will

    6.____

    A. forfeits his old security deposit and be required to pay another deposit
    B. have his old security deposit refunded and not have to pay a new deposit
    C. pays the difference between his old security deposit and the new one
    D. has to pay a security deposit based on the new apartment's rent 2

7. The Housing Administration will NOT require payment of a Security deposit if a tenant   7.____

    A. is, an Administration employee
    B. is receiving public assistance
    C. claims that payment will present a hardship
    D. indicates, in writing, that he will be responsible for any damage done to his apartment

8. Of the following, the BEST title for the above passage is: 8.____

    A. Security Deposits - Transfers
    B. Security Deposits - Policy
    C. Exemptions and Exceptions - Security Deposits
    D. Amounts - Security Deposits

Questions 9-11.

Terrazzo flooring will last a very long time if it is cared for properly. Lacquers, shellac or varnish preparations should never be used on terrazzo. Soap cleaners are not recommended, since they dull the appearance of the floor. Alkaline solutions are harmful, so neutral cleaner or non-alkaline synthetic detergents will give best results. If the floor is very dirty, it may be necessary to scrub it. The same neutral cleaning solution should be used for scrubbing as for mopping. Scouring powder may be sprinkled at particularly dirty spots. Do not use steel wool for scrubbing. Small pieces of steel filings left on the floor will rust and discolor the terrazzo. Non-woven nylon or open-mesh fabric abrasive pads are suitable for scrubbing terrazzo floors.

9. According to the passage above, the BEST cleaning agent for terrazzo flooring is a(n)   9.____

    A. soap cleaner   B. varnish preparation
    C. neutral cleaner   D. alkaline solution

10. According to the passage above, terrazzo floors should NOT be scrubbed with   10.____

    A. non-woven nylon abrasive pads   B. steel wool
    C. open-mesh fabric abrasive pads   D. scouring powder

11. As used in the passage above, the word *discolor* means, most nearly,   11.____

    A. crack   B. scratch
    C. dissolve   D. stain

Questions 12-15.

Planning for the unloading of incoming trucks is not easy since generally little or no advance notice of truck arrivals is received. The height of the floor of truck bodies and loading platforms sometimes are different; this makes necessary the use of special unloading methods. When available, hydraulic ramps compensate for the differences in platform and truck floor levels. When hydraulic ramps are not available, forklift equipment can sometimes be used, if the truck springs are strong enough to support such equipment. In a situation like this, the unloading operation does not differ much from unloading a railroad box car In the cases where the forklift truck or a hydraulic pallet jack cannot be used inside the truck, a pallet dolly should be placed inside the truck, so that the empty pallet can be loaded close to the truck contents and rolled easily to the truck door and platform.

12. According to the passage above, unloading trucks are

12.____

    A.   easy to plan since the time of arrival is usually known beforehand
    B.   the same as loading a railroad box car
    C.   hard to plan since trucks arrive without notice
    D.   a very normal thing to do

13. According to the above passage, which materials-handling equipment can make up for the difference in platform and truck floor levels?

13.____

    A.   Hydraulic jacks   B.   Hydraulic ramps
    C.   Forklift trucks   D.   Conveyors

14. According to the passage above, what materials-handling equipment can be used when a truck cannot support the weight of forklift equipment?

14.____

    A.   A pallet dolly   B.   A hydraulic ramp
    C.   Bridge plates   D.   A warehouse tractor

15. Which is the BEST title for the above passage?

15.____

    A.   Unloading Railroad Box Cars   B.   Unloading Motor Trucks
    C.   Loading Rail Box   D.   Loading Motor Trucks

Questions 16-19.

Ventilation, as used in fire-fighting operations, means opening up a building or structure in which a fire is burning to release the accumulated heat, smoke, and gases. Lack of knowledge of the principles of ventilation on the part of firemen may result in unnecessary punishment due to ventilation being neglected or improperly handled. While ventilation itself extinguishes no fires, when used in an intelligent manner, it allows firemen to get at the fire more quickly, easily, and with less danger and hardship.

16. According to the above paragraph, the MOST important result of failure to apply the principles of ventilation at a fire may be

16.____

    A.   loss of public confidence   B.   disciplinary action
    C.   waste of water   D.   excessive use of equipment
    E.   injury to firemen

17. It may be inferred from the above paragraph that the CHIEF advantage of ventilation is that it

17.____

    A.   eliminates the need for gas masks
    B.   reduces smoke damage
    C.   permits firemen to work closer to the fire
    D.   cools the fire
    E.   enables firemen to use shorter hose lines

18. Knowledge of the principles of ventilation, as defined in the above paragraph, would be LEAST important in a fire in a

18.____

    A.   tenement house   B.   grocery store
    C.   ship's hold   D.   lumberyard
    E.   office building

19. We may conclude from the above paragraph that, for the well-trained and equipped fire- 19._____
    man, ventilation is

    A. a simple matter   B. rarely necessary
    C. relatively unimportant   D. a basic tool
    E. sometimes a handicap

Questions 20-22.

Many public service and industrial organizations are becoming increasingly insistent that supervisors at the work level be qualified instructors. The reason for this is that technological improvements and overall organizational growth require the acquisition of new skills and knowledge by workers. These skills and knowledge can be acquired in two ways. They can be gained either by absorption-rubbing shoulders with the job or through planned instruction. Permitting the acquisition of new skills and knowledge is to be haphazard and uncertain is too costly. At higher supervisory levels, the need for instructing subordinates is not so obvious, but it is just as important as at the lowest work level. A high-ranking supervisor accomplishes the requirements of his position only if his subordinate supervisors perform their work efficiently. Regardless of one's supervisory position, the ability to instruct easily and efficiently helps to insure well-qualified and thoroughly-trained subordinates. There exists an unfounded but rather prevalent belief that becoming a competent instructor is a long, arduous, and complicated process. This belief arises partially as a result of the requirement of a long period of college preparation involved in preparing teachers for our school system. This time is necessary because teachers must learn a great deal of subject matter. The worker who advances to a supervisory position generally has superior skill and knowledge; therefore, he has only to learn the techniques by which he can impart his knowledge in order to become a competent instructor.

20. According to the above paragraph, a prolonged period of preparation for instructing is NOT 20._____
    generally necessary for a worker who is advanced to a supervisory position because

    A. he may already possess some of the requirements of a competent instructor
    B. his previous job knowledge is generally sufficient to enable him to begin instructing
       immediately
    C. in his present position there is less need for the specific job knowledge of the ordi-
       nary worker
    D. the ability to instruct follows naturally from superior skill and knowledge

21. According to the above paragraph, it is important for the higher-level supervisor to be a 21._____
    good instructor because

    A. at this level there is a tendency to overlook the need for instruction of both subordi-
       nate supervisors and workers
    B. good training practices will then be readily adopted by lower-level supervisors
    C. the need for effective training is more critical at the higher levels of responsibility
    D. training can be used to improve the supervisory performance of his subordinate
       supervisors

22. According to the above paragraph, the acquisition of new skills and knowledge by workers is BEST accomplished when

    A. the method of training allows for the use of absorption
    B. organizational growth and technological improvement indicate a need for further training
    C. such training is the result of careful planning
    D. the cost factor involved in training can be readily justified

22.___

Questions 23-25.

The organization of any large agency falls into three broad general zones: top management, middle management, and rank-and-file operations. The normal task of middle management is to supervise, direct and control the performance of operations within the scope of law, policy, and regulations already established. Where policy is settled and well defined, middle management is basically a set of standard operations, although they may call for high-developed skills. Where, however, policy is not clearly stated, is ambiguous, or is rapidly shifting, middle management is likely to have an important influence upon emergency policy trends. Persons working in the zone of middle management usually become specialists. They need specialist knowledge of law, rules and regulations, and court decisions governing their organization if they are to discharge their duties effectively. They will also have acquired specialist knowledge of relationships and sequences in the normal flow of business. Further, their attention is brought to bear on a particular administrative task, in a particular jurisdiction, with a particular clientele. The importance of middle management is obviously great. The reasons for such importance are not difficult to find: Here it is that the essential action of government in behalf of citizens is taken; here it is that citizens deal with government when they pass beyond their first contacts; here is a training ground from which a considerable part of top management emerges; and here also it is that the spirit and temper of the public service and its reputation are largely made,

23. According to the above paragraph, the critical importance of middle management is due to the fact that it is at this level that

    A. formal executive training can be most useful
    B. the greatest amount of action is taken on the complaints of the general public
    C. the official actions taken have the greatest impact on general attitudes towards the public service
    D. the public most frequently comes in contact with governmental operations and agencies

23.___

24. According to the above paragraph, the one of the following statements which is NOT offered as an explanation of the tendency for middle management responsibility to produce specialists is that

    A. middle-management personnel frequently feel that their work is the most important in an organization
    B. specialized knowledge is acquired during the course of everyday work
    C. specialized knowledge is necessary for effective job performance
    D. their work assignments are directed to specific problems in specific situations

24.___

25. According to the above paragraph, the GREATEST impact of middle management in policy determination would be likely to be felt in the situation in which   25.____

   A. middle management possesses highly developed operational skills
   B. several policy directives from top management are subject to varying interpretations
   C. the authority of middle management to supervise, direct, and control operations has been clearly established
   D. top management has neglected to consider the policy views of middle management

---

KEYS (CORRECT ANSWERS)

1.	C		11.	D
2.	C		12.	C
3.	D		13.	B
4.	A		14.	A
5.	C		15.	B
6.	D		16.	E
7.	A		17.	C
8.	B		18.	D
9.	C		19.	D
10.	B		20.	A

21.	D
22.	C
23.	C
24.	A
25.	B

TEST 2

Questions 1-2.

Metal spraying is used for many purposes. Worn bearings on shafts and spindles can be readily restored to original dimensions with any desired metal or alloy. Low-carbon steel shafts may be supplied with high-carbon steel journal surfaces, which can then be ground to size after spraying. By using babbitt wire, bearings can be lined or babbitted while rotating. Pump shafts and impellers can be coated with any desired metal to overcome wear and corrosion. Valve seats may be re-surfaced. Defective castings can be repaired by filling in blow-holes and checks. The application of metal spraying to the field of corrosion resistance is growing, although the major application in this field is in the use of sprayed zinc. tin, lead, and aluminum have been used considerably. The process is used for structural and tank applications in the field as well as in the shop.

1. According to the above paragraph, worn bearing surfaces on shafts are metal-sprayed in order to   1.____

   A. prevent corrosion of the shaft
   B. fit them into larger-sized impellers
   C. returns them to their original sizes
   D. replaces worn babbitt metal

2. According to the above paragraph, rotating bearings can be metal-sprayed using   2.____

   A. babbitt wire   B. high-carbon steel
   C. low-carbon steel   D. any desired metal

Questions 3-5.

The method of cleaning which should generally be used is the space assignment method. Under this method, the buildings to be cleaned are divided into different sections. Within each section, each crew of Custodial Assistants is assigned to do one particular cleaning job. For example, within a section, one crew may be assigned to cleaning offices, another to scrubbing floors, a third to collecting trash, and so on. Other methods which may be used are the post-assignment method and the gang-cleaning method. Under the post-assignment method, a Custodial Assistant is assigned to one area of a building and performs all cleaning jobs in that area. This method is seldom used except where buildings are so small and distant from each other that it is not economical to use the space-assignment method. Under the gang-cleaning method, a Custodial Foreman takes a number of Custodial Assistants through a section of the building. These Custodial Assistants work as a group and complete the various cleaning jobs as they go. This method is generally used only where the building contains very large open areas.

3. According to the passage above, under the space-assignment method, each crew *generally*   3.____

   A. works as a group and does a variety of different cleaning jobs
   B. is assigned to one area and performs all cleaning jobs in that area
   C. does one particular cleaning job within a section of a building
   D. follows the Custodial Foreman through a building containing large, open areas

4. According to the passage above, the post-assignment method is used mostly where the buildings to be cleaned are

    A. *large* in size and situated *close together*
    B. *small* in size and situated *close together*
    C. *large* in size and situated *far apart*
    D. *small* in size and situated *far apart*

4._____

5. As used in the passage above, the word *economical* means, most nearly,

    A. thrifty   B. agreed
    C. unusual   D. wasteful

5._____

Questions 6-9.

The desirability of complete refuse collection by municipalities is becoming generally accepted. In many cases, however, such ideal service is economically impractical and certain limits must be imposed. Some municipal authorities find it necessary to regulate the quantity of refuse, by weight or volume, which will be collected from a single residence or place of business at one collection. The purpose of the regulations is twofold: First, to maintain the degree of service rendered on a somewhat uniform basis; and, second, to insure a more or less constant collection from week to week. If left unregulated, careless producers might permit large quantities of refuse to accumulate on their premises over long periods and place abnormal amounts out for collection at irregular intervals, thus upsetting the collection schedule. Regulation is especially applied to large wholesale, industrial, and manufacturing enterprises which, in the great majority of cases, are required to dispose of all or part of their refuse themselves, at their own expense. The maximum quantities permitted by regulation should obviously be sufficient to take care of a normal accumulation at a household over the established interval between regular collections. In commercial districts, the maximum quantity limitations are often fixed on arbitrary bases rather than on normal production.

6. According to the above paragraph, many municipalities do not have complete refuse collections because

    A. it costs too much   B. it is difficult to regulate
    C. it is not a municipal function   D. they don't consider it desirable

6._____

7. According to the above paragraph, regulation by municipalities of the amount of refuse collected per collection from any one place of business does NOT contribute to

    A. accumulation of refuse by careless producers
    B. maintenance of collection schedules
    C. steady collection from one week to the next
    D. uniform service

7._____

8. According to the above paragraph, regulations by municipalities of refuse collection from certain enterprises helps to cut down

    A. accumulation of refuse for private collection
    B. the amount of refuse produced
    C. variation in the volume of refuse produced
    D. variation in collection service

8._____

9. According to the above paragraph, municipalities limit the amount of refuse collected in   9.____
commercial districts on an arbitrary basis rather than on the basis of a normal accumulation. This is *probably* done because

    A.   arbitrary standards are easy to establish and enforce
    B.   normal accumulation is different for each district
    C.   normal accumulation would require the collection of too much refuse
    D.   there is no such thing as a normal accumulation

Questions 10-13.

Modern office methods, geared to ever higher speeds and aimed at ever greater efficiency, are largely the result of the typewriter. The typewriter is a substitute for handwriting
and, in the hands of a skilled typist, not only turns out letters and other documents at least
three times faster than a penman can do the work, but turns out the greater volume more uni-
formly and legibly. With the use of carbon paper and onionskin paper, identical copies can be
made at the same time.

The typewriter, besides its effect on the conduct of business and government, has had a
very important effect on the position of women. The typewriter has done much to bring
women into business and government and today there are vastly more women than men typists. Many women have used the keys of the typewriter to climb the ladder to responsible
managerial positions.

The typewriter, as its name implies, employs type to make an ink impression on paper.
For many years, the manual typewriter was the standard machine used. Today, the electric
typewriter is dominant, and completely automatic typewriters are coming into wider use.

The mechanism of the office manual typewriter includes a set of keys arranged systematically in rows; a semicircular frame of type, connected to the keys by levers; the carriage, or
paper carrier; a rubber roller, called a platen, against which the type strikes; and an inked rib-
bon which makes the impression of the type character when the key strikes it.

10. The passage mentions a number of good features of the combination of a skilled typist   10.____
and a typewriter of the following, the feature which is NOT mentioned in the passage is

    A.   speed   B.   uniformity
    C.   reliability   D.   legibility

11. According to the passage, a skilled typist can   11.____

    A.   turn out at least five carbon copies of typed matter
    B.   type at least three times faster than a penman can write
    C.   type more than 80 words a minute
    D.   readily move into a managerial position

12. According to the passage, which of the following is NOT part of the mechanism of a man-   12.____
ual typewriter?

    A.   Carbon paper   B.   Paper carrier
    C.   Platen   D.   Inked ribbon

13. According to the passage, the typewriter has helped   13.____

    A. men more than women in business
    B. women in career advancement into management
    C. men and women equally, but women have taken better advantage of it
    D. more women than men, because men generally dislike routine typing work

Questions 14-18.

    Reductions in pipe size of a building heating system are made with eccentric fittings and are pitched downward. The ends of mains with gravity return shall be at least 18" above the water line of the boiler. As condensate flows opposite to the steam, run outs are one size larger than the vertical pipe and are pitched upward. In a one-pipe system, an automatic air vent must be provided at each main to relieve air pressure and to let steam enter the radiator. As steam enters the radiator, a *thermal* device causes the vent to close, thereby holding the steam. Steam mains should not be less than two inches in diameter. The end of the steam main should have a minimum size of one-half of its greatest diameter. Small steam systems should be sized for a 2-oz. pressure drop. Large steam systems should be sized for a 4-oz. pressure drop.

14. The word *thermal*, as used in the above paragraph, means, most nearly,   14.____

    A. convector   B. heat
    C. instrument   D. current

15. According to the above paragraph, the one of the following that is one size larger than the vertical pipe is the   15.____

    A. steam main   B. valve
    C. water line   D. run out

16. According to the above paragraph, small steam systems should be sized for a pressure drop of   16.____

    A. 2 oz   B. 3 oz
    C. 4 oz   D. 5 oz

17. According to the above paragraph ends of mains with gravity return shall be *at least*   17.____

    A. 18" above the water line of the boiler
    B. one-quarter of the greatest diameter of the main
    C. twice the size of the vertical pipe in the main
    D. 18" above the steam line of the boiler

18. According to the above paragraph, the one of the following that is provided at each main to relieve air pressure is a (n)   18.____

    A. gravity return   B. convector
    C. eccentric   D. vent

Questions 19-21.

    The bearings of all electrical equipment should be subjected to careful inspection at scheduled periodic intervals in order to secure maximum life. The newer type of sleeve bearings requires very little attention since the oil does not become contaminated and oil leakage is negligible. Maintenance of the correct oil level is frequently the only upkeep required for years of service with this type of bearing.

19. According to the above paragraph, the MAIN reason for making periodic inspections of electrical equipment is to   19._____

    A. reduce waste of lubricants
    B. prevent injury to operators
    C. make equipment last longer
    D. keeps operators "on their toes"

20. According to the above paragraph, the bearings of electrical equipment should be inspected   20._____

    A. whenever the equipment isn't working properly
    B. whenever there is time for inspections
    C. at least once a year
    D. at regular times

21. According to the above paragraph, when using the newer type of sleeve bearings,   21._____

    A. oil leakage is slight
    B. the oil level should be checked every few years
    C. oil leakage is due to carelessness
    D. oil soon becomes dirty

Questions 22-25.

There is hardly a city in the country that is not short of fire protection in some areas within its boundaries. These municipalities have spread out and have re-shuffled their residential, business and industrial districts without readjusting the existing protective fire forces; or creating new protection units. Fire stations are still situated according to the needs of earlier times and have not been altered or improved to house modern fire-fighting equipment. They are neither efficient for carrying out their tasks nor livable for the men who must occupy them.

22. Of the following, the title which BEST describes the central idea of the above paragraph is: 22._____

    A. The Dynamic Nature of Contemporary Society
    B. The Cost of Fire Protection
    C. The Location and Design of Fire Stations
    D. The Design and Use of Fire-Fighting Equipment
    E. The Growth of American Cities

23. According to the above paragraph, fire protection is inadequate in the United States in   23._____

    A. most areas of some cities   B. some areas of most cities
    C. some areas in all cities   D. all areas in some cities
    E. most areas in most cities

24. The one of the following criteria for planning of fire stations which is NOT mentioned in the above paragraph is:

    A. Comfort of firemen   B. Proper location
    C. Design for modern equipment   D. Efficiency of operation
    E. Cost of construction

24.____

25. Of the following suggestions for improving the fire service, the *one* which would BEST deal with the problem discussed in the paragraph above would involve

    A. specialized training in the use of modern fire apparatus
    B. replacement of obsolete fire apparatus
    C. revision of zoning laws
    D. longer basic training for probationary firemen
    E. reassignment of fire districts

25.____

Questions 26-30.

    Stopping, standing, and parking of motor vehicles is regulated by law to keep the public highways open for a smooth flow of traffic, and to keep stopped vehicles from blocking intersections, driveways, signs, fire hydrants, and other areas that must be kept clear. These established regulations apply in all situations, unless otherwise indicated by signs. Other local restrictions are posted in the areas to which they apply. Three examples of these other types of restrictions, which may apply singly or in combination with one another are:
NO STOPPING - This means that a driver may not stop a vehicle for any purpose except when necessary to avoid interference with other vehicles, or in compliance with directions of a police officer or signal.
NO STANDING - This means that a driver may stop a vehicle only temporarily to actually receive or discharge passengers.
NO PARKING - This means that a driver may stop a vehicle only temporarily to actually load or unload merchandise or passengers. When stopped, it is advisable to turn on warning flashers if equipped with them. However, one should never use a directional signal for this purpose, because it may confuse other drivers. Some NO PARKING signs prohibit parking between certain hours on certain days. For example, the sign may read NO PARKING 8 a.m. to 11 a.m., MONDAY, WEDNESDAY, FRIDAY. These signs are usually utilized on streets where cleaning operations take place on alternate days.

26. The parking regulation that applies to fire hydrants is an example of

    A. local regulations   B. established regulations
    C. posted regulations   D. temporary regulations

26.____

27. When stopped in a NO PARKING zone, it is advisable to

    A. turn on the right directional signal to indicate to other drivers that you will remain stopped
    B. turn on the left directional signal to indicate to other drivers that you may be leaving the curb after a period of time
    C. turn on the warning flashers if your car is equipped with them
    D. put the vehicle in reverse so that the backup lights will be on to warn approaching cars that you have temporarily stopped

27.____

28. You may stop a vehicle temporarily to discharge passengers in an area under the restriction of a   28.____

    A.   NO STOPPING - NO STANDING zone
    B.   NO STANDING - NO PARKING zone
    C.   NO PARKING - NO STOPPING zone
    D.   NO STOPPING - NO STANDING - NO PARKING zone

29. A sign reads "NO PARKING 8 a.m. to 11 a.m., MONDAY, WEDNESDAY, FRIDAY." Based   29.____
on this sign, an enforcement agent would issue a summons to a car that is parked on a

    A.   Tuesday at 9:30 a.m.   B.   Wednesday at 12:00.a.m.
    C.   Friday at 10:30 a.m.   D.   Saturday at 8:00 a.m.

30. NO PARKING signs prohibiting parking between certain hours, on certain days, are usu-   30.____
ally utilized on streets where

    A.   vehicles frequently take on and discharge passengers
    B.   cleaning operations take place on alternate days
    C.   NO STOPPING signs have been ignored
    D.   commercial vehicles take on and unload merchandise

KEYS (CORRECT ANSWERS)

1.	C		16.	A
2.	A		17.	A
3.	C		18.	D
4.	D		19.	C
5.	A		20.	D
6.	A		21.	A
7.	A		22.	C
8.	D		23.	B
9.	C		24.	E
10.	C		25.	E
11.	B		26.	B
12.	A		27.	C
13.	B		28.	B
14.	B		29.	C
15.	D		30.	B

BASIC FUNDAMENTALS OF GOOD GROOMING

TABLE OF CONTENTS

BASIC FUNDAMENTALS
OF GOOD GROOMING

INSTRUCTIONAL OBJECTIVES
1. Ability to appreciate the importance of good health habits.
2. Ability to understand the importance and relationship of good grooming habits to gainful employment.
3. Ability to dress in a manner suitable for obtaining and holding a job.
4. Ability to evaluate good grooming skills in relation to successful employment in public-service occupations.
5. Ability, with good grooming, to form positive attitudes toward personal pride and self-respect.
6. Ability to demonstrate a desire to improve personal appearance.
7. Ability to realize that poor posture affects both appearance and health.
8. Ability to accept positive suggestions on appropriate dress and cleanliness.

CONTENT
Introduction

Appearance is important in applying for a job and for working successfully on the job. This is especially true in public-service occupations. One's self-image is usually related to physical appearance.

Young workers are often self-conscious and lack a feeling of security. Their concern over their appearance directly affects their poise, self-confidence, and feeling of well-being.

Neatness and grooming are important for many reasons, but most of all for the feeling of personal pride and self-respect that they give the individual. These feelings are often reflected in general appearance, and may be the cause for vocational success or failure.

1. RELATIONSHIP OF GROOMING AND EMPLOYMENT

The pursuit of a career is one of the most important goals during an individual's life. Good grooming is an important step in the achievement of this goal. Good grooming affects appearance and vitality. An individual will be judged by the way he appears. For greater success in life, both on and off the job, it is important that a good impression is made.

When applying for a job, as well as in dealing with the public, the first impression is important. The first, and often the most lasting, impression an employer gets of the applicant is a visual one. Care in all areas of grooming is necessary to give a total picture of being well-groomed. *The individual who works at being well-groomed will have his appearance working for him.*

Employers expect their employees to present a neat and clean appearance at all times. The people who do the hiring must keep in mind the image of the agency they represent. If a person is hired, he is considered a part of that agency. If a person dresses poorly and is not groomed properly, or has poor personal habits, he will reflect poorly upon the agency. It must be remembered that certain agencies view their employees in terms of public relations. A poor representative of the agency or department can mean a loss of time and efficiency. In order to keep a job, a good appearance must be maintained, especially when serving the public.

In the employment interview, it does not matter what other qualities and abilities the person possesses; if the applicant does not measure up to the appearance standards set by the employer, he will be given no further consideration. Employment personnel point out that many people seeking a position lose out on this point alone-appearance. In the case of a public-service worker, this can be especially important. The agency managers realize that their workers will be dealing with the public, and that appearance will be a key to success of the agency as well as the employee. This is one of the major reasons for the personal interview required before employment in almost all public-service occupational fields. The moments which are spent in the employment interview are very important. The applicant has been given only a short time in which to sell himself and his services to the employer (sometimes represented by several people). No matter how impressive his letters or application, the physical appearance and the words used will either get the applicant a job or will bring defeat to his purpose.

2. RELATIONSHIP OF GOOD GROOMING AND GOOD HABITS

Good grooming, which is reflected in appearance, is dependent upon good habits. The employee who has developed good grooming habits may find that they make the difference when job advancement is being considered. Employers may use personal appearance as a sample of the kind of work that is done by an employee. In most cases a person who keeps himself clean and neat is the kind of person who will take his time to do a job well.

Self-concept

Self-concept is defined as the way an individual sees himself. The self-concept develops in response to the reactions of others, which in turn are a direct response to the individual's self-concept. The self-concept reflects how an individual feels about himself. Like any feeling, it may be partially unconscious, or based upon unconscious needs. The more realistic the self-concept, the better an individual will be able to control his personal relationships. A realistic self-concept may be developed by making an objective self-evaluation during which habits, attitudes, goals, interests, and aptitudes are analyzed.

Honesty in Self-Concept

Others may not see an individual as he sees himself; therefore, he should strive to relate his positive self-concept to them. By being honest when looking at himself, an individual may see things that he will want to change. When he does make changes in his self-concept by changing his appearance to others, he will build a healthy self-concept and a feeling of adequacy.

Each person is a special individual with his or her own unique qualities. Making the most of one's own special qualities is a key to success and happiness. An acceptance of the responsibility for one's health and appearance is mandatory. Care of one's skin and complexion, hair, teeth, breath, and posture is essential to a healthy self-concept.

A successful employee must evaluate himself and his own special qualities, emphasizing his assets. He should determine to make the most of his own special qualities and to minimize his liabilities. There are certain personal characteristics which are unchangeable, such as height, build, color and tone of skin, texture of hair, and features–deep-set eyes, big ears, large nose, dimples. However, looks may be changed by determining the best features, and utilizing the appropriate aids to make the most of these features. Each individual should set up his own self-improvement course in order to present a clean, neat appearance.

Positive Attitude Required in Self-Concept

Teachers may help students to change poor attitudes by encouraging them to adopt positive outlooks. A person must determine to make the most of every situation. Each experience can be as exciting and rewarding, or as dull or boring as a person makes it. Personality can also be improved by exercising enthusiasm. Students can be encouraged to give a little more of themselves by being the first to smile, to speak, or to offer to do a job.

People who will be working in public-service occupations cannot know what problems they might face in the future, and to prepare to meet these problems, they need to develop a greater understanding of themselves and a feeling of adequacy. They must attempt to discover their own interests, strengths, and abilities, and begin to understand how these traits are related to establishing personal and vocational goals. Through self-understanding, the workers will develop a sense of personal growth and worth. This sense of personal worth will usually manifest itself in a neat appearance.

Good Habits of Health

Good health is the result of cleanliness, proper nutrition, care of the body, and careful grooming. Physical changes of adolescence (the period of several years between puberty and early adulthood) are natural, and this calls for accepting responsibility for the care of one's health and appearance. It is a period of especially rapid growth, in which there are varying rates of change for different individuals. During this period of rapid change, glandular activities produce a rapid growth spurt, sexual maturation, emotional changes, and changes in eating and other living habits.

Good health habits are important during this period of physical and emotional change. Here is a list of good habits, with indication of their importance:

- Proper Diet - The right kinds of foods contribute to energy and to healthy blood; helps to build muscles and bones; and to provide vitamins which protect against disease.
- Proper Rest - The human body needs an adequate amount of sleep, although the amount depends on the individual—eight hours is the general average for the adolescent.
- Exercise - Exercise helps keep the body in good condition; aids blood circulation, breathing, digestion, and metabolism.
- Proper Elimination - This rids body of waste and harmful substances.
- Drinking Enough Water - Water aids in the digestion and absorption of foods, the carrying of foods to the body tissues, and the removal of body wastes; it also plays a basic part in regulating body temperature.
- Cleanliness - Dirt is the breeding place of disease and germs.

Good health habits go hand-in-hand with good grooming habits; both of these are essential for attractiveness. Good health habits affect overall general health and tend to improve the mental outlook and capacity for work. The result is energy and enthusiasm for greater job efficiency with less absenteeism.

Good Habits of Cleanliness

Cleanliness is important for social success as well as for health; cleanliness is imperative in order to make a good first impression as well as a lasting impression. Teachers realize that cleanliness may require a habit change; therefore, more than lecturing will be required.

The acquiring of a job may be the motivating factor required for the adoption of habits involving cleanliness as an indication of the quality of work to be produced by an employee. Students must be made to realize that cleanliness will be a large factor upon which their success in public service may depend.

Personal Grooming

Many students simply do not practice habits of cleanliness because they are unaware of how to achieve good personal grooming. Others do not have the facilities for keeping clean, and there are some who do not care. A teacher must give consideration to these facts when devel oping a grooming program for students.

General cleanliness can be achieved through a routine of regular bathing, care of skin and complexion, care of the teeth and breath, and for boys, may require daily shaving.

It is desirable, under normal conditions, to bathe regularly. It not only cleanses the body, but also serves several other functions. Bathing or showering acts as a tension release, body stimulant, or body regulator. The activity of the sweat glands, together with the bacteria present on the skin, produces perspiration wetness and subsequent odor. The offensive odor of bacteria may be controlled by using an underarm deodorant or antiperspirant. Antibacterial soaps also help combat this perspiration odor.

Care of Skin and Nails

Changes in the oil glands located on the face during the adolescent period of growth produce excess oils which contribute to the formation of acne. The face requires special washing so skin problems may be minimized. There are many excellent types of soap or lotion available for care of skin and complexion; the wise person will make himself aware of those available to him.

Nail care is often neglected by the adolescent; this, too, should be included as part of one's program for the achievement of personal cleanliness.

Care of the Mouth and Teeth

Clean teeth and fresh breath are important to an individual, both physically and socially. The variety of nourishing foods which promote general good health, also help in developing and maintaining healthy teeth. Teeth should be brushed in the morning, evening, and as soon as possible after eating. If brushing isn't possible, a food which has a detergent or cleaning action should be eaten, or water can be swished in the mouth. This is essential for the prevention of tooth decay and bad breath.

Toothpastes aid the toothbrush in cleaning food debris from the teeth and areas between the teeth. Dental floss is also helpful in removing small food particles. Toothpaste removes unsightly film, called *plac,* which tends to accumulate on the teeth and aids in the dislodging and destroying of odor-causing and decay-causing bacteria. The brushing of teeth should be done in the proper manner, as indicated by your dentist or school nurse, for greater efficiency. Attractive teeth and healthy gums are very important to one's overall health, grooming, and personal appearance; however, to have attractive teeth, a regular program of dental care should be followed in order to maintain this attractiveness.

Because cleanliness is a personal matter, chances are that one who is offensive will not be told such by others. This person may simply be avoided or talked about without his knowing. In either case, noticeable uncleanliness may jeopardize not only his personal reputation, but also his employment.

Good Habits of Hair Care

The grooming of hair can be a tremendous contribution to the overall appearance of an individual, particularly if the hair is:

- clean and lustrous
- becoming in style
- free from dandruff
- neatly combed

Care of the Hair

Care of hair should include a good haircut. Brushing is good for males as well as females. It distributes the natural oils and, like exercise, it stimulates circulation. Massaging maintains good circulation through the scalp tissues and about the hair roots.

Unclean hair has a noticeable odor; therefore, it should be shampooed as needed for cleanliness, but frequency of shampooing depends on the individual's hair and the hair style. Hair needs should be determined and a choice of shampoo should reflect these needs. A practice should be made of cleaning brushes and combs when hair is shampooed.

Many of these hair problems, which apply to both men and women can, and should, be dealt with, and controlled, to the extent possible, for best appearance and health:

- Dry hair
- Slow growing hair
- Split and dry ends
- Thin hair
- Oily hair
- Falling hair
- Fine, limp hair
- "Yellowed" or gray hair
- Very thick hair
- Dandruff

6

Hair Styling

Hair styles will depend not only on what is fashionable, but also on what is becoming to the individual. The proper choice of a style can be an asset to personal appearance. Hair styles are most becoming when the shape of the face, (oval, square, long, round, heart-shaped, etc.) is considered, for proper balance and proportion.

Each face shape is enhanced when a hair style which is most flattering to that shape is worn. Styling aids, such as permanents and hair sprays, can be used to aid in the achievement of good grooming.

Extreme styles for girls and length for boys are usually unacceptable by public-service or other employers. Excessive hair arrangements should, therefore, be avoided. Students must be aware of their own appearance and how their hair will "tell" something about them. Employees in public-service occupations must be conscious of the visual cues they give about themselves.

Good Habits of Posture

Posture is the foundation of one's appearance, and has a definite influence on the impression he makes. Poor posture is unbecoming and unhealthy; good posture helps to develop poise and improves body functioning. Well-fitted clothing and shoes help to maintain posture through body balance.

The outline, following, indicates the basis for good standing and sitting posture. These general "guidelines" would be of assistance in acquiring a healthy and attractive posture.

<u>Good sitting posture</u> is achieved by these habits:

- Sit back so that hips touch back of chair
- Keep feet flat on floor
- Sit tall
- Keep chest out, with neck and head in line with upper back
- When writing, lean forward from the hips, maintaining the correct alignment of the back, neck and head

<u>Good standing posture</u> is attained through consistent attention to these details:

- Keep feet parallel and slightly apart, with toes pointed straight ahead
- Stand with knees easy, not bent or forced back
- Hold abdomen in by contraction of abdominal muscles
- Keep back as flat as possible
- Stand with hips firm and tucked under body
- Keep shoulders relaxed and down, shoulder blades pressing slightly together
- Be proud, stand with head high, chin slightly in, and back of neck pushed slightly backward
- Keep weight evenly distributed on each foot, and most of the body weight on the balls of your feet

188

Posture will affect a person's appearance, the way he feels, his health, and his job efficiency. It may be accepted by an employer as an overt demonstration of an employee's willingness to work.

3. RELATIONSHIP OF DRESS AND SUCCESS

Clothing is a means of communication. The first visual impression of a person is based almost 90 percent on the appearance of his clothing. Students, employees, and all others need to develop an awareness of the necessity for neat, clean, and well-fitted clothing for job success. Some individuals lack the ability to choose styles which are appropriate for their jobs.

Trends in color and style have changed drastically and will continue to change; therefore, there exists a need to help people develop good taste in dress. The public-service employee must have, and put to practice, a knowledge of pleasing color combinations and appropriate styles. While the relationship between clothing management and appearance is obvious, many workers fail to realize the impact that it has upon job efficiency. Inappropriate dress may be an office distraction, or may even prevent getting the job in the beginning.

Common Sense in Clothing Selection

Common sense is the major factor in deciding what clothing is appropriate for the job interview, as well as the job itself. In order not to detract from one's self, conservative and tasteful clothing should be chosen. The type of clothing which will be worn on the job should also be worn for the interview, except when a uniform or special protective clothing is required. Outer winter garments should not be worn in the presence of the interviewer.

Personal comfort must also be considered when choosing clothing. It is wise for a person to dress in a manner which allows him to forget his clothing so that attention can be given to more important matters.

Students should learn what is suitable to wear for every occasion; clothes worn to a party or to school may be conspicuous when worn on the job. A large wardrobe does not insure that a person is well-groomed; the choice of what is worn is the determining factor.

Criteria for Wardrobe Selection

Attention to the following data (given in outline form) may be useful in acquiring the ability to choose appropriate dress:

Remember elements in design:

- Color
- Texture
- Line
- Shape

These elements should be harmonious or mutually complementary.

8

Remember principles in design:

- Unity
- Balance
- Dominance
- Contrast
- Proportion
- Rhythm

These principles largely determine the appropriateness of a particular style of dress.

Pay attention to lines:

- Vertical
- Curved
- Horizontal
- Diagonal

The type of lines selected as basic to clothing styles should be proportionate to the other elements of design and the shape of the individual's figure.

Consider figure features:

Pay attention to problems of different figure types, and coordinate features with the elements and principles of good design.

People come in different sizes and shapes. These differences should be considered, and used to the individual's advantage in selection of a wardrobe.

Care of Clothing

Clothes should be kept clean and well-pressed. It is of little importance whether clothes are new or old; however, it makes considerable difference if they are unclean. It is not necessary nor required that a great deal of money be spent on clothing; but inexpensive neatness can mean the difference between getting and keeping a job, or losing it.

Under special conditions of working, the employer may give a clothing allowance to the employee for purchase of clothing for use on the job, and some employers may reimburse the employee for clothing purchased for special use. Many jobs require uniforms, and some employers will furnish and launder them. When a uniform is to be worn, care must be taken to insure that it is clean and pressed, and that all the accessories are in order. It is important to always have an extra uniform ready if something should happen to the one being worn.

Appropriate Dress Helps on the Job

The standards set by the particular public-service agency should be a guide when considering clothing and accessories. For example, agencies may have regulations against wearing of mini-skirts in the office. Necklaces, rings, bracelets, may present a hazard on the job in that they could get caught in the equipment.

Good clothing management can have an effect on job success in its ability to promote promptness and neatness on the job. The prearranging of clothing can save time.

A person who is dressed appropriately will fit well into the working situation and will have a personal feeling of well-being which will be reflected in his successful employment.

4. SUMMATION

Acquiring and keeping a job, whether in public-service or some other occupation, is one of the most important goals of any individual. How he sees himself, that is, his self-concept, influences how he looks and how others see him. In applying for a job, a person has only a few minutes to present himself. In those few minutes, the employer forms an impression. For greater success in life, it is important that a good impression be made. Good grooming affects appearance and vitality and will help to make that good impression.

In order to be a well-groomed individual, one must practice good health habits, such as proper diet, rest, and exercise, drinking sufficient water, elimination of body waste, and cleanliness. Cleanliness is a basis for good grooming. It is desirable to bathe as regularly as possible, and give special care to complexion, nails, teeth, and hair. Hair should be properly cut and extreme styles should be avoided.

Whether on the job or looking for a job, an individual should wear clean, neat, well-fitted clothes. They should be comfortable so that he does not have to be concerned about how he looks or feels and is free to think about more important things. It is also important that an employee comply with the standards set by the agency for which he works in the matter of dress. In addition, the foundation of a person's appearance is his posture. Good posture helps to develop poise and has influence on the impression one makes.

STUDENT LEARNING ACTIVITIES

- View pictures of job applicants and select the ones that you would hire for positions of: social worker, teacher's assistant, recreational aide, secretary, employment counselor, forestry aide, fireman. Discuss the reason for each selection.
- Discuss personal experiences related to poor grooming and wrong first impressions.
- Prepare checklists for phases of grooming.
- Set up a self-improvement program which focuses on a trait for improvement in grooming.
- View the film *A Time and a Place* and write comments on how appearance affects behavior for discussion after the film.
- Submit questions on good grooming skills for class discussion.
- Participate in a student panel moderated by the school nurse or physician on health habits for teenagers.
- Discuss effects of rest, relaxation, and hygiene on job efficiency.

- Discuss in small groups the effect of proper and improper diet on health, the way we look, the way we feel, the way we act.
- Discuss, "How it feels to work or sit near someone who isn't clean."
- Role-play a situation in which long hair would make a difference, as for instance, getting or not getting a job.
- Bring in pictures of attractive hair styles for display.
- Discuss the effect of posture on a person's appearance and the way he feels, and on his health and job efficiency.
- List various types of job families in public service and the particular type of grooming practices required for each.
- View pictures of employees on various jobs, and discuss types or appearance of clothing worn.
- Listen to your local school principal or a personnel officer from a local public-service agency speak on what is expected of a prospective employee.
- Write an essay on the following sentence: "A first-class appearance is a letter of introduction you can write for yourself."

TEACHER MANAGEMENT ACTIVITIES

- Prepare for discussion a series of pictures of job applicants, demonstrating such various personal appearances as:

> Man with three days' growth of beard,
> Man with open collar and tie hanging loose,
> Lady in business suit; in formal wear,
> Man with long hair and sport shirt,
> Man in neat, clean clothes, shaven,
> Girl in a mini-skirt or bare midriff,
> Girl in pants suit or simple dress,
> Boy in faded blue jeans and sweatshirt,
> Boy in sport shirt and casual pants.

- Encourage students to discuss personal experiences related to poor grooming and wrong first impressions.
- Set up a checklist for all phases of grooming.
- Supervise the setting up of programs which focus on traits for self-improvement.
- Arrange to have the school nurse or physician moderate a student panel on health habits for teenagers.
- Lead a discussion on how rest, relaxation, and hygiene affect job efficiency.
- Lead a discussion on the effect of proper and improper diet on health, appearance, and actions.
- Invite a beautician and a barber to speak on the proper care of skin, hair, and nails.
- Organize the class into groups to debate such subjects as: "Whether or not a person is clean is his or her own business," "How a student can improve his personal grooming," etc.
- Lead discussions on various topics, such as, "What do we communicate through clothing?" "How does posture affect health and job efficiency?" "How does it feel to sit or work next to someone who isn't clean?"
- Have students role-play a situation in which long hair made a difference; for instance, in obtaining a public-service job.

- Have students list types of jobs familiar in public-service and the particular grooming practices required.
- Have students view pictures of employees on various jobs and discuss types and appearance of clothing worn.
- Invite the principal or a public-service agency personnel officer to speak on what is expected of a prospective employee.
- Have the students write an essay on what the following sentence means to them: "A first-class appearance is a letter of introduction you can write for yourself."

EVALUATION QUESTIONS

Public service managers realize that their workers will be dealing with the public. As workers are considered a part of the agency that hired them, their appearance reflects upon the agency that they represent.

Two top-level jobs at the front desk are open. As public service manager, you must select two workers for these jobs.

All of the following people have the necessary skills and qualifications to advance, and all of them have expressed a desire to be promoted. Which two workers would you select?

- Mary misses many working days. She is a picky eater. She dates often and usually does not get to bed before 1:00 a.m. Mary's hair is dull and her skin is oily. Although Mary is well dressed, her posture is poor.
- John does not care to spend money on clothes because he believes in saving his money. He often wears clothes that are slightly soiled. His teeth are dirty and at times his breath has an unpleasant odor. John feels that these things are unimportant and that he should not change his appearance to please others.
- Susan is a shy girl who feels she is poor at most things. Susan is very thin. Her choice of clothing is not flattering to her. Although she has good features, she feels she is unattractive.
- Jack belongs to a motorcycle club. His nails are dirty and he does not shave often. His shoulder-length hair is dirty and unkempt. As he does not believe in bathing, he has a strong body odor. Jack wears tight black pants, a black leather jacket, and high-heeled boots to work. Jack believes he should be free to dress as he wishes.
- Sam has many outside interests. He enjoys active sports and keeps his body in good shape. He believes in eating the right foods and getting the proper amounts of rest and exercise. Sam has excellent posture.
- Sally is a single girl who is very concerned about her looks. Sally goes on dates after work so she wears plunging necklines, short, tight dresses, and heavy jewelry. She has a very fancy hair style.

ANSWER KEY

Answers will vary on this test. The instructor may wish to have a discussion after the test, with students justifying their selections. Students may be evaluated on the soundness of their judgment.

BASIC FUNDAMENTALS OF INTERPERSONAL RELATIONSHIPS

TABLE OF CONTENTS

BASIC FUNDAMENTALS OF
INTERPERSONAL RELATIONSHIPS

INSTRUCTIONAL OBJECTIVES

1. Ability to distinguish between formal and informal behavior.
2. Ability to identify the important factors in communicating with people.
3. Ability to understand how defense mechanisms affect communication with others.
4. Ability to identify the roles played in effective person-to-person communication.
5. Ability to acquire the human relations skills needed for getting along with others both on and off the job.
6. Ability to establish greater personal effectiveness with others so as to develop better cooperation and superior-subordinate relationships in public-service working situations.
7. Ability to recognize the mutual dependence of individuals on each other.
8. Ability to form positive attitudes toward the worth and dignity of every human being.
9. Ability to become aware of how feelings affect one's own behavior, as well as one's relationships with other people.
10. Ability to use an understanding of human relationships to effectively work with people.
11. Ability to improve communications with others by developing greater effectiveness in dealing with people in the world of public service.

CONTENT

INTRODUCTION

Perhaps the single most important skill that a public-service worker, or anyone for that matter, needs, is the ability to get along with other people. "Person-to-person" relationships are the building blocks of all social interactions between two-individuals. If there is one essential ingredient for success in life, both on and off the job, it is developing greater effectiveness in dealing with people.

The skill of the teacher is critical to the success of this unit. He should establish a permissive and non-threatening group climate in which free communication and behavior can take place. The importance of this unit cannot be over stated. The overall objective is to establish greater personal effectiveness with others and to develop better co-operative and superior-subordinate relationships in the public-service occupations. Obtaining greater "self-awareness" is a large part of this goal. Because interpersonal relations are affected by a variety of factors, some attention should be given initially to basic rules of conduct and behavior on the job.

1. ## INTERPERSONAL CONDUCT AND BEHAVIOR ON THE JOB
Most public-service agencies have clearly defined rules and regulations. The behavior of the public-service worker is often guided by the established proce-

dures and directives of that individual agency. In many cases, even individual departments or units will have procedures manuals, which regulate conduct and office work.

Formal Organization of the Office

At one point or another, most public-service employees either work directly in an office, or come in frequent contact with other people working in an administrative or staff office. Students should become familiar with the organizational structure of the occupational groups in which they are planning on working. A park worker, for example, must know about the organization of the Parks Department—what kinds of staff or administrative services are provided, what about training, what are the safety rules, what goes into personnel records, etc. Preparing a flow chart of the relationships between different positions in a particular agency is one way of learning about the organization of that office or agency.

Office as a Setting for formal and Informal Relations

It is necessary to become aware of the different kinds of social relations shared with co-workers and the public. Some co-workers, for example, are seen only at work, and others are seen socially after work and/or on weekends. Factors that determine which co-workers become *personal* friends and which are just *work* friends should be considered and discussed.

On the other hand, a public-service worker usually has more formal relationships with the public with whom he comes into contact. Consider the relationships of the preschool teacher's aide and his students, the library helper and his library patrons, the police cadet and the general public, etc. In each of these cases, the public expects the public-service worker to help them with a particular service.

Although the distinction between formal and informal social relationships is not always clear, one should be sensitive to the fact that both kinds of relationships affect the behavior of the public and the public-service employee, Normally, the very organization of the public-service office helps to create a social climate for developing working relationships of a formal nature, and personal relationships with co-workers and the public which are of a more impersonal nature.

Office Behavior

Specific kinds of behavior relate to these formal and informal relationships with other people. Typically, the formal relationship is well prescribed and regulated by procedures or directives. The license interviewer, as an example, has specific questions to ask, and specific information to obtain from the applicant. Their relationship can be described as formal or prescribed by regulation. On the other hand, other office behavior can best be described as informal and non-prescribed (or *free*). Interpersonal relations in this case are often more personal and relaxed by their very nature.

3

2. INTERPERSONAL COMMUNICATION - THE MEANING

Interpersonal communication can be defined as a two-way flow of information from person-to-person. One cannot Study human relations without examining the constant relationships that man has with other people; the individual does not exist in a vacuum. Most of man's psychological and social needs are met through dealings with other people. In fact, one psychiatrist (Harry Stark Sullivan) has developed a theory of personality based upon interpersonal situations. This viewpoint, known as the *Interpersonal Theory of Psychiatry,* claims that personality is essentially the enduring pattern of continued interpersonal relationships between people. This interpersonal behavior is all that can be observed as personality.

Importance of Face-to-Face Contacts

The very phrase. *Public Service Occupations,* suggests frequent face-to-face contacts with not only the general public, but with co-workers as well. With possibly a few exceptions, practically every public-service employee encounters frequent person-to-person contacts both on and off the job. The ability to get along with people is a very important part of public-service work.

Listening Techniques

Effective listening is a critical part of interpersonal communications. Listening is an active process, requiring not only that one must *pay attention* to what is being said, but that one must also *listen* for the meaning of what is being said. Almost one-half of the total time spent communicating, (reading, writing, speaking, or listening) is spent in listening.

Even though people get considerable practice at listening, they don't do too well at it. Many studies have shown that, on the average, a person retains only about 25 percent of a given speech after only 10 minutes have elapsed. Most people forget three quarters of what they hear in a relatively short period of time. Clearly, people need to improve their listening skills if they are to become more effective in their relations with other people.

3. FACTORS IN INTERPERSONAL COMMUNICATION
There are a number of components that affect the person-to-person relationship. Some of the factors common to both the sender and the receiver in a person-to-person communication are:

The Attitudes and Emotions of the Individuals

For example - two people are shouting and screaming at each other - how effective is their interpersonal communication?

○ *The Needs and Wants of the People Communicating*

Both the sender and receiver have unique desires, some open, and some hidden from the other person. These needs can and do strongly influence interpersonal relationships.

○ *The Implied Demands of the Sender and Receiver*

An important factor in interpersonal communications involves requests or demands. How are these demands handled? What are some typical responses to demands? These factors are common to both the sender and the receiver in interpersonal relations and affect the individual behavior of the people communicating.

The Choice of Words of the Conversant

One's choice of words can have a direct bearing on the interpersonal communication. The vocabulary one uses in interpersonal relationships should be appropriate for the occasion. For example, a preschool teacher's aide would not use the same vocabulary in talking to a three-year-old, as she would in talking to the preschool teacher.

How Each Sees the Other

The process of communicating from person-to-person is greatly influenced by the perception that the sender and receiver have of each other. The feelings that a person has toward the other person are reflected in his tone of voice, choice of words, and even in his *body language*. A reference book mentioned in the resource section of this unit, *How to Read a Person Like a Book*, deals with the importance of body language in person-to-person relationships.

The Right Time and Place

Another factor that may be important in interpersonal relationships is the timing of the communication. For example, one of the first things a supervisor should do if he wants to talk over a problem with his subordinate, is ask the question: "Is this the right time and place?" Problems should not generally be discussed in the middle of an office, where other employees, or the public, can hear the discussion. Personal problems should be discussed only in private.

The Effect of Past Experience

In general, the quality of the person-to-person transaction will depend upon the past experience of the individuals. Human beings have acquired most of their opinions, assumptions, and value judgments through their relationships with other people. Past experience not only helps to teach people about effective interpersonal relationships, it is also often responsible for the irrational prejudices that a person displays. A strong bias usually blocks the interpersonal relationship if the subject of the communication concerns that particular bias.

The Effect of Personal Differences

An additional factor in interpersonal communications involves the intelligence and other personal differences of the people communicating. An example of such a personal difference is the *objectivity* of the people involved, as compared with their *subjectivity*. One person may try to be very fair and objective in discussing a point with another person, yet this other person is, at the same time, taking everything personally and being very subjective in his viewpoint. It is almost as if an adult was talking to an angry child.

Such differences can impede the communications flow between two people. In fact, all the factors mentioned in communications should be examined as to whether they block or facilitate interpersonal relationships. *The most effective interpersonal relationships are those that are adult-like in their character.*

4. DEFENSE MECHANISMS IN INTERPERSONAL RELATIONS

Defense mechanisms are attempts to defend the individual from anxiety. They are essentially a reaction to frustration - a self-deception.

Causes for Defense Mechanisms

In order to help understand some of the causes for defense mechanisms, remember the basic human needs:

- *Biological or physiological needs* - hunger, water, rest, etc.
- *Psychological or social needs* - status, security, affection, justice etc.

Fear of failure in any of these basic needs appears to be related to the development of defense mechanisms; attitudes toward failure, in turn, originate out of the fabric of childhood experience. The social and cultural conditions encountered during childhood determine the rewards and controls which fill one's later life. These childhood experiences, and their resultant consequences, affect personality development, the individual's value system, and his definition of acceptable goals.

Individuals who are dominated by the fear of failure may react by using one of these defense mechanisms:

- *Rationalization* - making an impulsive action seem logical.

- *Projection* - assigning one's traits to others.

- *Identification* - assuming someone else's favorite qualities are their own.

Results of Use of Defense Mechanisms

A common factor to all defense mechanisms is their quality of *self-deception*. People cling to their impulses and actions, perhaps disguising them so that they become socially acceptable. Their defense mechanisms can be found in the everyday behavior of most normal people and, of course, have *direct influences* on interpersonal relationships.

A person, for example, who is responsible for a particular job makes a mistake, and the work doesn't get done. When confronted with the problem by his supervisor, the individual puts the blame on someone or something else. This is a very common form of a defense mechanism.

Defense mechanisms can sometimes have *negative influences* on interpersonal communications. They can contribute to the individual forming erroneous opinions about the other person's motives. These mechanisms can alter the perceptions and evaluations made about the individual by other people, Ways to understand these mechanisms must be sought; one solution is to become more aware of the common defense mechanisms, and to become less defensive through greater acceptance of others.

5. THE INFLUENCES OF ROLE-PLAYING IN INTERPERSONAL RELATIONS

Everyone wears a mask and plays a certain role or roles in life. Even if the role one plays is to be himself, that particular form of behavior can still be considered a role. As a public-service employee, one's role is to serve the public. This can be done in a number of ways. Some of the factors involved in public-service roles will be mentioned below:

Exploring Superior-Subordinate Relations

Public-service employees are accountable for their actions. From the entry-level public administrative analysis trainee, to the President of the United States, every public servant must be accountable to either an immediate supervisor, a governing body, or to the public itself. Entry-level public-service employees gain experience and get promoted, but they continue to be subordinates and responsible for their actions, even though they also become supervisors and have people working for them.

Simulation exercises can be developed which will examine the perceptions of the superior by the subordinate. *Authority* and *power* factors may enter in here, as the superior also perceives the subordinate in a particular way. *Dominance* and *need* factors are at work in superior-subordinate relationships, and the style of leadership used (*autocratic, democratic,* or *lassiez-faire*) is a form of leadership role.

Peer relationships can be explored through simulation exercises. The ways in which co-workers perceive each other and the resultant effect on cooperation is one area to be examined. Ways to establish a climate or environment for effective, cooperative relations should be sought.

It is desirable also to simulate, for better comprehension, interpersonal communications with the general public. Role-playing techniques, which permit the exploration of person-to-person relationships, are highlighted in the following section on simulation exercises.

Interpersonal Relations Achieved Through Simulation

The preparation of students for entry-level public-service occupations must include an opportunity to experience meaningful interpersonal relations. Public-service employees, whether office or field workers, experience personal relationships with other people every day. The initial success of the public-service worker will depend in large measure upon his ability to interact effectively with others in the office or field. Accordingly, a principle objective of simulation exercises for entry-level public-service education is to have the student acquire the necessary interpersonal relations skills that make for success in all public-service occupations.

When developing a model public-service simulation with the principal objective being to improve favorable interpersonal relations, certain criteria must be established. These criteria may be stated as follows:

- *Interpersonal relations must be the principal component of the simulation*. Provision must be made for students to interact with others in an office interpersonal setting so that they may work and communicate effectively with one another.

- *The simulation must be as realistic as possible*. Realism can best be accomplished by simulating an actual public-service operation in as many areas as possible.

- *Originality must play an important part*. Model simulations, currently in use, must not be copied in an effort to maintain simplicity.

- *The simulation must be interesting*. Students must be motivated to participate in the simulation and to be enthusiastic about its operation.

- *The simulation must be unstructured*. Provision must be made to allow for an awareness of events as they take place. Students must learn to cope with a situation without prior knowledge that the situation will occur.

In order for the teacher to determine if the model public-service simulation developed has, in fact, improved interpersonal relations, the simulation must be evaluated in terms of meeting the established objectives.

6. ## MEASURING INTERPERSONAL RELATIONS

Survey of Interpersonal Values

A valid and reliable instrument for measuring interpersonal relations, such as the *Survey of Interpersonal Values,* may be used for this purpose. This instrument is intended for grades 9-12, and is designed to measure the relative importance of the major factored interpersonal value dimensions. These values include both the subject's relations with others and others with himself. The value dimensions considered are:

- *Support*--being treated with understanding, encouragement, kindness, and consideration.

- *Conformity*--doing what is socially correct, accepted, and proper.

203

- *Recognition*--being admired, looked up to, considered important, and attracting favorable notice.

- *Independence*--being able to do what one wants to do, making one's own decisions, doing things in one's own way.

- *Benevolence*--doing things for other people, sharing, and helping.

- *Leadership*--being in charge of others, having authority or power.

A pretest on interpersonal values is administered before the model public-service simulation actually begins, and the same test is administerd as a post-test after a stipulated period of time. By comparison of results, and through the use of applicable statistics, the gain in behavior modification in interpersonal relations can be determined, as a result of using the model public-service simulation.

Analysis of Interpersonal Behavior

Public-service employees should be aware of their own needs, and of the needs of other people. They should be able to recognize situations or behavior calling for professional help, and be able to refer people to such appropriate help. New employees must be able to use their knowledge of person-to-person relationships to effectively work with people.

In order to become more effective in interpersonal relationships, students must gain an understanding of:

- *Self-evaluation* - to be able to assess their own strengths and weaknesses.

- *Group Evaluation* - as a class to be able to evaluate other individuals' competencies in interpersonal communications.

- *Correction of own self-perception* - to be able to do something about the knowledge and attitudes formed by adjusting their individual behavior.

STUDENT LEARNING ACTIVITIES

- Define formal and informal social behavior.

- List the important factors in interpersonal communication.

- View and discuss the film strip, *Your Educational Goals, No. 2: Human Relationships*.

- Role play in alternate supervisor-subordinate relationships practicing effective interpersonal communication.

- Write an essay on "Defense mechanisms affect interpersonal relationships."

- View the film, *The Unanswered Question,* and discuss human relationships afterwards.

- Listen to a discussion of structured interpersonal communications and evaluate the effectiveness of the person-to-person relationship.

9

- In small groups, discuss the ways in which people are mutually dependent on each other,

- Use simulation exercises to practice interpersonal relations.

- List the different kinds of roles and games played in interpersonal communications.

- Debate the statement: *Understanding person-to-person relations is one of the most important skills a person can acquire for success in life.*

- Discuss how understanding interpersonal relationships can help a person to effectively work with people.

- Define the role of recognizing one's own feelings in relation to others.

TEACHER MANAGEMENT ACTIVITIES

- Have the students define formal and informal social behavior.

- Show transparencies on interpersonal relations, *(Social Sensitivity lour Relationship with Others)* and discuss concepts afterwards.

- Assign written exercises on the important factors in interpersonal communication.

- Set up role-playing exercises on subordinate-supervisor roles in effective interpersonal communication.

- Encourage small-group discussions of the ways people are mutually dependent on each other.

- Show a movie on human relationships *(The Unanswered Question)* and discuss key points afterwards.

- Separate the class into teams to debate such statements as: Understanding interpersonal relations is one of the most important skills a person can acquire for success in life.

- Encourage individual study and reading in interpersonal relationships.

- Assign an essay on the worth and dignity of man in interpersonal relations.

- Bring in public-service workers who deal with others to talk to the class about the value of effective interpersonal communications.

05

Evaluation
Questions

Fill in the crossword puzzle below.

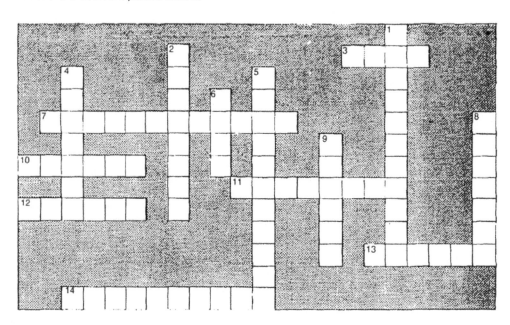

ACROSS:

3.   A strong prejudice or _____ can block good relationships.
7.   Being abie to do what one wants to do satisfies the need tor _____.
10. One's _____ of words should be correct for the occasion.
11. Friends usually have an _____ relationship.
12. In talking over problems with others, is important.
13. Everyone needs to feel _____.
14. _____ is assigning one's traits to others.

DOWN:

1.   We _____ when we try to make our actions seem logical.
2.   When we assume someone's qualities as our own we _____ with that person.
4.   Individuals _____ when they do what is socially proper.
5.   When we attract favorable attention, we gain _____
6.   Some people have a strong _____ of failure.
8.   _____ mechanics help to protect a person from anxiety.
9.   A public service worker usually has a _____ relationship with the public.

Answer Key

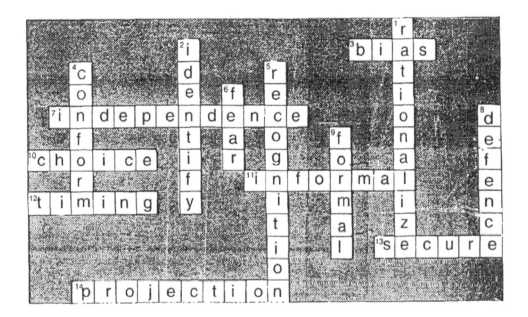

Made in the USA
Las Vegas, NV
03 October 2024

96221961R00129